THE WAR GENERATION

Kennikat Press

National University Publications

Series in American Studies

General Editor

James P. Shenton

Professor of History, Columbia University

The War Generation

Veterans of the First World War

Stephen R. Ward, Editor

James M. Diehl   Michael A. Ledeen

Donald J. Lisio   Robert Soucy

National University Publications

KENNIKAT PRESS • 1975

Port Washington, N.Y. • London

Manufactured in the United States of America

Published by
Kennikat Press Corp.
Port Washington, N.Y./London

Library of Congress Cataloging in Publication Data

Main entry under title:
The War generation.

(National university publications)
Includes bibliographical references and index.
1. Veterans—Addresses, essays, lectures.
2. Veterans—Societies, etc.—History—Addresses,
essays, lectures. I. Diehl, James M. II. Ward,
Stephen R.
UB356.W37   355.1'15   75-15596
ISBN 0-8046-9101-0

CONTENTS

THE WAR GENERATION

When troubles rise and the War is nigh,
God and the Soldier is the cry.
When War is over and the troubles righted,
God is Forgotten and the Soldier slighted.

—Traditional verse

STEPHEN R. WARD

INTRODUCTION

In a century that has already witnessed two world wars, two major conflicts in Asia, and countless smaller military enterprises, a legacy of millions of men who served their individual countries in the armed services survives as a continual reminder of national policies won and lost. As citizens they were expected to go willingly, or by force if necessary, to bear arms in defense of their nation's interests. Most interrupted schooling, jobs, and family responsibilities to accept the obligation. Once thrown into the scene of combat, they observed first-hand the holocaust of battle, the waste of human life, and forged a bond of comradeship which only the environment of prolonged terror could create. When the fighting ended, they returned to civilian pursuits to be honored by some, pitied by others, and forgotten by most.

Over the centuries returning war veterans have aided in causes bent upon disruption of the state. Julius Caesar settled ex-legionnaires on land in the empire, partly as repayment for services rendered and partly to keep them available, away from the center of political power, if he needed them. The houses of Lancaster and York made use of veterans of the French wars in the civil conflicts of fifteenth-century England. Napoleon recalled his demobilized army when he escaped from Elba. The use and abuse of veterans throughout history by politicians, ex-generals to ex-corporals, and others has been a common theme, yet our understanding of the veterans' role in the upheavals in which they participated is vague. This volume of essays proposes to investigate the activities, philosophies, and organizations of ex-servicemen who fought in the First World War and who emerged into peacetime societies of five major belligerents of that war: Britain, the United States, France, Italy and Germany.

3

The First World War was the first of its type in the history of warfare. Nations mustered an entire generation into a war of attrition which lumbered on without result. The extended conflict resulted in astronomical casualty lists which staggered the imagination of even the most prescient observers. Long wars produce an adverse effect upon combatants and noncombatants alike, but the 1914–18 war laid a unique heritage upon the survivors. The static fronts in almost every theater of combat, frustration with the lack of progress, isolation from reality among the soldiers, trench warfare, and suicidal assaults against formidable defensive bulwarks introduced a special psychology to the whole course of the war. Trench warfare pitted opposing forces in such close proximity that a feeling of mutual hostility sometimes developed toward all those who remained outside. It was this type of unrelenting peril not often experienced in warfare that left its mark on a generation of young survivors.

This war generation had been born in the last two decades of the nineteenth century, a time of great change in most countries. Syndicalism, economic stress, political instability, and a host of domestic and foreign crises had dominated the period leading up to the outbreak of war. The ideologies of the Left made advances in pre-1914 Europe, but the end of the war signaled a reaction from the Right in the form of fascism and totalitarianism. The war also toppled most of the monarchies, and in their place new democratic governments struggled to survive. Discharged servicemen, many of whom had observed political discontents and upheavals develop within their own ranks during the war, emerged into societies struggling with extremes. In this environment of uncertainty the role of ex-servicemen became a source of concern to those who sought stability, and a source of potential power to those who encouraged disruption.

The authors of these essays were asked to analyze the activities of war veterans during and after the First World War. A broad latitude was suggested to allow each essayist opportunity to uncover facets which he deemed most significant. The principal theme, however, is that of the war's impact upon this generation of veterans and, in turn, the impact these men had on the aftermath of war. This theme should result in a better perception of veterans as a group within a society and a fuller understanding of the interwar period. In a comparative setting the theme and goals are most clearly presented. More questions than answers may result, however, from this study. For example, if the nature of the First World War provided commonality of stimulus for all participants, was there a commonality of response? Did a monolithic body of men, regardless of nationality, emerge from this war stamped out of a single mold and endowed with collective insights occasioned by their participation in the war? Or were they, in fact, products of their particular national experiences whose actions throughout the interwar era should be judged against that background rather than against the experiences of war?

The answers to these questions are not easy generalizations; but it should be noted that most of the contributors agree that the actions of veterans were determined more by their national experiences than by the impact of the war experience. One needs only to contrast the openly activist Italian and German ex-servicemen with their generally passive British and American counterparts to reach that conclusion. The turmoil present after the war in the first two countries differed markedly from the relative domestic tranquility of the latter two.

Many generalizations have been made regarding the topic of veterans in texts and monographs dealing with the interwar period. One impetus for this work stems from an article in the *Revue française de science politiques* by René Remond entitled "Les ancien Combattants et la politique." This 1955 article surveyed the French, German, and American veterans' experiences following the First World War, pointing out ideological similarities. Remond concluded, quite correctly, that organizations of veterans enlisted only a minority of eligible ex-servicemen. However, among the several organizations, regardless of nationality, he observed a single thread of conservatism. He proposed two hypotheses in answer to that observation: one, that outside parties, particularly capitalist and industrialist interests, aided veterans' groups and won them over to the conservative cause; and second, that a "veterans' spirit" was present within organizations which took them naturally toward rightist ideology. Remond argued that the second hypothesis was the more plausible. Those who joined organizations were themselves nostalgic for the former military life and sought to perpetuate it. The "military way" then became the standard not only for military affairs but for civilian life as well. Quick, forthright decisions, obedience to orders, and selfless commitment to higher causes became purposeful aspirations for the society at large. This approach proved antagonistic to parliamentary procedure and democratic rule, but veterans' organizations, according to Remond, tended to view society in this manner. He concluded that while veterans often claimed to be apolitical, "the veteran mentality is indeed one of the modern components of the psychology of the man of the Right."

Remond's arguments were doubtless meant to encourage further study of the political persuasiveness of the Right among veterans. The essays in this volume both support and contradict his theories. In each nation organized veterans embraced rightist causes, but a closer analysis reveals that some organizations and movements of veterans supported the causes of the Left. This feature was particularly observable in Europe during and immediately after the war. Only a minority of veterans inclined to the Left, but these examples challenge previously held beliefs. Left-leaning organizations rejected the "military way" and advanced the "unity of the trenches" idealism with which they sought to create a better society by transplanting the brotherhood and comradeship ideal into postwar society. The conclusion might be drawn, then, that rightist veterans used both the concepts of the "military way" and the "unity of the trenches" to solidify support, while those of the Left spoke of unity and comradeship but used it in the broader idealistic context and as an example of the spirit which could produce a more perfect society in peacetime.

There were several similarities among ex-servicemen, regardless of nationality. One example was the rise of leaders who presented themselves as the embodiment of the war generation. Personalities as diverse politically as Oswald Mosley in Britain, Adolf Hitler in Germany, Henri Barbusse in France, and Gabriele D'Annunzio in Italy emerged in the postwar period to direct their comrades. The interesting feature is that all used similar rhetoric, albeit expounding differing political views, to develop veterans' support behind them. The element of activism was another important similarity. In every country incidents of militancy occurred, either initiated by veterans on their own behalf or joined by them in support of other causes. They showed a willingness to contest government decisions or, in some instances, to bring down the establishment. Specific acts of militancy varied only from country to country at different times. Italian, British, and German veterans experienced a militant period immediately following the war, while French and American veterans carried out disruptive tactics well into the 1930s.

Another consistent feature among veterans, regardless of nationality, was the penchant to become factionalized. All countries produced several veterans' organizations with varying goals and beliefs. Each of these organizations struggled to advance membership and generate causes that would place it first. This rivalry brings into question whether a true sense of comradeship actually existed. Unity within a given organization was far more prevalent than a united front of veterans within a nation. In Germany, for example, ex-servicemen appeared united against the Weimar Republic, yet disagreed as to how it should be dismantled. In France, the point is made that during the riots of 1934 Parisian veterans turned against the Daladier government yet failed to secure the support of their former comrades in the provinces.

There are as many differences among veterans of the 1914–18 war as there are similarities, although the differences are more subtle than sharply defined. In practically every instance discharged servicemen reflected the national condition of the interwar period. There was greater radicalism among them in Germany and Italy than in Britain and America because veterans were drawn into the domestic conflicts of their separate national environments. The D'Annunzio-Mussolini struggle described in the Italian essay shows clearly how two sides vied for a single body of men after the war. On the other hand, American veterans experienced very little divisiveness. Several British organizations were formed initially but then united in 1921 to form the British Legion, while the French and Germans maintained several organizations into the 1930s. Differences can also be seen on the matter of political participation. The Germans, French, and Italians took more political gambles than British and American veterans. The latter two acted politically, as will become evident, but their positions were more tentative and less partisan. One will find it more valid to compare individual national experiences than to make overall generalizations. Italian veterans reacted in a certain manner to their circumstances while Americans responded to their own national conditions. One of the principal themes that emerge in this work is that veterans reflected the social, economic, intellectual, and political divisions within their individual nations. The war experience may have set them apart as a separate group, but the comment in the French essay that French veterans were more conditioned by the Third Republic than by the First World War holds true for the others as well.

While outside forces often determined the thrust of most veterans' movements, there were also internal forces that unified them. Unity could be most easily achieved on issues that dealt solely with pensions, bonus payments, treatment of disabled men, and the belief that the state and public owed them more gratitude than they received. Each essay discusses governmental treatment of ex-servicemen, and the point is made that governments generally failed to comprehend the magnitude of their responsibilities toward veterans after the war.

Ironically, German veterans of the Weimar era received the best treatment of those surveyed in this volume. Governments also failed to understand the potential force that united veterans could bring to bear upon national policy. The immediate postwar period provided the best opportunity for veterans to affect policy, and the worst was over if governments survived the challenge. The depression of the thirties brought forth another crisis which allowed a rekindling of the veterans' spirit, and unity was forced on internal and external issues that challenged the state. Again, stable governments were able to survive while weaker ones (the Weimar Republic in particular) did not. Throughout the interwar period efforts were made to tie internal unity into international organizations. Henri Barbusse proposed an international union of ex-servicemen shortly after the war, and the former Allies organized the Fédération Interalliée des Anciens Combattants in the mid-1920s. Both these groups sought to improve international relations through a body of united veterans. The latter organization not only demonstrated the universal ideal for peace expressed by those who experienced war, but also the general trend of the times reflected in the Locarno Pact of 1925. This type of progressive desire on the part of ex-servicemen was indeed typical up to the outbreak of the Second World War. It belies, in part, the belief that veterans must always be classed as conservative and reactionary. Few wanted to return to the pre-1914 world. Perhaps some of their solutions must now be judged as reactionary, but at the time they seemed visionary. Above all, they believed that their generation deserved an opportunity to lead the country. Statements cited by several contributors indicate that the war generation thought the older generation should relinquish its leadership to younger men with vision.

These essays are meant to stimulate inquiry and to offer interpretations on a topic that has often been subjected to superficial generalizations. No attempt has been made to survey the entire interwar period or to cover all facets of veterans' activities within that period. Instead, each author has attempted to focus upon events, ideologies, and personalities that shaped the veterans' experience in their particular country. There is general agreement among the contributors that unity among veterans proved difficult to sustain as the war experience receded into the past. Consequently, their impact upon the interwar period was limited to those moments in which they challenged the state on issues that affected them as civilians and veterans. Greater unity among them resulted in those countries that lacked stable governments and thus enabled a grievance group, such as veterans, to develop a broader spectrum of support from which to pressure for change. What is imparted in these essays, then, is not only a study of veterans, but in the wider context, a case study of group action and its effect upon the national community.

ONE   STEPHEN R. WARD

GREAT BRITAIN:
Land Fit for Heroes Lost

For all its experiences with wars during its long history, Great Britain found many aspects of its participation in the First World War unprecedented—none more so than that of its employment of manpower. Traditionally, its role in past Continental conflicts, most notably the wars of the French Revolution and Napoleon, had stressed the contributions of superlative seapower, finance, and a small expeditionary force. But in 1914, accepting the guidance of Field Marshal Lord Kitchener, it offered its allies not only its preponderant seapower but also a mass army fashioned on the Continental scale as well. To mobilize the manpower required, it resorted successively to two methods: first, voluntary recruiting; and then, as the crisis of the war became more acute, conscription. Never in history had any nation rallied so many men by free volunteering. But inevitably in 1916 it was forced to break with precedent and impose conscription. Yet even before conscription was instituted, and before the war ended, Britain began to face another burden it had never experienced. Returning soldiers—volunteers and conscripts—began to flow back to civilian life. Whereas the military establishment had been staggered by the rapid expansion of recruits, the civilian establishment reeled under the quantitative impact of veterans returning from Britain's most devastating conflict.

As early as 1915 servicemen began returning to find a rude shock awaiting them. Both government and public were unprepared to assist their ex-servicemen in readjusting to civilian life. Most of the men discharged during the war had suffered wounds that disqualified them from further combat duty. They required special care and assistance. Recruiters had made enticing promises, assuring those who enlisted in the wave of patriotic enthusiasm that their country would adequately compensate them. Yet those who returned found that preparations had not been made to assist the growing number of men who had become the casualties of a long war. A small staff of army personnel administered veterans' rehabilitation in the buildings of Chelsea Hospital (dating from the seventeenth century), and the impact of army casualties overwhelmed it. Here hospital administrators had become accustomed to administering on the small scale of the old professional army, and their compassion toward those who represented a new breed of civilian enlistees proved sadly deficient. As one man associated with administration of pensions wrote, "It was thought necessary to guard against malingering in the old Army, [and] the general rule was to give the benefit of the doubt to the state rather than the man."[1]

Unlike most of Europe and America, Britain had had no previous experience with mass civilian armies. Like the commanders in the field, who contended with the tactical and strategic implications of a mass army, the government at home failed to grapple with growing numbers of returnees from the front. Those who were disabled soon realized that the government which had so avidly encouraged enlistment proved incompetent to minister to those who suffered the consequences of war. During the first two years of the war, neither the army nor the government had projected programs to rehabilitate disabled men, secure employment for them, or establish training centers for the limbless ex-servicemen. Those who returned during the early years of the war were treated in the manner of their predecessors —the professional army of the past. The realization that Britain had placed an army of civilians in the field had not yet been accepted. Old army men had remained passive and accepted whatever might be doled out; but the new army of citizens refused to suffer quietly.

In early 1916, under pressure to secure manpower for the army and in order to establish procedures for selective induction of military manpower from war industries, Parliament passed two conscription acts, a significant departure from Britain's historic reliance upon a volunteer army. Compulsory service virtually eliminated the dilemma whether to serve or not to serve. Moreover, as one writer suggests, the draft "brought first-hand experience of the horrors of war, not just to a couple of million volunteers and horny-handed professionals, but willy-nilly to twice as many ordinary unadventurous civilians—one in three of the adult male population.''[2] It also removed the responsibility of service from individuals and imposed it upon the government. The excuse could no longer be offered that men who joined the army did so at their own risk. The state had assumed the burden of after-care for those who served in the armed forces, although at first it did not appear to recognize this responsibility.

James M. Hogge, a Liberal member of Parliament for East Edinburgh, was one of the first to call attention to the effect of conscription on those servicemen who had been disabled in the war. Before the war he had been associated with B. Seebohm Rowntree's statistical surveys of poverty in England, and this experience had alerted him to the conditions of life often experienced by dependents whose husbands and fathers had enlisted. In 1915 he sponsored the Civil Liabilities Act, which provided payment by the state of debts incurred by servicemen whose army pay did not match their expenses incurred prior to enlistment.[3] At the same time he inaugurated a column in the *Edinburgh Evening News* in which he answered queries regarding payments and gratuities available to servicemen and their families.[4] Most M.P.s had not bothered with these matters, assuming that the army took care of its own. Hogge, on the contrary, rightly believed that the size of the army and the scope of the war had touched every home in Britain. He recognized the special consequences of war for the civilian population, particularly for those who joined the services. He believed that the state, not the army, must accept responsibility for the welfare of ex-servicemen and their dependents. The conscription acts, which he had opposed, convinced him that the state had assumed a moral and legal obligation to those who volunteered or were compelled by statute to serve in the armed forces.

When David Lloyd George formed his coalition government in December, 1916, he invited Hogge to join the newly formed Ministry of Pensions in a subordinate capacity. By that time Hogge was recognized as the best-informed M.P. in regard to pensions, rehabilitation of ex-servicemen, employment opportunities, and all matters regarding the rights of veterans. Lloyd George, however, did not offer him the portfolio. Instead, the post went to George N. Barnes, a Labor M.P., in order to afford balance for the composition of his 1916 coalition.[5] It was pointed out later that ''on his merits he [Hogge] ought to have been the Minister of Pensions, and would have been but for the requirements of political strategy."[6] But Hogge was denied the post, and he refused a subordinate role.

Hogge sensed the extent of disenchantment building among veterans in 1916. Already one small organization of ex-servicemen had been formed in Blackburn, called the Blackburn Society (later to be called the National Association of Discharged Sailors and Soldiers), and other local groups were being formed to work for the improvement of benefits and pensions for ex-servicemen. One month after he rejected Lloyd George's offer, Hogge formed his own organization, the Naval and Military War Pensions League. The organization proposed to eradicate inequalities that appeared in granting and administering pensions, to organize all ex-servicemen and their dependents, to protect their future interests, and to represent those interests in Parliament.[7] The announcement of the new League was greeted with apprehension, especially by those who sought to keep veterans' issues out of politics. In addition, many disliked Hogge because of his radical politics and penchant for unpopular causes. He supported Scottish nationalism, opposed conscription, and openly associated with conscientious objectors. He and his constant companion in these causes, William R. Pringle, M.P., drew hostility (i.e., "Progge and Hingle," "reprehensibles of the House," and the like) from many quarters. Hogge inflated his unpopularity by associating with veterans and organizing them into a league that might result in an American-style Grand Army of the Republic on British soil.

Virtually alone, James Hogge established the pattern for organized veterans' activities in Britain that continue to the present day. He derived his precedents from the experiences of trade-union pressure politics and earlier models of European and American veterans' groups. Neither the army nor the government had made conscientious efforts to improve conditions among ex-servicemen; therefore, Hogge planned to initiate improvements through pressure applied to Parliament. During the first months of 1917 Hogge spoke throughout the country and established new League branches. He warned that veterans' pensions would be "one of the biggest questions of the immediate future."[8] He insisted that ex-servicemen should not become charity cases supported by local philanthropy and inadequate royal warrants issued at the pleasure of the monarchy. Veterans were entitled to pensions, and Parliament must be pressured to make pensions a statutory right for all disabled ex-servicemen. The League planned to inform the public of conditions among ex-servicemen and their families, but in 1917 the progress of the war itself completely absorbed both the government and the public as well. It was difficult for a small segment of society to generate support and interest. Veterans needed a sensational issue in order to expose the government's neglect of its returning heroes, most of whom were disabled. Fortuitously for Hogge and ex-servicemen, the government provided them with an issue.

On the western front the offensive tactics—especially the Somme battle—of 1916 had taken a tremendous toll of lives, and replacements had become difficult to secure by early 1917. Neville Chamberlain, then acting as director of national service, suggested that the Military Service Acts (conscription) be amended to allow a special review of all men born between 1895 and 1898 to determine whether all those eligible were serving in the armed forces.[9] The War Cabinet quickly authorized such a bill, and it was placed before Parliament.[10] Many of Britain's youth had been rejected in the course of physical examinations during 1914 and 1915 when standards were high, and the bill, the Military Service (Review of Exceptions) Bill, authorized medical tribunals to examine all eligible men with an eye to induction into the service. Hogge raised objections in Commons and attempted to attach an amendment calling for the statutory right of pension; but it failed, and the bill became law on April 5, 1917.[11]

The Review of Exceptions Act provoked an immediate response from ex-servicemen, who organized demonstrations against the law and the manner in which it was implemented. The government planned to recall all men under 31, including those who had already served. Those who were employed in munitions factories and government offices retained their exemptions. The undercurrent of discontent that had been building for two years finally erupted. London's East End became the center of activity, and the local ex-servicemen's club organized a protest demonstration at Trafalgar Square a few weeks after the law was passed. Hogge addressed the demonstrators and disclosed that one ex-soldier had been ordered to report to his local medical tribunal when he had only one eye.[12] In fact, tribunals recalled many veterans, most of whom had been officially declared disabled. Nevertheless, Sir Auckland Geddes, director general of recruiting, issued instructions that "there is not a man who is able to make a living in ordinary life who cannot be employed in the Army somewhere,"[13] and zealot tribunal members followed his instructions by declaring disabled men fit for service.

Hogge wasted no time in exploiting the controversy over the Review of Exceptions Act. Soon after the Trafalgar Square demonstration he and Pringle, together with veterans from Poplar (London), formed a new organization called the National Federation of Discharged and Demobilized Sailors and Soldiers, which replaced Hogge's League.[14] It accepted the purposes of the League completely but used the Review of Exceptions Act as a rallying issue to enroll members to lobby for the law's repeal. It organized demonstrations, held open meetings, sent members into movie houses to speak during intermissions, and tub-thumped the cause throughout the country. The campaign produced a slogan, "Every man once before any man twice," that coupled condemnation of the act with the government's alleged favoritism toward its civilian employees.[15] Hundreds joined the new organization, but the government refused to repeal its act.

In early June, however, a by-election was called at Abercromby (Liverpool), and Conservatives nominated as their candidate Lord Stanley, eldest son of Lord Derby, the new secretary of state for war. Stanley, then serving in the army, announced his candidacy on June 14, but the predicted uncontested by-election became a two-way contest when Frank Hughes, a one-legged former army private sponsored by the Federation, entered the race.[16] Hughes's appearance in the campaign produced consternation among Liverpool Conservatives and misgivings in London. For a time Derby considered withdrawing his son's name rather than have him face the prospect of encountering angry ex-servicemen at the polls.[17] For Hogge the by-election presented a unique opportunity to expose the government's ungracious behavior toward ex-servicemen. Lord Derby, not his son, became the center of attention. Hogge claimed that it was Derby who "has climbed to his position by breaking every pledge he has made, and we are going to fight him on his home ground."[18] Derby became the symbol of both the government and the army, the two institutions primarily responsible for the unsatisfactory treatment of veterans.

Liverpool was a fortified city in the Derby political fiefdom of Lancashire. The Federation's candidate proved inept and unpromising, but the issue he represented transcended his personal limitations. The government had become estranged from its former soldiers, and Hughes characterized his campaign as a battle of democracy against privilege and called attention to soldiers' dependents who pleaded for bread while war profiteers waxed rich.[19] The Federation's campaign succeeded in attracting the War Cabinet's attention. The Cabinet first conceded that those veterans who had served overseas and were discharged on medical grounds would be exempted from examination.[20] Then two days before the Abercromby poll, Andrew Bonar Law, chancellor of the exchequer and Leader of the House of Commons, secured the Cabinet's approval for a committee of inquiry to investigate the implementation of the Review of Exceptions Act.[21] This announcement, declared one of Liverpool's leading Conservatives, had "a wonderfully good effect [on the election outcome]."[22]

Hughes lost the by-election, but ex-servicemen had won their first battle with the government. A committee of inquiry, meeting shortly after the by-election, substantiated charges that had been leveled against the tribunals. Disabled men had been called before tribunals, and orders had been issued to search for malingerers who had been unjustifiably discharged. The committee's recommendations were quickly implemented; medical review boards and examinations were removed from War Office control and placed under civilian management.[23] The army had failed to recognize that it was dealing with a citizen army whose veterans had generated sufficient criticism and publicity to effect a reversal of policy that discriminated against them. The success of the first engagement encouraged Hogge to suggest that war veterans could "take into their hands the destinies of the Empire at any moment they chose to do so,"[24] but such euphoric predictions, in time, proved unjustified. Yet a limited victory had been achieved through the pressure of a new organization that proposed to mobilize public opinion on behalf of ex-servicemen and to improve benefits for those who had risked their lives in the trenches.

The Federation rapidly expanded into a significant organization. Even though Hogge was a Liberal, he kept the organization nonpartisan. To some it appeared that he planned to launch a powerful movement that might threaten established political institutions. But the coalition spirit dominated wartime politics and many frowned upon factional activities. Nevertheless, while the consequences of one large veterans' organization might be advantageous to its members, government leaders disliked the prospect of one or two large groups dominating the postwar period. Hogge's presence seemed especially ominous because he was a radical. Therefore, a new organization, associated with Lord Derby, emerged to counter the Federation.

Derby's apprehension with regard to the mood of ex-servicemen in 1917 had been building for some time. The unpleasant experience at Abercromby was for him but one example of a new condition within the army which he detested. He respected the old army as an institution because professionals knew their place and one could depend upon disciplined troops. He revealed his contempt for the attitude of the new army in a memorandum to the War Cabinet in July:[25]

> In view of the fact that the Army of today is by no means as highly disciplined as that in existence before the war, and also that classes of men serving at the present moment include individuals of every shade of education and opinion, it is probable that the movement to encourage soldiers to take part in political questions will be fanned by certain factions for their own ends.

Derby found it difficult to accept the new conditions. Instead of a professional institution closely scrutinized by Parliament, the army had become a microcosm of the whole society. He realized that the army's character had changed, but he refused to sanction attempts by self-interested politicians to stir up veterans who appeared to offer easy prey to the machinations of demagogues. A clear threat had been presented, and Derby acted quickly to curtail it.

A few weeks after Abercromby, Derby and two other Conservative M.P.s, John Norton-Griffiths and Wilfred Ashley, projected a new organization more in keeping with their political philosophy. Their proposal was presented for approval to the Army Council, which replied that "the formation of an organization of this character would serve the useful secondary purpose of countering the activities of the promoters of other associations amongst soldiers and ex-soldiers which avowedly have for their object an organized opposition to authority."[26] In addition to securing Army Council support, Derby alerted the War Cabinet to his plans.[27] He then enlisted Liberal and Labor M.P.s to endorse the new group. In November the Comrades of the Great War was officially constituted at Mansion House, London, in ceremonies that included the Lord Mayor, several peers, and army officers.

British ex-servicemen had been organized in unprecedented fashion even though another year would pass before the war ended. Political figures representing the major parties had lent their support and, in some cases, dominated the groups. The Comrades was not an official government organization, but its intentions soon emerged, as one former Comrade admitted, "to keep us nicely dusted."[28] The conflict over control of veterans mirrored the struggle taking place in British society as a whole. The Comrades associated with privileged classes who were endeavoring to maintain their political and social superiority, while the Federation and Association represented the egalitarian forces within the society, which sought to undermine control by the feudal structure. The approaches of Hogge and Derby personified the conflict. Hogge urged veterans to place their grievances before Parliament and the public, while Derby favored a paternalistic approach. Nevertheless, both men appeared to be altruistic in their motives, even though personal disappointments motivated their initial participation in veterans' affairs. Baser motives, however, drew two other men, Horatio Bottomley and Noel Pemberton-Billing, into the movement.

Bottomley's association with the servicemen's community began early in the war. As publisher of *John Bull,* a national weekly newspaper devoted to sensationalism and addressed to working-class Britons, Bottomley wrote a column devoted to answering service-related problems encountered by servicemen and their families. His column antagonized the army at first, because he published letters from servicemen criticizing government policy and army life. It was soon realized, however, that servicemen vented their frustrations through these letters and were usually placated by the thought that *John Bull* was working to solve their problems. Bottomley's image as the servicemen's friend was well established by 1917. He portrayed himself as a tireless worker on behalf of servicemen, although skeptics produced a 24-page blank pamphlet, entitled "What Horatio Bottomley Has Done for His Country and the Wounded Soldiers."[29]

In late 1917 Bottomley sought to advance himself as a leader in the veterans' movement. When the Comrades was formed, open rivalry developed among the three organizations. The competition offered Bottomley an excellent opportunity to ingratiate himself. He published a series of articles in *John Bull,* purporting to expose the Comrades as the vehicles of a plot by privileged classes to undermine pressure tactics employed by the Federation. Soon after the articles appeared, Bottomley began negotiations with the Federation, promising it £2,000 annually provided that he be allowed to control the organization's treasury and establish a consultative committee with "civilian representation."[30] The Federation at first accepted the offer to meet the Comrades' challenge. This marriage of convenience soon faltered, however, because of personal and political differences between Hogge and Bottomley. Hogge's pacifist nature contrasted sharply with Bottomley's rigid patriotism. It soon became apparent to Federation members that Bottomley sought only to dominate the organization for his own personal aggrandizement. Within a few months Bottomley's money was returned, and the Federation narrowly escaped an ill-fated association.

Another individual who flirted with the veterans' movement was Noel Pemberton-Billing. He had been elected to Parliament in 1916 as an Independent from East Hertfordshire following a career in the Royal Navy. In 1917 he founded the Vigilante Society to improve the morals of the country and to assure "purity in public life." During the summer of 1918 he was sued for libel by a dancer named Maud Allen, and the trial provided Britons with comic relief from the arduous war. In his society's periodical he had accused Miss Allen of perverting prominent Englishmen by giving a dance known as "The Vision of Salome" and organizing what Pemberton-Billing described as "the cult of the clitoris."[31] During the trial he claimed further that the Germans kept a list of 47,000 Englishmen who were morally corrupt. Many political and prominent personalities were listed. He asserted that the Germans used this information to secure military secrets. The trial created a sensation, and Pemberton-Billing was acquitted. Many considered him a hero even though he was discredited by most of his colleagues.[32]

Throughout 1918 he attended several meetings of the Federation and expressed the opinion that the veterans' movement would become a powerful force in the future. To this end he formed the Silver Badge Party in the summer of 1918. His association with this organization was kept secret, and only evidence from those who knew him linked him to the organization.[33] Nevertheless, the party's views were closely tied to those of the Vigilante Society. It favored imperialism, announced publicly that all members must be born of British parents,[34] and it was secretly antisemitic.[35] The relationship between Hogge and Pemberton-Billing remains vague; but in 1918 Hogge began calling for veterans' candidates to contest the first general election after the war, and Pemberton-Billing evidently decided to form a separate veterans' party for that purpose. The Silver Badge party emerged in the summer of 1918 as a party of conservative, activist veterans seeking entrance into Parliament to express their viewpoint.

The arrival of the Silver Badge party raised to four the number of distinct veterans' organizations, none of which had been formed by veterans themselves. The Association could claim grassroots origin, but even it had begun with Trades and Labor Council support. Two of the four groups were led by men considered untrustworthy by the establishment. Bottomley's unsuccessful attempt to join with the Federation exemplified veterans' susceptibility to exploitation by personalities of questionable repute. Derby left the Comrades to the trusted leadership of Wilfred Ashley, but political activism among the rest aroused suspicion and prompted governmental surveillance of ex-servicemen in 1918 to discover the motivations behind their activities.

Actually, veterans were only one of several groups monitored by government intelligence agents. German spies, Bolshevik sympathizers, Independent Labor party members critical of the war effort, anticonscriptionists, and many others came under scrutiny of the Special Intelligence Branch of the Home Office. Several reasons seemed to prompt surveillance of ex-servicemen. The association with Hogge and other radicals no doubt bothered many who, as the Army Council had done, warned against "promoters" of an organization "which avowedly have for their object an organized opposition to authority." Opinions were expressed that radicals had infiltrated the veterans' movement and were distorting the crusade for improved benefits into a political issue. One report sent to the War Cabinet read:[36]

> There is a determined attempt among the extremists to capture the Discharged Soldiers' Federation, and the demand for better allowances should be very carefully watched, for if they succeed in getting the soldiers and their wives to back them, they will be a very numerous and dangerous body.

Political involvement among organized ex-servicemen was neither desired nor to be tolerated. Those who observed veterans' activities became worried and therefore overracted by spying on the movement. Close surveillance had been maintained of army morale throughout the war, and a watchful eye on veterans seemed logical. Furthermore, the Bolshevik scare emerged in 1918. Aside from the precedent of events in Russia, Workers' and Soldiers' Councils had been formed in several British factories, and activism among veterans suggested a similar development there. A growing opinion that veterans would undermine political stability after the war stirred politicians to action. One M.P., Montague Barlow, who had served on committees dealing with problems of ex-servicemen, expressed apprehension that higher pensions would soon become a political issue. He told the House of Commons in July, 1918, that if this eventuated, politics in the postwar period would follow the same course as in the United States in the 1870s and 1880s.[37] Later he warned the War

Cabinet that "the danger is that bodies of discharged men will go from one candidate to another at the election and put their support to the highest bidder in the matter of pensions."[38] Activism among veterans, whether it hinted at revolution or simply meant participation in political pressure tactics, portended unpleasant prospects for those who observed the trend in 1918. Revolution was not necessarily feared, but American-style organized pressure suggested grim prospects. Barlow's remarks in Commons spurred his colleagues to agree to a moratorium on discussion of pensions during the next general election. The resolution was approved over Hogge's objections, 132–34, but its passage did not prevent veterans from making pensions an issue.[39]

By mid-1918 the Federation had begun plans to contest certain constituencies as soon as a general election was called. Some candidates would be supported by the National Executive Council while others would be nominated and financed by local Federation branches. When Lloyd George dissolved Parliament a few days after the Armistice, therefore, the Federation was prepared to act. It was joined by the Association and the Silver Badge party in proposing nearly fifty candidates throughout Britain. Most of the prospective candidates were combat veterans, although some nonveterans were suggested as well. By nomination day on December 5 the number had been reduced to twenty-nine men contesting English constituencies only, but the Silver Badge party failed to nominate a single candidate.[40]

This so-called coupon election of 1918 returned Lloyd George as leader of a coalition government. Yet, for all their efforts, veterans succeeded in electing only one member to Commons, Robert Barker, running under the Association banner. They had participated in the constitutional process and had pled their cause before the electorate. Even though the percentage of electorate casting votes was the lowest in twentieth-century British history (58.9 percent), British voters clearly indicated that postwar unity was more important to them than the needs of interest-group candidates. Despite defeat, ex-servicemen again counted victories on issues such as the statutory right of pension. The argument put forth to the electorate emphasized that if workers received compensation for injuries on the job, then disabled servicemen deserved compensatory allowances as well. Candidates who faced veterans in the constituencies conceded this principle, and even those not facing veterans' candidates agreed that as soon as Parliament convened they too would support it.[41]

The end of the war signaled a new pattern of activity among veterans. Britain had won the war, but the long conflict had damaged the economic and social fabric of the country. Lloyd George promised during the election to make Britain a "land fit for heroes to live in," but his government was unable to provide it. Those who remained in the army disapproved of the structured demobilization procedure the government had planned, and rioting broke out among the troops in the first two months of 1919. The plan was then altered, but for the demobilized soldiers it represented yet another example of bureaucratic bungling which their discharged predecessors faced during the war. The discontent expressed over the demobilization process signified a radical temper among soldiers that promised future difficulties. The combination of an unpopular demobilization scheme, administrative confusion regarding absentee general election ballots which resulted in only 20–30 percent voting among servicemen, Bolshevik and socialist agitation, and disappointment at conditions found at home, sparked defiance among them.

The majority of returning servicemen in 1919 expected to resume careers left behind when they enlisted or were drafted. While the government offered gratuities and limited unemployment payments to demobilized servicemen, it had not prepared programs in areas of education, apprenticeship, and employment assistance. Many who took jobs in the economic boom of 1919 lost them when the boom ended in early 1920. Young men who had been conscripted or had dropped out of school to join suffered most from the industrial conditions of the 1920s. For the next ten years these two groups contained the highest incidence of unemployment. Lloyd George had hoped to revive Britain's agricultural production by settling thousands of veterans on small farming projects, but this scheme failed. Emigration to other parts of the empire proved more successful, and by early 1921 over 42,000 ex-servicemen had emigrated, primarily to Canada and Australia.[42] But these programs did not alleviate domestic unemployment, and few solutions were forthcoming. Separation pay and an unemployment donation for twenty-six weeks following demobilization became the only sources of income. By March, 1919, over 300,000 veterans received out-of-work donations.[43] In May the War Cabinet decided to extend the donation an additional thirteen weeks to ameliorate discontent, and further extensions came later in the year for the same reason.[44]

Disillusionment settled in quickly for a large portion of returning servicemen. Instead of jobs, new opportunities, adequate housing, and other benefits, too many of them found the lines at the local labor exchanges crowded with former comrades. Some believed that a collective idealism had been developed in the trenches and that veterans would emerge dedicated to changing society. Perhaps more correctly, there was a collective antipathy, as C. G. F. Masterman had suggested, toward "meddling politicians" and those who had mismanaged the army and reconstruction.[45] Nevertheless, these were the survivors who had offered more of themselves than any British generation before them, and they deserved to lead the country in the postwar period. E. L. Woodward suggests, however, that this generation, which was his, was denied its proper role:[46]

> I knew well enough that for my generation, and particularly for those of us who had been in the army, the war was an experience likely to dominate the rest of our lives. . . . I thought the future was in our hands; that we should get the support of those immediately younger than ourselves; that our elders would listen to us, and, for very shame, be ready to give us a directing control over the management of affairs. These hopes have been disappointed. . . . The men who came back from the war have counted for less, perhaps, in the political life of their country than any generation during the last two or three centuries.

Woodward's evaluation represented his personal view, but his belief that his generation had somehow been denied opportunity to lead was shared by many of his comrades.

For both practical and idealistic reasons, veterans became discontented. Those who wished to express their disenchantment in truculent fashion found an excellent outlet in 1919. The syndicalist spirit of direct action, manifest in strikes, shutdowns, and boycotts, encouraged veterans to become radical. Revolutionary fever was everywhere, and prospects for revolution in Britain had not been so promising since the Chartist period in the early nineteenth century.[47] George Lansbury, editor and publisher of the *Daily Herald,* wrote that "in London we found ourselves surrounded with *agents provacateurs* and spies. I attended three secret meetings of ex-soldiers and officers; at each of these proposals for secret arming and secret organising for revolution were proposed."[48] Reports from the Home Office's Special Branch confirmed the surge of radicalism.

The increased number of incidents, not only among veterans but among other groups as well, caused the Home Office to establish a new Directorate of Intelligence in the spring of 1919 devoted to full coverage of revolutionary movements. The Directorate began submitting weekly reports to cabinet ministers, entitled "Report on Revolutionary Organisations in the United Kingdom."[49] One of the first crises that confronted it grew out of the formation of the Soldiers', Sailors' and Airmen's Union. The organization was inspired by the *Daily Herald,* whose opposition to British intervention in Russia prompted several attempts to sow insurrection in the army. The SSAU proposed that Derby men* still in service who had enlisted for a period not to exceed six months after hostilities ended should demobilize themselves on May 11.[50] Quick response by the Directorate of Intelligence stopped the attempt, but the incident exposed the extent of syndicalism within the service ranks.[51]

In the same month two new veterans' groups emerged, in London and Glasgow. The first called itself the National Union of Ex-Servicemen, which had been formed from the Federation's radical fringe in London's East End. The Federation had depended upon this area for much of its manpower in London demonstrations during the war, but the organization's determination to remain nonaligned politically caused a splinter group to form. The NUX proposed to join with the Labor party so as to unite ex-servicemen with a party committed to social change. Unlike those groups formed prior to the armistice, the NUX pointed to the need for change in the society as a whole rather than improvements for veterans as a distinct group. They stated:[52]

> We are ex-servicemen, *but we are also citizens,* and we realise that our general interests are inseparably bound up with the general interests of the people as a whole. We shall therefore support the Labour party in its efforts to improve conditions under which all people—including ourselves—must live.

The NUX represented the first attempt by veterans to form an organization without assistance from outside groups or political personalities. It was begun by two former Federation men, A. E. Mander and John Beckett, both of whom were Labor party supporters but independent of the party organization.

The same was true of the second organization, the International Union of Ex-Servicemen (or International Ex-Servicemen's Union)

---

*Derby men were serving-age personnel who attested their willingness to serve in the armed forces in 1915. Lord Derby was responsible for the program, and many enlisted under this scheme prior to the passage of conscription.

which was formed by dissident Federation members in Glasgow. The IUX received aid from such nonveterans as suffragist Sylvia Pankhurst and a Scottish revolutionary named John Maclean, but it began as a grassroots organization. Unlike the NUX, the IUX favored revolution; it proposed to become a "revolutionary socialist organisation [standing] alone among ex-service organisations in this country in its determination to fight for the overthrow of the capitalist system. . . ."[53]

The creation of these groups emerged from the belief that the older, prearmistice organizations had not pressed their demands for a new order after the war. The NUX and IUX charged that the prearmistice groups were controlled by the establishment and led by nonveterans. In 1919, however, changes were taking place. The Comrades' membership began to challenge the authority of its executive, and the Association dismissed its labor representatives. Hogge became the assistant whip of the Independent Liberal party and left the leadership of the Federation to a veteran, T. F. Lister. The Federation experienced a strong push from its members to take direct action. In May a demonstration was held in Hyde Park on behalf of improved benefits for disabled men. After several vehement speeches, the men began marching toward Westminster and Parliament. Police threw up barricades and battled with demonstrators for almost an hour. When order was finally restored, a deputation presented a list of grievances to James Hogge. A few days later an indignant House of Commons debated the grievances, and Hogge was chastised by his colleagues, who leveled allegations of demagoguery and of picking the pockets of ex-servicemen against him. One ex-soldier M.P., Austen Hopkinson, a Federation member who had contested the 1918 election as an Independent, warned the Commons that the organization had become a "huge, shapeless, menacing mass without policy and without ideals, a prey to ambitious politicians and on the verge of collapse into anarchy."[54]

Some evidence of anarchy could be found within the veterans' movement in 1919, but lack of direction plagued it more. Too many interlopers, for good reasons and ill, had intruded their personalities in the organizations. The temporary swing to the left in 1919 came naturally in a period of general unrest, but neither the NUX nor the IUX produced notable results. The IUX formed only thirteen branches, centered in the economically depressed area of the Clyde River in Scotland.[55] The NUX aligned with the Labor party in December, 1919, but only as an auxiliary organization.[56] The socialists simply missed their opportunity. Walter Kendall writes in *The Revolutionary Movement in Britain, 1900–21*:[57]

> If socialist influence had existed within any of the services, if there had been, for example, a common front between the soldiers and sailors in 1918–1919, if the soldiers and sailors had launched a coordinated movement, or established links with any of the trade union struggles pending, then the whole future of the state might well have been called into balance.

But the socialists and trade unionists failed to secure an alliance. Differences between servicemen and the Independent Labor party had erupted during the war because the ILP had not supported the war effort. Workers' and Soldiers' Councils, formed in 1917 and 1918, were poorly organized and promptly suppressed by the government.[58] Relations between trade unions and veterans deteriorated rapidly in 1919, and ill will continued throughout the 1920s. Many job-conscious unions refused to admit new memberships until the economy showed signs of improvement. Apprenticeship programs and training for ex-servicemen were curtailed for fear that new men would dilute the work force. Finally the Labor party itself failed to seize the initiative to win veterans, as evidenced by its lax attitude toward the NUX. This mistake was not repeated during and after the Second World War.

The summer and fall of 1919 marked the high point of radicalism and disruptive tactics among ex-servicemen. The Federation, NUX, and IUX boycotted nationwide peace celebrations in July in order to draw attention to conditions among disabled men. In several towns and cities where peace celebrations were held, riots and arson blighted the festivities. The Directorate of Intelligence reported that "during the past week there have been signs from every part of the country of a spirit of discontent and unrest that may break out with serious consequences at any moment."[59] Apparent government apathy, unemployment, and alienation prompted disorders and gave rise to schemes that preyed upon the unsatisfactory conditions veterans faced. The NUX sponsored a "back pay" issue, which would offer a bonus to ex-servicemen if accepted by Parliament. To raise the money to implement this panacea, it proposed a war tax on profiteers and landlords who had accrued wealth while servicemen were fighting and dying to defend them.[60] The NUX even took the issue into a by-election in Manchester, where the Labor candidate promised to push "back pay" through Parliament. Neither he nor the issue succeeded, but political analysts were quick to point to the danger of demagogic promises in campaigns and reminded readers of similar practices followed by American politicians in the 1880s.[61]

Finally, in late 1919, the government produced its long-awaited reforms for treatment of ex-servicemen: pensions were made a statutory right; programs were inaugurated to hire disabled men and train them for new positions; labor exchanges were ordered to give veterans preferential treatment; local war pensions committees were directed to include veterans as members; and many agencies, public and private, were asked to assist ex-servicemen. Most of the grievances put forth by the prearmistice groups were redressed. Veterans submitted testimony to the Select Committee on Pensions, and it accepted most of their suggestions. By the end of 1919 passion had cooled among a majority of veterans. Issues remained, but the government no longer viewed appeals to the public with indifference. In 1920 only a few acts of radicalism took place. The IUX occupied vacant houses, took over a few public buildings and labor exchanges, but mass demonstrations and direct-action episodes declined. Even so, one intelligence agent wrote that the potential for violence among ex-servicemen remained. "In the event of rioting," he wrote, "for the first time in history the rioters will be better trained than the troops."[62]

By 1920 all veterans' organizations suffered from lack of interest and finances. Trade declined, and industrial production slowed as the postwar boom ended. Six separate organizations (an Officers' Association was founded in 1920) could offer nothing new in the way of grievances and issues that would keep the membership alive. Further separateness and isolation foreshadowed the demise of the entire movement. In the spring of 1921, after several months of negotiations, the Association, Comrades, Federation, and the Officers' Association united to form the British Legion. The NUX and IUX refused to join and disbanded by the end of the year.

The period 1916–21 represented the most significant phase in the history of British veterans. For the first time ex-servicemen had organized to promote their own interests and, in some cases, the interests of society at large. They had made a lasting impression on the public and government in terms of grievances that required attention. The Great War had brought change in several areas of society, and the fact that a new special-interest group had emerged from the war was ultimately recognized as healthy and proper. The separate organizations had often pursued different issues and goals, but similarities among them far outweighed differences. Rivalry in recruiting followers and the pursuit of new issues kept the movement lively, but by mid-1920 membership declined as interest waned, and the enthusiastic campaigns for increased benefits, rehabilitation of the disabled, employment, and other issues lost out to civilian concerns of family, job, and home.

When the British Legion emerged in 1921, competition ended and it became the veterans' spokesman. Field Marshal Haig, who retired from the army with an earldom, became president, and the Prince of Wales, also an ex-serviceman, became patron. The choice of Earl Haig was probably wise, but he disliked political activism. Further, he distrusted the conscript, as a communiqué in 1917 reveals:[63]

> The influence of these men and their antecedents generally are [sic] not such as to foster any spirit but that of unrest and discontent; they came forward under compulsion and they will depart the Army with relief. Men of this stamp are not satisfied with remaining quiet, they come from a class which like to air real or fancied grievances, and their teaching in this respect is a regrettable antidote to the spirit of devotion and duty of earlier troops.

He insisted that politics and partisanship, except on those matters dealing with ex-servicemen, must end if the Legion was to survive. Members of earlier organizations agreed to bury the divisions of the past and avoid controversy in the future. The organization began with only 18,106 members in the first year, and it required a concerted drive for membership to increase it to over 100,000 by the next year. Once during the interwar period (1938) membership exceeded 400,000, or approximately 10 percent of all eligible veterans.[64] Other organizations, such as the Labor League of Ex-Servicemen (1927) and the Limbless Ex-Servicemen's Association (1932), were formed, but none offered a threat to the Legion's predominance. It became a consensus organization, which avoided controversial domestic and foreign issues. A House of Commons branch was formed in 1922 with member M.P.s from each party. The M.P.s maintained party discipline, except on a few occasions when party policy on veterans' issues differed from the Legion position.[65]

Conditions in Britain in the 1920s were not conducive to the development of a forceful veterans' movement. By the time the British Legion was founded, many of the hard legislative battles had been fought—and mostly won. Legion leadership did not develop significant new issues even though many activists from the predecessor organizations had joined it. On the occasion of the general strike in 1926, some members of the Legion leadership issued a call for members to be prepared to assist the government, but they received a strong reprimand from working-class members.[66] After that incident the organization's leadership declined to issue statements that might alienate sections of the membership. Its loyalty to Britain was presupposed, and no campaigns displaying excessive patriotism or supernationalism characterized it. The Legion and ex-servicemen in general reflected the society of the 1920s that preferred Stanley Baldwin and "safety first" to David Lloyd George's dynamism. Apathy settled upon them as it did on the rest of society. Few politicians made promises of special treatment, and Legion political arm-twisting was kept minimal. Contemporary writers disagreed as to whether veterans would become converts to Labor or reactionaries; however, when predictions were tested, veterans spread themselves across the political spectrum. The war had changed very few politically—it only reinforced views previously held. One writer noted that though many had suggested that the war would bring about a "fusion of the classes," it was remarkable "how quickly the heroes of the trenches have again become 'the lower classes.'"[67] The decade following the war produced few examples of veterans taking a role in British affairs or having any impact on the society. Assimilation seemed far more characteristic of the war generation than any other trait.

One interesting development that affected this generation was the legend or myth of the Lost Generation. Proponents claimed that a whole generation of British talent and leadership had perished in the war. The notion developed that the cream of British manhood had volunteered in the early stages of the war and that few had survived the holocaust. This belief reflected both England's preference for elitist leadership and its reaction against lackluster military direction during the war. Even David Lloyd George, hardly a protagonist of aristocratic rule, perpetuated this thesis in his memoirs when he wrote that "the volunteers of 1914 and 1915 were the finest body of men ever sent to do battle for Britain. Five hundred thousand of these men, the flower of our race, were thrown away on a stubborn and unintelligent hammering away at what was then an impenetrable barrier."[68] Britain mourned this loss perhaps more than any other country participating in the war, even though her percentage of combat deaths was lower.[69]

This thesis persists even today, but the tedious reiteration of it during the interwar period placed a heavy burden on the survivors.[70] Veterans agreed that their lost comrades should be memorialized, but questioned whether the nation should devote so much of its time and treasure to the dead, while survivors stood in unemployment lines. A Labor M.P. named Jack Jones was ushered out of the House of Commons in 1922, shouting, "You are a dirty lot of dogs slobbering over dead soldiers and starving the living ones,"[71] and Peter Deane wrote in a 1930 article in the *Nation* that "we talked of the Lost Generation, and made sure that it was lost. . . . We neglect the survivors as though they did not exist, and keep our pity for the dead who have no need of it."[72] Another veteran, Robert Graves, whose *Goodbye to All That* still ranks as one of the best autobiographies of disillusion, harbored similar feelings. He wrote:[73]

> I also suggested that the men who had died, destroyed as it were by the fall of the Tower of Siloam, were not particularly virtuous or particularly wicked, but just average soldiers, and that the survivors should thank God they were alive, and do their best to avoid wars in the future. . . . The ex-service men had not been too well treated on their return, and liked to be told that they stood on equal terms with the glorious dead.

The Legion exploited public lamentation for the dead by embarking on an enterprise that memorialized the fallen and assisted the living. The project began with the idea of selling poppies on Armistice Day in commemoration of those who had died. John McRae's famous wartime poem "In Flanders Fields" set the tone for the project, and the Legion began its first sale in 1921 with great success. Receipts grossed over a half million pounds annually, and over half went to schemes benefiting ex-servicemen throughout the country.[74] The sale of poppies kept the Legion solvent, and it provided a constant source of income that advanced the organization and financed programs to assist veterans and their families.

Some of the money gathered went to unemployment assistance, yet it proved insufficient to compensate increasing joblessness among ex-servicemen. A revival of trade promised by postwar politicians never materialized. By the late 1920s 80 percent of the unemployed between the ages 30 to 34, and 58 percent of the total unemployed, were veterans.[75] Efforts were made to institute compulsory employment of veterans, as was common among several European countries, but the government resisted. Parliament even refused to require private enterprise to employ a percentage of disabled men, although a scheme of voluntary employment called the King's National Roll was instituted. Britain's economic shortcomings never reached crisis proportions, but ex-servicemen experienced more than their share of the misery caused by the economic doldrums of the 1920s. Those who had hoped that war's end would bring a brighter future found instead a bleak period of economic stagnation and political lethargy. The flood of war books in the decade after the war ended represented only one articulated symptom of a generation discouraged by the world it had inherited. British veterans were not the only former soldiers to feel discontented, but their total integration into civilian life prevented them from doing anything about it.

The world depression of the 1930s worsened conditions in Britain, although the impact never staggered her as much as it did other countries which had reached greater heights of prosperity in the 1920s. Unemployment never fell below one and a half million in the interwar period, and after ten years statistics on unemployed veterans ceased to be singularly significant in the face of unemployment among the general population. Young men who had come of age in the 1920s faced even greater hardships than those who had served in the war. Ramsay MacDonald's Labor government assumed office in 1929, promising to cure unemployment. The prime minister appointed a special task force under the Lord Privy Seal, J. H. Thomas, to find solutions quickly. One of the members of Thomas's committee was an ex-serviceman, Oswald Mosley, chancellor of the duchy of Lancaster. The committee produced nothing tangible, and its inaction motivated Mosley to offer his own solutions, including early retirement. When his scheme was rejected by the party in May, 1930, he resigned his post. Unemployment soared to two and a half million by the end of the year, and Britain seemed headed for a crisis.

Oswald Mosley was born into an aristocratic family in 1896 and educated at Winchester and Sandhurst. He joined the Royal Air Force in 1915, served with distinction, and was invalided out in 1916. An aristocrat who survived the war, he entered Parliament as a Conservative in the election of 1918, only to become an Independent in 1920. In 1924 he joined the Labor party and was considered by many to be one of its most talented young members. But his confrontation with the party in 1930 marked a turning point in his career. Had he swallowed his pride and stayed with Labor, he might well have reached the heights of political power, as did his successor to the post of chancellor of the duchy of Lancaster, Clement Attlee, another ex-serviceman. Instead, Mosley struck out on his own and formed the New party to contest the election of 1931; but this venture failed. The New party had initially attracted many outstanding young Englishmen, including Harold Nicolson; but the next year, inspired by Italy's experience under Mussolini, Mosley formed the British Union of Fascists to provide the authoritarian power to carry out changes he believed were urgently needed.[76]

The BUF did not enlist veterans exclusively, although it was, as one writer suggests, "a movement of youth. . . . They saw themselves as the postwar generation come to sweep away the corruption of the past and often referred to themselves as a movement of ex-servicemen."[77] According to Mosley, veterans expected progressivism following the First World War. The social program outlined by Lloyd George found favor among them, but it was frustrated by older politicians who stood in the way of young men and new ideas. In a 1921 speech as president of the League of Youth and Social Progress, Mosley gained attention by referring to elder politicians as "these old dead men with their old dead minds embalmed in the tombs of the past."[78] The "safety first" psychology of the 1920s, he declared, represented an anachronism in a world that had changed dramatically. The economic crisis of the early 1930s proved that the old ideas no longer worked. Mosley had joined the Labor party because it stood for progressive thought; but when hard decisions were needed, it too failed to produce a "new deal." The one recourse left seemed to be to break away from the shackled political system and change Britain by novel means. Mosley thought that the ingredients necessary to generate support lay open to him in 1932. The country had reached a crisis in its economy, and new leadership was needed. His former comrades suffered from unemployment, lack of housing, and the general disregard of the rest of society. As their leader, he would at least fashion the land fit for heroes.

Among the earliest converts to Mosley's movement were veterans who had played an active role in earlier veterans' groups. John Beckett, a former Labor M.P., had served as a local leader in the Federation and later cofounded the National Union of Ex-Servicemen. Another veteran, Henry H. Beamish, had been associated with the Silver Badge party and was a Federation candidate in the election of 1918. Beamish, according to Colin Cross's work on British fascism, was responsible for developing the issue of antisemitism in the BUF, and as a former Pemberton-Billing lieutenant he came to the BUF with sufficient experience. Other veterans in leadership positions included Geoffrey Dorman, Charles Bethnick-Budd, Arnold Leese, and G. K. Chesterton. The movement developed its strongest support in London's East End, where the Federation and NUX had originated and thrived. On many issues the IUX and NUX shared similar philosophies with the BUF. Although politically poles apart, the organizations held that Britain's social order must be altered and that veterans must play a leading role in effecting change. All were antiestablishment. "This is the generation," Mosley reminded his former comrades, "which faced 1914, which in four years made an effort which staggered the world. . . . THIS IS OUR GENERATION NOT THEIRS. We have fought and conquered while they muddled and destroyed."[79]

Mosley tried to rekindle the spirit of unity that had developed in the ranks of the army during the war. His fiery speeches in open-air forums offered a spectacular witness to his ability as an orator, demagogue or not. He called upon ex-servicemen and the public at large to initiate a national renaissance. His leadership and his generation, he promised, would replace mediocrity and lethargy. "Through and beyond the failure of men and of parties [he told them], we of the war generation are marching on and we shall march on until our end is achieved and our sacrifice is atoned."[80] He pointed to the menace of communism, the need for economic reforms and a rebirth of national spirit. His artful presentation of the argument charmed some veterans and younger men into following him. Like Hitler, he offered uniforms, food, and living quarters for his paramilitary organization known as the Blackshirts. The organization provided protection for him during mass rallies and public meetings, but bully tactics carried no appeal in Britain and soon discredited the movement. In 1936 the government passed and enforced the Public Order Act which forbade political uniforms and processions of the type Mosley had organized. In 1940 he and several hundred followers were interned.

Oswald Mosley represented the politicized activism of disillusionment. The movement he set in motion openly called upon former comrades to change the fabric of the society which they had defended over a decade earlier. "This was the most complete companionship I have ever known," Mosley wrote, "except in the old regular army in time of war. . . . We were banded together by the common danger of our struggle and the savage animosity of the old world toward us."[81] Yet despite Mosley's enthusiasm, the BUF never exceeded 20,000 members and declined rapidly as international threats and domestic criticism made it an unpopular movement by the late 1930s. The stable British could no more accept the demagoguery of the Right than they could tolerate the tyranny of the Left. Furthermore, Britain did not experience the great economic and political crises that other countries faced during the 1920s and 1930s. Attempts to generate a crisis, as in the case of Mosley, failed to convince the great majority of British people. The threat of communism in England was far less than Mosley imagined at the time; but if the economic crisis had worsened and unemployment had increased, the opportunity for the success of his movement, he believed, might have been enhanced.[82]

It is reasonable to conclude that although Mosley embodied certain features common among ex-servicemen—a unifying experience, aspirations for a better society, and justice for their common cause—he placed too much reliance on the theory that war had shaped his former comrades into a generation of men perpetually angry at a world they did not make. Indeed, the opposite resulted. Veterans remained inner-directed from the inception of their earliest organizations and continued this policy in the British Legion. Organized veterans, those who continued to hold to the "unity of the trenches" ideal, rejected issues and positions not directly related to their interest groups. The two exceptions, the NUX and IUX, flourished momentarily in the highly charged atmosphere of immediate postwar Britain, but ultimately succumbed when their causes failed to enlist large memberships. The British Legion accepted inner-direction because the full membership willed it so. The Legion advocated peace and advanced its cause through international organizations of veterans, but this policy followed government overtures along the same line. By the time Mosley issued his challenge to his generation to save Britain from itself, the great majority of veterans neither believed him nor cared to solve Britain's dilemma in the manner he proposed.

The impact of British veterans on their country and on their times was therefore minimal. This result was predictable in a country where constitutional processes were well established and the desire for order was uppermost in the citizens' minds. From the beginning veterans proposed to educate the public and the government on their responsibilities to those who defended them. Though many orators and writers proposed that veterans deserved the right to determine Britain's future in the postwar period, veterans themselves opted for assimilation rather than leadership. Some might suggest that this conclusion supports the assertion that all the leaders died in the war; but if that were true, one must account for survivors such as Attlee, Eden, Macmillan, Mosley, Graves, Sassoon, Dalton, and countless others who assumed leadership roles, deferred in the case of three prime ministers, to the post–Second World War period. Former trade-union leader and cabinet minister John Burns put it correctly when he designated the new army of the First World War "the people in khaki."[83] They were citizens first. The military mystique in Britain, if it existed, lost its charm during the Cromwellian era. Even the persuasive powers of an Oswald Mosley could induce no more than a handful to follow him. Veterans were periodically pulled left and right, but in the end, as with the rest of the country, they eschewed extremist solutions. They did not ask for much in return for their services, and they did not get much. They were promised homes but did not receive them. They were promised full employment but did not obtain it. They were promised a "land fit for heroes to live in," but they knew better than to expect it. It was left for another war generation to reap what its predecessors had sown.

NOTES

1. Arthur Griffith-Boscawen, *Memoirs* (London: John Murray, 1925), p. 196.

2. Arthur Marwick, *The Deluge* (New York: Norton, 1970), pp. 79–80.

3. *Papers by Command,* Cd. 8249, Regulations Made by the Civil Liabilities Committee (HMSO, 1916), p. 1.

4. *Edinburgh Evening News,* October 29, 1928. Obituary.

5. Thomas Jones, *Lloyd George* (Cambridge: Harvard Univ. Press, 1951), pp. 97–98.

6. *The Ex-Service Man,* September 25, 1918.

7. *The Times,* January 16, 1917.

8. Ibid., January 22, 1917.

9. War Cabinet Minutes, W.C. 39, appendix 1, January 19, 1917 (Cab. 23/1).

10. Ibid., W.C. 55, 4, February 5, 1917 (Cab. 23/1).

11. Parliamentary Debates, House of Commons, 92 (March 29, 1917), 643.

12. *The Times,* April 23, 1917.

13. Cd. 8617, Select Committee on the Military Service, *Review of Exceptions Act* (HMSO, 1917), p. xii.

14. Graham Wootton, *The Official History of the British Legion* (London: Mac-Donald & Evans, 1956), p. 2.

15. Interview between the author and J. R. Griffin, November 7, 1966, London. Griffin served as general secretary to the Federation and later to the British Legion.

16. *Liverpool Echo,* June 21, 1917.

17. Stanley Salvidge, *Salvidge of Liverpool* (London: Hodder & Stoughton, 1934), pp. 158–59), and Randolph Churchill, *Lord Derby, King of Lancashire* (New York: Putnam, 1960), p. 276.

18. *The Times,* June 25, 1917.

19. *Liverpool Echo,* June 22, 1917.

20. W.C. 166, 1, June 20, 1917 (Cab. 23/3).

21. W.C. 169, 14, June 26, 1917 (Cab. 23/3).

22. Salvidge, p. 160.

23. Cd. 8617, pp. 9, vi.

24. *Stratford Express,* July 25, 1917.

25. War Cabinet Paper, G.T. 1522, July 26, 1917 (Cab. 24/21).

26. Army Council Minutes, War Office Papers, precis 878, August 1, 1917 (W.O. 163/22).

27. W.C. 222, 5, August 22, 1917 (Cab. 23/3).

28. Interview between the author and A. Kennedy Hunt, April 22, 1967, Cardiff, Wales. Hunt was the organizer of the Comrades' Plymouth branch in 1918.

29. Julian Symons, *Horatio Bottomley* (London: Cresset Press, 1955), pp. 167–68, 191. Bottomley was convicted of fraud in 1922 and sent to prison for five years.

30. Minutes, National Executive Council, National Federation of Discharged and Demobilized Sailors and Soldiers, March 5, 1918.

31. Anon., *Verbatim Report of the Trial of Rex v. Noel Pemberton-Billing* (London: Imperialist Press, 1918), pp. 481, 22.

32. A. J. P. Taylor, *English History, 1914–45* (New York: Oxford Univ. Press, 1965), p. 103.

33. Interview between the author and J. R. Griffin, November 21, 1966, London. The silver badge was issued to ex-servicemen to be worn on civilian clothes as recognition of honorable discharge.

34. *The Times,* November 30, 1918.

35. Pemberton-Billing's own antisemitism is documented in several public statements and pamphlets. In 1919 he published two pamphlets, entitled *The Jews' Who's Who* and *Jewry Uber Alles;* cf. Home Office, Directorate of Intelligence, "Report on Revolutionary Organisations in the United Kingdom," Cabinet Paper C.P. 70, November 6, 1919 (Cab. 24/92). In addition, H. H. Beamish, treasurer of the Vigilante Society, and the Silver Badge party's secretary were brought to court on a libel suit by Jewish M.P., Sir Alfred Mond, for placing a poster in a store window which read, "Sir Alfred Mond is a traitor—he allotted shares to the Huns during the war"; cf. *The Times,* December 6, 1919.

36. Home Office, Special Intelligence Branch, "Fortnightly Report on Pacifism and Revolutionary Organisations in the United Kingdom and Morale Abroad," War Cabinet Paper, G.T. 6079, October 21, 1918 (Cab. 24/69).

37. *Parl. Debs.,* House of Commons, 108 (July 10, 1918), 333.

38. War Cabinet Paper, G.T. 6284, letter from Montague Barlow to Andrew Bonar Law, November 13, 1918 (Cab. 24/69).

39. *Parl. Debs.,* House of Commons, 108 (July 10, 1918), 401.

40. See my article "The British Veterans' Ticket of 1918," *Journal of British Studies,* 8 (November, 1968): 162.

41. Graham Wootton, *The Politics of Influence* (Cambridge: Harvard Univ. Press, 1963), p. 206.

42. *Parl. Debs.,* House of Commons, 138 (February 28, 1921), 1436.

43. 18th Abstract of Labor Statistics as quoted in A. C. Pigou, *Aspects of British Economic History, 1918–25* (London: Macmillan, 1947), p. 218.

44. W.C. 574, 2, May 30, 1919 (Cab. 23/10).

45. C. G. F. Masterman, *England after the War* (New York: Harcourt, Brace, 1923), p. 20.

46. E. L. Woodward, *Short Journey* (London: Faber & Faber, 1942), p. 114.

47. Walter Kendall, *The Revolutionary Movement in Britain, 1900–21* (London: Weidenfeld & Nicolson, 1969), p. 187.

48. George Lansbury, *My Life* (London: Constable, 1928), p. 189.

49. Basil H. Thomson, *The Scene Changes* (London: Collins, 1939), p. 421.

Thomson held the post of director of intelligence in this period.

50. *Daily Herald,* May 9, 1919.

51. See my article "Intelligence Surveillance of British Ex-Servicemen, 1918–20," *Historical Journal,* 16 (March, 1973): 184–85.

52. *Statement of Aims and Policy,* pamphlet 1 (NUX), n.d. [1919].

53. *Workers' Dreadnought,* 6 (January 3, 1920): 1591.

54. *Parl. Debs.,* House of Commons, 116 (May 28, 1919), 1270-78.

55. Directorate of Intelligence *Report,* G.T. 8192, September 18, 1919 (Cab. 24/88).

56. *Glasgow Herald,* December 25, 1919.

57. Kendall, p. 194.

58. The army was instructed to use King's Regulation 451, which prohibited soldiers from taking part in demonstrations and political meetings. The War Cabinet planned to stop a large Workers' and Soldiers' Council meeting in August, 1917, with this regulation; cf. W.C. 207, 1, August 8, 1917 (Cab. 23/3).

59. Directorate of Intelligence *Report,* G.T. 7790, July 24, 1919 (Cab. 24/84).

60. *Commonweal,* May 3, 1919. An ex-M.P., R. L. Outhwaite, devised this scheme, which the NUX adopted. Outhwaite evidently gleaned most of his ideas from Henry George's *Progress and Poverty.*

61. *Manchester Guardian,* September 24, 1919 and *The Times,* October 7, 1919.

62. Directorate of Intelligence *Report,* C.P. 1830, September 2, 1920 (Cab. 24/111).

63. War Cabinet Paper, G.T. 6874, October 3, 1917 (Cab. 24/75).

64. Wootton, *Official History,* appendix 5, p. 305.

65. Brunel Cohen, *Count Your Blessings* (London: Heinemann, 1956), p. 62. Cohen lost both legs in the war and played an important role in founding the British Legion. He was a member of Parliament during most of the interwar period.

66. Wootton, *Official History,* pp. 89–90.

67. T. H. Proctor, "The Motives of a Soldier," *International Journal of Ethics,* 31 (October, 1920): 45.

68. David Lloyd George, *War Memoirs, 1918* (Boston: Little, Brown, 1936), p. 336.

69. Walter F. Willcox, "Military Losses in the World War," *Journal of the American Statistical Association,* 23 (September, 1928): 305.

70. This belief is expressed in many works covering the interwar period. Reginald Pound's *Lost Generation* (London: Constable, 1964) is a clear defense of the premise and typical of the generally held belief. An argument against it is included in Corelli Barnett's *The Collapse of British Power* (New York: Morrow, 1972), pp. 425–28.

71. *The Times,* November 29, 1922.

72. Peter Deane, "The Tragedy of the Survivors," *Nation and Atheneum,* 48 (October 18, 1930): 103.

73. Robert Graves, *Good-bye to All That* (Garden City, N.Y.: Doubleday, 1957), 2nd rev. ed., p. 318.

74. Wootton, *Official History,* appendix 13, p. 317.

75. R. C. Davison, *The Unemployed* (London: Longmans Green, 1929), p. 94.

76. Nigel Nicolson (ed.), *Harold Nicolson: Diaries and Letters, 1930–1939* (New York: Atheneum, 1966), pp. 114–15.

77. Colin Cross, *The Fascists in Britain* (New York: Barrie & Rockliff, 1963), p. 67.

78. Sir Oswald Mosley, *My Life* (London: Nelson, 1970), pp. 101, 128.

79. Cross, pp. 120, 128.

80. Mosley, p. 70.

81. Ibid., p. 306.

82. Ibid., pp. 308–10.

83. British Museum, *John Burns Diary,* January 7, 1919.

TWO   DONALD J. LISIO

UNITED STATES:
Bread and Butter Politics

American doughboys of the Great War left the field of battle in triumph and with a special sense of identity reserved only for those who had undergone the unique experiences of war. Unlike those earlier soldiers who had "liberated" Cuba and the Philippines at the turn of the century, they were battle-toughened veterans returning home from a world war which many believed had saved democracy. Of course, thousands had never left the United States, but they too had trained in earnest for combat, and whether the mud in which they had crawled was foreign or domestic, the experiences of army rigors made a deep and lasting impression on them. For many the war had been the greatest adventure of their lifetime, a youthful crusade of lasting importance. Without any doubts the nation at first hailed them as victorious heroes, the proud warriors who had saved the Allies, strengthened democracy, insured peace for future generations, and brought glory and honor to the nation.

This euphoria was short-lived. Soon after the armistice President Wilson's disastrous demobilization policies quickly promoted a sharp recession. Thousands of soldiers were suddenly discharged, war contracts canceled, and the war prosperity gave way to a sharp if somewhat brief recession. Not long after the homecoming parades the soldiers' return to civilian life became a rude and bitter experience.[1]

At the same time Attorney General A. Mitchell Palmer promoted a national panic by massive arrests and deportations of "aliens" and "radicals" who, he insisted, were internal subversive forces bent upon fostering communism, revolution, or other antidemocratic activities. The red scare of 1919–20 seared the nation with the fear that its enemies were closer at hand than they had realized. Race riots, red hunts, housing shortages, and unemployment contributed to a mood of disillusionment and anger. That mood soon became more deeply entrenched as opponents of Wilson's internationalism and the League of Nations rent the country and accelerated the souring reaction toward the costly war and its futile results.[2]

Returning to civilian life was a more difficult transition than was generally appreciated, especially for men who had suddenly acquired a new, potent sense of identity. First as brave warriors and then as heroes they felt a special duty to promote and preserve the love of country which had nourished them during difficult times of military life. Shocked and angered by the intense transitional dislocations, they joined in the new crusade against "foreign" ideologies, aliens, and radicals. They and their buddies had fought, had been wounded, and had died to defeat these elements. The Bolsheviks were especially hated, not only for their ideology but also because they had pulled Russia out of the war and thus allowed the Germans to throw many more thousands of troops against the western front. Many American soldiers had been killed or wounded as a result.[3]

Patriotism was a very serious subject to the ex-soldiers. Yet, as usual, it was difficult to define. The concoction usually included love of country and its democratic heritage mixed with devotion to capitalism and belief in the moral superiority of American people. As often as not, however, the veterans' definition of patriotism—much like that voiced by other groups—emerged in negative terms, emphasizing that which the veterans' organizations opposed, feared, or hated.[4] The Veterans of Foreign Wars, for example, took direct action against radical meetings, while the Legion opposed strikes by organized labor, and both launched vigorous Americanization programs in the public schools.[5] Little, if anything, was said against the Ku Klux Klan, which flourished in the 1920s, perhaps because the beliefs and hatreds expressed by these organizations were often too similar to warrant fine distinctions. Keeping foreign ideas and elements out of the public schools, deportation of radical aliens, respect for the flag and for the ideals of the nation blended into a virulent jingoism.[6] Thus, veterans both reflected and promoted this unfortunate wave of misdirected fervor, and to it they added a special ingredient of their own.

Because they had trained for war and had fought for democracy, they conceived of themselves and of their organizations as especially qualified to pass upon and promote the definitions, practices, and rituals of patriotism. War was abhorrent to them, yet they also considered it an indisputable fact of life. Therefore, rather than supporting pacifists' efforts to insure peace, they advocated a strong, ever-ready defense. Pacifist groups flourished in the 1920s and 1930s, and to many of the men who had fought in the world war, they were, almost by definition, un-American. Veterans' groups suggested that the ex-servicemen, more than ordinary citizens, were the real experts on war and peace, and they denounced the "dubious patriotism" of pacifists who suggested alternative avenues of international relations. Only a strong army, navy, and reserve force would avoid the woeful lack of preparation and hasty training which had proven so costly in the war.[7]

The veterans advertised these attitudes with Preparedness Day parades and Memorial Day extravaganzas, which rivaled the traditional Fourth of July celebrations. Another favorite tactic was the surge of marches staged to counter and to detract from the radical May Day celebrations. Great pressures were brought on local officials to prevent or seriously impede the May Day demonstrations. Indeed, the suppression of "radicalism" and fomenting of proper attitudes became consuming goals for many ex–fighting men. Parades in villages and cities stressed the virtues of martial spirit, heroism, and love of country, which the veterans strove to inculcate in the youth of the nation.[8]

Much, of course, has been written about the superpatriotic activities of veterans' groups. Yet their effectiveness is difficult to assess. Undoubtedly they helped to promote the immigration restriction laws of the 1920s, yet these discriminatory laws stopped far short of the Legion's demand for a complete ban on all immigration for five to ten years and a lengthening of the naturalization process. Equally evident was their spirit of intolerance toward "radical" ideas, assemblies, and demonstrations. Most successful apparently was the intense pressure on public educators to Americanize the nation's youth in ways acceptable to them.

Yet one must be careful not to ascribe too much influence to the veterans. Organizations such as the KKK, National Civic Federation, DAR, and a host of lesser superpatriot groups were also active in promoting the same concepts and fears. In the two decades between the two great wars, the Legion and the VFW as often reflected as molded attitudes. Moreover, the hatreds and intolerance sanctioned and popularized by the federal government through the Espionage Act of 1917, the Sedition Act of 1918, and the Creel Committee can hardly be underestimated in their long-term influences. Nor had the actions of Attorney General Palmer done anything to counter or reduce these attitudes. The Sacco–Vanzetti case of the 1920s, the Mooney case of the 1930s, and the continuing trials of the Scottsboro boys symbolized the lasting imprint of the earlier hysteria and the widespread fears and hatreds at every level of American society.

While the veterans' organizations certainly supported and perpetuated a narrow, intolerant superpatriotism, and must not be excused for their misguided zeal, many of their efforts to lead the nation were repeatedly and decisively defeated. The American people and Congress continually rebuffed a strong army and navy and the Legion's special appeal for universal military training.[9] Lip service to patriotism and colorful parades aroused enthusiasm, and the harassment of unpopular groups remained in vogue, but other issues which were especially important to the veterans received very little support.

In fact, during the 1920s and 1930s Congress drastically reduced the armed forces and refused to consider universal military training seriously. Instead, world arms-limitation treaties and efforts to outlaw war became genuinely popular. The United States joined in international treaties limiting its naval forces, while President Hoover vigorously put forth a host of further arms-limitation measures at the Geneva Disarmament Conference in 1932.[10] By the middle and late thirties as European democracies crumbled in the wake of economic catastrophe, and during the rise to power of militant Fascists and Nazis, the Legion and VFW supported the neutrality acts designed to prevent United States entry into still another world war, though defense continued to be their chief refrain.[11] It was the events in Europe and the Far East, not the veterans' foresight, which finally moved the nation toward some degree of preparedness. By 1940 the veterans' groups united in their opposition to the neutrality acts. Yet, as in World War I, the United States entered World War II woefully unprepared.

For all the publicity, ballyhoo, and jingoism promoted by the Legion and the VFW, there is considerable evidence that many of their most important demands were not especially popular during the 1920s and 1930s, except among their own immediate constituency. It was one matter to attend patriotic picnics and denounce communism, but as with their demands for expensive defense programs, the nation's political leaders also opposed the still more expensive legislation for veterans' benefits. Too often veteran legislative power has been exaggerated.

Liberals and radicals attacked the vets for their anti–civil libertarian positions and their smug jingoism. At the same time many conservatives increasingly joined in the attack, but for different reasons. Their complaints centered on bills for veterans' benefits, which they considered extraordinarily expensive. Indeed, liberals and conservatives alike soon denounced the one-time heroes as "mercenaries of patriotism."[12] And to many ex-servicemen who sought pensions and hospital benefits, the nation seemed to respond with the attitude "better dead than in bed." Thus, while few opposed the ex-doughboys' loud and fervent jingoism, at the same time many abhorred the benefits which they sought.

Ironically, it was these very expensive benefits which were the most progressive and just measures advocated by veterans' groups, measures for which they were to fight their longest, toughest, and most successful battles. In the halls of Congress, on the bread-and-butter issues of veteran benefits, the Legion and the VFW revealed the central purpose for their existence and made their most lasting and positive contribution to the nation. Locked in an ideologically naive view of patriotism and its enemies, they nonetheless became tough-minded legislatively, and in the field of veterans' benefits they awakened the nation to the ongoing expenses of war.

Congress knew at the outset of World War I that more adequate provisions for the care of veterans was essential. In contrast with its actions in previous wars, especially the Civil War and the Spanish-American War, Congress quickly passed special legislation in 1917 to provide life insurance for all veterans willing to pay the low-cost premiums. It also guaranteed that wounded and disabled veterans would have hospitalization and pension benefits upon their return.[13] Unfortunately, medical knowledge and education in 1917 was in an admittedly deplorable state, and the army's hastily contrived medical-records system was so inadequate that disabilities often went unrecorded and legitimate benefits were thus denied.[14]

Moreover, laws providing for hospitalization and pension benefits were often written without knowledge of the types of medical problems likely to arise during the war. Even if one were not actually wounded, life in the trenches was a unique nightmare, and sickness and disease proliferated. What in fact constituted a legitimate basis for hospitalization was thus often vague and ill defined, especially for those diseases encountered during the war which did not necessarily manifest themselves until after the soldier had been discharged. This was true of such diseases as tuberculosis, neuropsychiatric disorders, and ailments of a "constitutional nature."[15]

In addition to having complicated medical problems, the disillusioned and frustrated returnee often felt quite sensitive about the low pay scale which Congress had enacted. Civilians during the war had prospered, the nation was obviously enormously wealthy, and the veteran came to believe that his pay for risking his life and bearing the hardships of the war should be roughly equivalent to the scale which industrial workers had received. The American Legion agreed. Formed in France in 1919 by General Pershing to keep morale high during the slow, vexing process of returning home, the Legion sought chiefly to promote the welfare of veterans of the world war. While not aligning itself with either political party, the Legion, like the smaller and more exclusive Veterans of Foreign Wars, could hardly escape the political battles which the GAR, United Confederate Veterans, and United Spanish War Veterans had had to fight earlier. Congress and the American people could be generous to veterans, but past experience had demonstrated that they had to be convinced that the costs of war did not stop when the fighting ended. Indeed, the far larger, long-term costs were only beginning, and the veterans were determined that they would not be forgotten.

The demand for pay equalization, often referred to by its opponents as a "bonus," was a reasonable and just one. Led by the highly popular national commander Hanford MacNider of Iowa, the Legion demanded that Congress provide an additional $1.25 per day for overseas duty and $1.00 per day for each day of service in the states. With over 4 million men in the armed forces, the payment, estimated at $3 to $5 billion, was undeniably an expensive one, requiring either a temporary increase in taxes or heavy deficit financing.[16] Nonetheless, after the recession of 1920–21 the nation could clearly have afforded to pay the bonus. Indeed, after Harding's appointee Charles R. Forbes and his friends had stolen some $250 millions from the Veterans' Bureau and had encouraged corruption in the building of veterans' hospitals, it was understandable that the ex-soldiers increasingly came to believe that the government was more ready to praise them than it was to care for them.

The high cost of the proposed "bonus" motivated Wilson's secretary of the treasury, William Gibbs McAdoo, and his successor, Andrew Mellon, to persuade both Democratic and Republican presidents against the legislation.[17] However, neither McAdoo nor Mellon

realized the degree to which this issue would unite veterans in per-
fecting a congressional lobby of immense influence. Congressmen
who were also Legionnaires or members of the VFW were naturally
helpful. However, the legislative success depended more on
congressmen's fear of the highly organized network of local Legion
posts, which averaged eight thousand veterans to every congressional
district in the nation, on the political power this represented, and on
the Legion's skilled lobbyist John Thomas Taylor. A natty dresser,
with spats, walking cane, stentorian voice, and an expert's knowledge of congressional procedures and voting records, Taylor became
a lobbyists' legend during the two decades between the wars. He
knew how every congressman had voted on every piece of legislation
favored or opposed by the Legion. More important, he knew to
whom he should talk at the proper time and level of power and how
best to convince them of the justness of the veterans' cause.[18] It was
the bonus that proved to be the new organization's crucial test. Soon
it became a crusade which launched the Legion into the thickets of
partisan politics and won for it the devotion and membership of hundreds of thousands of veterans.

Twice Congress passed the bonus, and twice it was vetoed, first
by Harding and later by Coolidge. Each time Andrew Mellon stood
out as the single most powerful opponent of the bill. Dubbed by his
party as the greatest secretary of the treasury because of his successes
in steadily reducing taxes for the wealthy, he argued against the
bonus on the grounds of high taxes and fiscal irresponsibility. Finally, however, in 1924, after exerting strong pressure, the veterans
succeeded in winning congressional approval of a bill which in effect
established an endowed life-insurance policy for each veteran based
on the $1.25 per day for foreign service and $1.00 per day for
domestic service. But it was not to be payable until 1945. Rather
than raise the money through taxes, Congress created a sinking fund
which would accumulate an excess of the three to five billion dollars
needed by means of compounded interest. The average payment
would be approximately one thousand dollars for each veteran, yet
because one had to wait twenty years or die before receiving it, the
veterans quickly dubbed it the ''deathbed'' bonus. Still, the bill provided a shrewd compromise, and Congress easily overrode the expected presidential veto. This was a major victory which added to the
prestige of the Legion and demonstrated the political power and skill
of the new lobby.[19]

From 1924 until 1929 Republican leaders created an ''era of good feelings'' among the major veterans' organizations.[20] Influential Republicans such as Hanford MacNider, Ogden Mills, and other Legion officials found little to criticize and much to praise. Legislative successes won the Legion an increasing membership. From 609,407 in 1925 it grew to 794,219 by 1929, the year that Herbert Hoover became president.[21] Hoover valued the ex-soldiers and recognized the Legion's power. Highly influential Legion stalwarts were sometimes Hoover's allies as well. The president, for example, appointed his friend MacNider as his minister to Canada, and Ogden Mills became his assistant secretary of the treasury.

The president had witnessed and had been touched by the great suffering of the war. As the director of the European relief administration, the Quaker pacifist had developed a profound respect and admiration for the American Expeditionary Forces. Unfortunately, his one term in office marked a sharp and ironic end of the good feelings between veterans and Republican administrations.

In reality, Hoover did more to enlarge and improve upon the quality of veteran benefits than any of his predecessors, yet he was the most unpopular president in the period between the wars.[22] A shy man with little speaking ability or political charisma, he had become the most important cabinet officer in the administrations of both Harding and Coolidge. He was the expert organizer and administrator who had turned the Commerce Department into an innovative force in government, and who earned the respect of virtually all who knew him, including the immensely influential Washington press corps. After his landslide defeat of Al Smith in 1928, when many of the hatreds and stresses in American life boiled to the surface, Hoover soon faced the unprecedented, baffling depression of the 1930s and, in addition to many other problems, an increasingly hostile and militant veterans' lobby.

As soon as he became president, Hoover ordered sweeping reorganization of the veteran bureaucracy. The three inefficient agencies that had administered veterans' affairs were consolidated into the new Veterans' Administration headed by the exceptionally efficient and knowledgeable former General Frank T. Hines. In forcing the reorganization, Hoover antagonized some veteran leaders by allowing his good friend Secretary of the Interior Ray Lyman Wilbur to argue against a consolidation bill before a public hearing. Wilbur, like Hoover, favored consolidation, but wanted the new agency in the Interior Department, not under the direction of Hines. Nonetheless, despite the misleading appearances of opposition, Hoover worked quietly behind the scenes to insure consolidation under Hines and with the new agency to promote much greater efficiency and service. The initiative for the reorganization had been Hoover's, but his loyalty to his friend momentarily cast an unnecessary shadow on his relations with veterans.[23]

In addition, Hoover ordered Hines to undertake a thorough study of the numerous inequalities which resulted from the log-rolling, haphazard manner in which Congress had passed bills for the various competing veterans' lobbies. Hoover was shocked by the inconsistencies, injustices, and lack of equity which characterized the extremely complicated laws governing veterans' benefits.[24] He sought to establish guidelines which could help Congress formulate new laws insuring fair and just treatment for all veterans. To this end he established a committee which recommended that future veteran legislation be based on three criteria: a minimum of ninety days of service, treatment and pensions for disabilities which were service-connected, and free treatment for veterans who had nonservice-connected ailments if they could establish measurable need by proving that they had not earned enough money to pay income tax.[25]

In 1930, when Hoover publicized these criteria as justification for his veto of a pension bill for Spanish-American War veterans, the Congress and veterans' organizations erupted in unexpected, unrestrained fury. The first two criteria, ninety days of service and service-connected disability, were noncontroversial, but veteran leaders denounced the need clause as insulting, a "pauper's oath" which offended the dignity of the nation's heroes. Congress agreed and quickly overrode the veto. Thus at the very time that Hoover was expanding hospitalization and pension benefits, increasing efficiency and service to the veterans, and seeking to bring order and generous equity out of the legislative tangle of veteran laws, he appeared to many veterans to be a mean-spirited ingrate.[26]

In fact, Hoover had hoped to avoid what he believed would become a strong public backlash against too much aid. As the 1930 congressional election approached and the Great Depression worsened, congressmen introduced over forty veteran-benefit bills, including one to pay the full bonus immediately. Immediate payment abandoned the previously agreed upon skillful compromise, which would have increased the veterans' total payment through compounded interest. Instead, the new enthusiasm demanded the full amount, scheduled to be accrued by 1945, fifteen years ahead of that and during the nation's worst economic crisis. Yet this time the Legion did not support the bonus. It was satisfied with the earlier compromise and advocated other measures of its own.[27]

The principal bill of 1930 was one which sought to increase greatly the number and variety of diseases which could qualify as service-connected and, equally important, to extend the presumption that these diseases were service-connected to the present date. Until then special enumerated diseases had been designated for benefits only if they had been diagnosed by 1925. The popular Rankin bill which had been amended in committees many times, was the most costly veterans' legislation yet introduced. Because of its cost and numerous inequities both Hoover and Veterans' Administrator Hines could not believe that either Congress or the public would allow it. Yet the Legion and especially the VFW brought all their considerable pressure to bear, and passage seemed certain.[28]

Several aspects of the bill disturbed Hoover. First, the veterans who developed diseases after the arbitrary presumption date would not be eligible for benefits. The new date was as medically unsound as the earlier presumption date, and the bill was clearly inequitable. Second, the pension rates were extraordinarily high, and third, the bill was vaguely worded. It allowed for diseases of "a constitutional nature," and even service-connected obesity would qualify.[29]

As the depression worsened, Hoover had repeatedly insisted on economy in government and cutbacks in federal expenditures. Veterans commanded an inordinate proportion of the annual federal income, a fact which infuriated the National Association of Manufacturers and the National Economy League, an extremely vocal, conservative, bipartisan watchdog of spending.[30] Liberals would soon join the opposition, preferring a general relief program instead.[31] Hoover favored liberalizing hospital and pension benefits but on a more limited and equitable basis. Yet Congress was determined to pass the Rankin bill with its arbitrary deadline and preferred diseases, and if necessary override his veto.

Caught in a difficult position, Hoover decided on a legislative maneuver which would greatly reduce the cost of new benefits by lowering monthly pension amounts, especially for those with nonservice-connected infirmities, yet at the same time abandoning the sacrosanct service-connection restriction which had disallowed any benefits to many veterans in the past. The substitute bill would extend greater equity to all veterans of the world war, dropping entirely the listed diseases and arbitrary dates. Thus, in a complicated series of moves, Hoover introduced his own bill which granted hospital and pension eligibility to all world-war veterans—regardless of the nature of the disease, or the cause, or date of disability. It was the most liberal and equitable bill, and furthermore, in discarding any pretense of service-connected causes, it departed radically from prior legislation. This and its expense brought disavowals of responsibility even from the American Legion, which feared a backlash against its own pet bills. Nonetheless, Hoover's disability act was a sensible compromise, and Congress had little choice but to accept it.[32]

By the middle of 1930, therefore, Hoover had provided most generously for the veterans. New laws provided total annual benefits of $675.8 million, a figure that represented 16 percent of the annual federal income to only 4 percent of the population.[33] But ironically, few, if any, realized that the 1930 Disability Act was Hoover's bill. Partially this resulted from his behind-the-scenes substitution of his own bill in place of the Rankin measure as well as his inability to practice politics artfully. Yet at the same time he could not reveal his generosity to veterans during a crisis when he was insisting on strict economies. Thus, few ex-servicemen recognized him as a benefactor. Instead, they continued to think of him as aloof and uncaring. Indeed, the VFW took full credit for the legislation and then promptly supported the most dramatic veteran crusade: Congressman Wright Patman's bill to pay immediately the full value of the bonus.[34]

Hoover feared that the full payment of the bonus would retard economic recovery by draining off billions of dollars into government bonds. Rather than a fiscal policy which would encourage people to invest their hoarded dollars in the stock market, Patman's first bonus bill as well as others introduced in both houses would require the sale of government bonds to raise the money. Because government bonds were safer investments than stocks, Patman's bill, the president believed, would drastically curtail the flow of money back into the stock market and other more productive channels. While this line of economic thought is no longer tenable, it was the conventional wisdom of the day, with both liberals and conservatives in agreement.[35] Twice Hoover personally addressed the American Legion national conventions on his opposition to the immediate payment of the bonus.[36] In both instances the Legion conventions supported him, but the VFW and Wright Patman, the evangelical populist from Texas, would not be dissuaded.[37] Indeed, against Hoover's determined opposition they convinced Congress to pass, and then override his veto of, a bill allowing the veterans to borrow up to 50 percent of the face value of the bonus. It was a major legislative defeat for the beleaguered president, but it did not end the bonus controversy.[38]

Even before the passage of the loan bill, Hoover believed that the veterans had received more than generous treatment from his administration. In this belief he was undoubtedly correct. Had times been prosperous, Hoover's record suggests that he might have favored full payment, but under the circumstances he could not bring himself to support further veteran benefits. By 1932, during the steady decline in federal income, the nation was allotting one-fourth of its annual budget for veteran benefits. Federal annual income had dropped to less than $2 billion, yet the bonus would require an expenditure of $2.4 billion.[39]

But, even with the passage of the bonus loan bill, many unemployed veterans were still not satisfied. In the spring of 1932, after the House Ways and Means Committee shelved Wright Patman's newest bill, which would pay the remaining 50 percent or full amount of the bonus by simply printing the additional money and thus inflating the currency, a group of angry veterans from Oregon began a march on Washington which soon took on the character of a crusade and captured the imagination of a depression-weary nation. When news of the march made national headlines, thousands of other veterans joined in the trek toward the capital, until by late June as many as twenty thousand had assembled in Washington.

Officially Hoover remained aloof. He refused to greet the men or provide the slightest public recognition, yet he was privately far more helpful to the destitute petitioners than previous historians have realized. For two months he allowed the protesters to occupy federal parks, federal buildings scheduled for demolition, and the broad mudflats of the Anacostia River where the bulk of the men and women and their families lived in army-supplied tents or erected crude huts and shacks.[40]

Fortunately, the Washington police chief, former Brigadier General Pelham D. Glassford, befriended his former comrades-in-arms, and provided the organization, fund-raising, and helpful assistance which allowed for a peaceful protest. However, congressmen were far from pleased with the incessant lobbyists. Finally, to settle the issue, the House voted to pass the bonus bill, but on June 16 the Senate overwhelmingly defeated it. More aid to this small percentage of the population when thousands of nonveterans and their families were in equal need did not seem just. Indeed, many senators concluded that rather than depression relief, the bonus represented special-interest pleading. Certainly the men had deserved the payment after the armistice, especially when the nation had experienced constant economic growth during most of the twenties. But now America had to turn to the greater priority of relief for all the poor and needy. And liberal senators feared that passage of the $2.4 billion bonus would galvanize conservatives into a coalition against the national relief legislation still pending before the Congress.[41]

The bonus march was the most dramatic event of the 1932 election campaign. Hoover was patient with the protesters, even sponsoring legislation to provide transportation loans back to their homes after Congress had adjourned. Some influential Republican leaders believed the president to be much too lenient, but he insisted on allowing the long, embarrassing lobby even though he would not officially recognize its existence.[42] Finally, one month after the defeat of the bonus bill and several days after Congress had adjourned—when there was no longer any hope of passage—the president agreed to begin a limited evacuation of the remaining eight thousand protesters by repossessing federal buildings along Pennsylvania Avenue scheduled earlier for demolition. The result was a long series of blunders, the outbreak of a riot on July 28, and subsequently the tragic dispersal of the bonus marchers by troops, tanks, cavalry, and tear gas.

My article published in 1967 established that Hoover had not intended to drive the protesters from the capital. Indeed, he had a much more limited objective, even placing the troops under civilian control of the police chief, and limiting their actions to clearing the thousands of veterans and curious spectators from the downtown riot area. Unfortunately, following first a brief but intense brick battle and then a second confrontation in which a badly battered policeman drew his revolver and fatally wounded two of his attackers, Hoover received intense pressure by police officers and other administration officials to call upon the army for assistance. This he finally and reluctantly did, but only after carefully restricting the responsibility of the troops. However, General Douglas MacArthur, the army chief of staff, whom Hoover placed in charge of supervising the troops, deliberately disobeyed the president's written and repeated verbal orders not to drive the veterans out of their largest settlement located across the Anacostia River and far from the riot site. MacArthur cleared this and other camps and drove the frightened men and their families out of the city and into the night. It was the classic time for the military man to take control, a time of great stress, confusion, and uncertainty.[43]

MacArthur attempted to justify his disobedience on the grounds that he had faced an "incipient revolution" of communists and radicals. Confused and stunned by the swift sequence of events, Hoover accepted these reassurances from MacArthur and Secretary of War Patrick J. Hurley. Both were trusted advisers, and Hoover had personally appointed MacArthur chief of staff over several senior officers. Hoover was angry with the disobedience but eventually came to believe that MacArthur had acted as the circumstances dictated. Accordingly, the president accepted that the situation had been far more serious than he had realized, and he could not bring himself to think that both MacArthur and Hurley would deliberately mislead him.Several days later, however, after Hoover had publicly supported his subordinates, accounts of the rout became less hysterical and less favorable to the president, and once again he had second thoughts. He even requested MacArthur and Hurley to explain to the press what "really did happen," but both refused. This exchange still remains relatively unrecognized. Hurley and MacArthur insisted that Hoover was a hero who had put down a communist revolution, that the action was justified, that such a public statement would only raise undue doubts in the midst of the campaign, and that he had little to worry about from a few radical critics and "crackpots."[44]

Hoover's decision to accept the repeated assurances of his two advisers resulted in his personal as well as political tragedy. Hurley and MacArthur had claimed proof of their charges, but the proof was not forthcoming. Intense investigations by the FBI. Army Intelligence, Immigration Bureau, Metropolitan Police, Secret Service, and the attorney general's office failed to uncover any evidence of communist responsibility or proof of a plot to topple the government. In fact, the evidence revealed that while communists were present in the crowd at the riot site, only one of them was reported involved in the brick battle, and it was the angry veterans, not the reds, who were responsible for the confrontation.[45]

The tragedy of Hoover's bonus crucible was simply that the "facts" known to him soon after the event did not correspond to reality, or even a relatively accurate approximation of reality. Yet for reasons unknown to historians, though probably because he trusted his advisers and was seared by his critics, he believed the proadministration distortions and allowed them to continue while protecting Hurley and MacArthur. In so doing, he did not serve the nation in the highest traditions which he himself advocated. For that matter, he also served himself poorly and failed to clarify the historical record. Very soon he reaped the bitter consequences.

Understandably, Hoover's critics and all the veterans' organizations launched a scathing attack upon him. Believing that the callous president had suddenly ordered the army to drive out the veterans and their families, and further incensed over his claim of communist inspiration and domination, they lashed back at him with a fury which destroyed his previous reputation as an honest and basically decent man. Some critics even erroneously charged that Hoover had diabolically plotted to provoke the riot and then ordered the rout so that he could center his campaign on the issue of law and order and pose as the savior of the republic. The American Legion, which had officially refrained from endorsing the bonus, was now greatly angered. The VFW had led the bonus fight and had publicly censured Hoover for his cruel and inhumane use of troops. Legionnaires meeting in Portland, Oregon, several weeks later were now also expected to support the bonus bill and perhaps even to join with the VFW in censuring Hoover personally.

The president and his chief advisers were especially shaken by the vehemence of the nationwide outrage. Unable to prove a communist coup, Attorney General William D. Mitchell, with Hoover's support, next sought to prove to the Legionnaires that a large percentage of those involved in the rioting and resistance were not veterans, but criminals, radicals, and communists. The flimsy "white paper," presented to the Legion at its national convention in September, 1932, misused statistics regarding arrest records of veterans who had earlier returned home, and by tortured, circuitous logic tried thereby to prove that a large percentage of the veterans who had remained in Washington at the time of the riot were "criminals." Attorney General Mitchell's report distinctly compounded Hoover's blunders. Police Chief Glassford easily disproved these newest charges, and the veterans' fury intensified. Skillful Hoover lieutenants stopped the Legion short of censuring the president, but it did overwhelmingly endorse immediate payment of the bonus.[46]

The controversy galvanized the veterans for their most determined and successful legislative battle. Legion and VFW membership soared as angry members of both organizations applied intense pressure on Congress to pay the $2.4 million bonus. However, Roosevelt also opposed the bonus, and while he too realized the power of the veterans and the benefit of the rout in further smoothing his path to the presidency, he was more determined than Hoover to stop the veteran lobby.

FDR had consistently informed the public that the bonus could not be paid until the budget was balanced and the government had sufficient funds.[47] He had attacked Hoover repeatedly during the campaign for spending too much money, unbalancing the budget, and allowing waste and inefficiency in government. And in one of his first acts as president he forced through Congress the Economy Act of 1933, which so severely cut veteran benefits that even his strongest veteran supporters could not condone the unexpected and doubtlessly unfair nature of his response.[48]

Roosevelt's action resulted more from his ignorance of the complexities and inequities of veteran legislation than from deliberate callousness. He was incensed over Hoover's willingness to grant nonservice-connected pension and hospital benefits, but he did not know that Hoover had been forced to abandon the principle of service-connected benefits in order to insure some degree of fairness and equity and to avoid certain passage of a still more expensive and inequitable bill. However, the veterans lost no time in educating the new president. FDR's drastic and hastily conceived economies had actually removed legitimate benefits to veterans with service-connected disabilities as well. So severe were the numerous cuts that within weeks the president and his advisers received reliable information from trusted friends who pointed to the enormity of the blunder and the need to rescind entire sections of the act. This Roosevelt accomplished by a continuing series of executive orders which eventually eliminated the worst abuses.[49]

Meantime, a second bonus march materialized. Fueled by the new sense of indignation, this protest contained many more commnists than the first march. Aided by the experiencd and efficient Veterans' Administrator Frank T. Hines, Roosevelt managed the second march with great finesse and dispatch. Unlike Hoover, who allowed the men to camp in the district, Roosevelt isolated them at Fort Hunt, Virginia, where they were provided with food, tents, bedding, and transportation. Within a relatively short time FDR created jobs for the marchers and other unemployed veterans in what eventually became the Civilian Conservation Corps. The second march therefore ended peacefully, as did two even smaller bonus marches in 1934 and 1935. However, the question of immediate payment of the bonus, the continued restoration of all prior benefits, and the extension of pensions to widows and dependents remained very much in the forefront of the veterans' demands.[50]

Between 1933 and 1935 the Legion and the VFW worked incessantly to secure congressional passage of the bonus. As in the early twenties, the bonus was again a crucial test of veteran strength, a battle which both organizations now believed was just, and which they could not afford to lose. Aided by the continuing zeal and hard work of Wright Patman in the House, the veterans won congressional approval in 1935. This time, however, FDR assembled the entire Congress to hear his reasons for vetoing the bill. Just as he had warned the Legion in a 1933 personal address to stay out of partisan politics, he again repeated his opposition to special class legislation at a time when the nation was in deep depression. Like Hoover, FDR was angered and somewhat alarmed by the veterans' special sense of identity, the evangelical nature of their righteousness, and by their conviction that their demands took precedence over the needs of other Americans who were equally, if not more, destitute.

Congress upheld the president's veto, but the next year, 1936, it again passed the bonus, and this time Roosevelt wrote a lame veto message which, as expected, was quickly overridden. Veteran power had gained a stunning victory. Moreover, by 1939–40, FDR approved a series of executive orders which restored the vast majority of the benefits which the Economy Act of 1933 had eliminated. In the case of the Spanish-American War veterans, he even dropped his opposition to pensions for veterans with nonservice-connected disabilities. FDR yielded gracefully, because he came to understand the complexities of veterans' needs as well as their political muscle. Yet he did so reluctantly and served both the nation and the veterans with his opposition. For while the ex-servicemen enlightened him and the American people to the fact that war costs do not stop when the firing is over, Roosevelt had drawn a line for them as well.[51]

In the middle and late 1930s, as European dictators appealed to veteran identity and military glories, FDR, like Hoover, insisted upon restraining the tendency to view veteran needs as somehow more important than the needs of their fellow citizens. Indeed, Roosevelt remained far more aloof from the veterans than Hoover. Neither was much influenced by their continual jingoism. Roosevelt, for example, recognized the Soviet Union, and Hoover pushed hard for success at the Geneva Disarmament Conference.

Veterans were influential between the wars, but they were by no means as powerful as they wished to believe. Indeed, an important private study by Wright Patman reveals that congressmen who had voted against the bonus in 1932 and again in 1934 had no difficulty achieving renomination in the Democratic primaries in 1936, despite repeated veteran threats of retaliation at the polls. Congress responded favorably in part because many believed in the justness of the veterans' cause, because of the impact of the rout of the bonus marchers which created a sympathetic attitude toward veteran causes, and no doubt because some feared the political potential of the well-organized and locally potent opposition at the polls. Yet the Patman study further demonstrates that the veterans' political power must not be overemphasized.[52]

Throughout the 1920s and 1930s veterans' organizations grew in power, and despite their jingoism they taught the nation an important lesson about war, and in turn learned from two determined presidents. Unlike Harding and Coolidge, who vetoed the bonus during prosperous times, Hoover and Roosevelt faced the task of restraining militant organizations during the worst depression in American history. Of the two, Hoover was the more knowledgeable and generous, but ironically, because he was a poorer politician, he received less credit. And after the rout of the bonus army and his disastrous defense of it, Hoover received the hatred of millions of veterans. FDR opposed veteran pressures for much the same fiscal and social reasons. As a superior politician, however, he succeeded in toning down the sense of special identity, superiority, and expectation of special privilege that characterized many veteran crusades between the wars.

In the final analysis one must conclude that while the veterans' organizations contributed to a narrow, bigoted superpatriotism, their chief positive impact was in educating the Congress and the American people to the fact that wars are far more costly than many like to consider. Veteran agitation during the 1920s and 1930s served to remind Americans that wars embarked on with an initial flush of patriotic fervor often breed a growing sense of disillusionment, and former heroes are all too often quickly and easily forgotten. The ex-doughboys refused to be abandoned, however, and following World War II Congress would demonstrate that it had learned this lesson well.

NOTES

1. For a good summary see David A. Shannon, *Between the Wars: America, 1919–1941* (Boston: Houghton Mifflin, 1965), pp. 15–25.

2. Ibid., pp. 25–30, 79–81; Robert K. Murray, *Red Scare: A Study of National Hysteria, 1919–1920* (Minneapolis: Univ. of Minnesota Press, 1955), pp. 87–104.

3. Roscoe Baker, *The American Legion and American Foreign Policy* (New York: Bookman Associates, 1954), pp. 25–29.

4. Ibid., p. 4; "Another Warning to the Legion," *Literary Digest*, 53 (Dec. 27, 1919): 18–19; Cyrus LeRoy Baldridge, "Is the American Legion American?" *Scribner's Magazine*, 100 (Sept., 1936): 134–38; Marcus Duffield, *King Legion* (New York: Cape & Smith, 1931), pp. 157–71.

5. Baker, p. 32; Dorothy Culp, *The American Legion: A Study in Pressure Politics* (private ed., Chicago: Univ. of Chicago Libraries, 1942), pp. 14–17; "Another Warning to the Legion," 18–19; Duffield, pp. 267–97; William Gellerman, *The American Legion as Educator* (New York: Teacher's College, Columbia Univ., 1938), pp. 87–130, 200–235; "Americanizing Americans as the Legion Does It," *Literary Digest*, 76 (Jan. 13, 1923): 42–44; author interview with James E. Van Zandt, Apr. 14, 1972. Van Zandt had long been active in VFW affairs and served as commander-in-chief from 1933 to 1936. He told of the VFW's efforts to impede or disrupt May Day parades.

6. Baker, p. 267; Murray, pp. 88–90. The citations in fn. 5 also support this conclusion. The best scholarly analysis is Rodney G. Minott, *Peerless Patriots: Organized Veterans and the Spirit of Americanism* (Washington, D.C.: Public Affairs Press, 1962). See esp. pp. 54–89.

7. Baker, pp. 78, 110–21; Gellerman, pp. 169–96; Duffield, pp. 144–55.

8. Interview with James E. Van Zandt; Richard S. Jones, *A History of the American Legion* (Indianapolis: Bobbs-Merrill, 1946), pp. 236–44. Also see citations in nn. 5 and 6, and Minott, pp. 90–101.

9. Author interview with Warren MacDonald, special assistant to the administrator of veteran affairs, Apr. 6, 1972. For years MacDonald was research director for the American Legion. Also see Baker, pp. 12–13; Sylvanus Cook, "The Real American Legion," *Nation*, 125 (Sept. 7, 1935): 224-25; Minott, pp. 91-95.

10. For a detailed examination of Hoover's arms-reduction policies, see John Richard Wilson, "Herbert Hoover and the Armed Forces: A Study of Presidential Attitudes and Policy" (Ph.D. diss., Northwestern Univ., 1971), especially pp. 132–33.

11. "To Save America for Democracy," *Foreign Service* (Sept., 1938), 5. *Foreign Service* was the official magazine of the VFW. Also see Baker, pp. 156–57; James E. Van Zandt to Franklin D. Roosevelt, November 15, 1935, president's personal file, Franklin D. Roosevelt Library, Hyde Park, N.Y. (hereafter cited as FDRL).

12. For example see Andrew W. Mellon to Willis C. Hawley, February 13, 1931, presidential papers, p.p. 298, Herbert Hoover Presidential Library (hereafter cited as HHPL). Also see "Bonus Raid," *Nation*, 132 (Feb. 18, 1931): 170; "Mercenaries of Patriotism," *New Republic*, 46 (Feb. 25, 1931): 30–31; Katherine Mayo, *Soldiers What Next?* (Boston: Houghton Mifflin, 1934). Accounts which exaggerate veteran legislative powers include Duffield; Gellerman; Culp; Mayo.

13. For a good summary of congressional legislation passed in the 1920s, see Arthur L. Hennessy, "The Bonus Army of 1932" (Ph.D. diss., Georgetown Univ., 1955), pp. 10–87. Also see Jones, pp. 165–80; and Roger Daniels, *The Bonus March: An Episode of the Great Depression* (Westport, Conn.: Greenwood, 1971), pp. 37–39.

14. The best case for the inadequacy of medical records is made in "A Pension for Disabled World War Veterans," *Foreign Service* (Aug., 1930), 6.

15. There is at the HHPL a vast amount of correspondence and reports on medical and pension inequities. For example, Hoover to Frank T. Hines, Apr. 12, 1930, PP 296, HHPL. Also see "Brief of Major Inequities in Veteran Legislation" and

"Chronological Resumé of Veteran Laws 1861–1932" in pp. 286A, HHPL. Another excellent summary of veteran benefits is David R. B. Ross, *Preparing for Ulysses. Politics and Veterans during World War II* (New York: Columbia Univ. Press, 1969), pp. 12–25.

16. See n. 13. Also see Baker, pp. 12–18; Culp, pp. 2–3, 14–17; Marcus Duffield, "The American Legion in Politics," *Forum,* 85 (May, 1931): 257–65; Ralph R. Perry, "The American Legion in Politics," *Outlook,* 124 (Jan. 14, 1920): 62–63.

17. See n. 13.

18. Among the best sources on the Legion's role in the bonus fight is the Adjusted Service Certificate file at the American Legion National Headquarters in Indianapolis, Indiana [hereafter cited as ALP]. The file on John Thomas Taylor is also extensive.

19. See n. 13. Also see correspondence in Records of the Treasury, secretary's correspondence, Soldier's Bonus, RG 56, National Archives (hereafter cited as NA).

20. Jones, p. 140.

21. Baker, p. 16. Also see Daniels, pp. 41–64.

22. See "Chronological Resumé of Veteran Laws 1861–1932;" Frank T. Hines to Herbert Hoover, Sept. 13, 1930, PP 284, HHPL.

23. Herbert Hoover to Frank T. Hines, April 12, 1930, PP 296; "Minutes of the Committee to Coordinate Veteran Affairs," PP 56; U.S. Congress, House, Committee on Expenditures in the Executive Departments, Hearings on H. R. 6141, *Consolidation of Veteran Affairs,* 71st Cong., 2nd sess., Jan. 8, 1930, pp. 43, 46, 62. Also see William A. Du Puy to Ray Lyman Wilbur, May 9, 1929, Wilbur papers, HHPL; and Edwin S. Bettelheim to Walter Newton, Jan. 20, 1930, PP 157, HHPL.

24. Herbert Hoover to Frank T. Hines, Apr. 12, 1930, PP 296, HHPL. For an extensive analysis of Hoover's relations with the veterans, see Donald J. Lisio, *The President and Protest: Hoover, Conspiracy, and the Bonus Riot* (Columbia, Mo.: Univ. of Missouri Press, 1974), pp. 1–50. Daniels also deals with the veterans, but because we disagree on so many points I have not cited our differences.

25. "Minutes of the Committee to Coordinate Veteran Affairs," PP 56, HHPL;

26. Herbert Hoover, "Message to the United States Senate, May 28, 1930, Veto of S. 476, Spanish-War Veterans' Pension Bill;" George H. Woods to C. B. Hodges, PP 207, HHPL. There are numerous letters of protest in this box.

27. Jones, pp. 145–48; U. S. Congress, Senate, *Congressional Record,* 71st Cong., 2nd sess., 1930, 72, pt. 11: 12055–56.

28. O. L. Bodenhamer to Royal' C. Johnson, telegram, June 30, 1930, PP 296; Frank T. Hines to Hoover, June 21, 1930 and June 25, 1930, PP 284, HHPL.

29. Herbert Hoover, "Message to House of Representatives, June 26, 1930, Veto of H. R. 10381," PP 284, HHPL.

30. In 1932 the National Economy League was especially incensed. See National Economy League, "Declaration of Purposes, June 29, 1932," PPF 1998, HHPL.

31. See n. 12.

32. U. S. Congress, House, *Congressional Record,* 71st Cong., 2nd sess., 1930, 72, pt. 11: 11828–42, 12460–62; U. S. Congress, Senate, *Congressional Record,* 71st Cong., 2nd sess., 1930, 72, pt. 11: 12058–61, 12198–99, 12387–418. Also see Hoover to Grenville Clark, July 12, 1932, PP 296, HHPL.

33. For a summary of benefits see "Veteran Relief," memo, Apr. 8, 1931, PP 296; Hines to Hoover, Sept. 13, 1930, PP 284, HHPL. Also see United States Bureau of the Census, *Historical Statistics of the United States, Colonial Times to 1957* (Washington, D.C.: U.S. Government Printing Office, 1960), pp. 7, 711, 738, 740.

34. Edwin S. Bettelheim, "A Pension for Disabled World War Veterans," *Foreign Service* (Aug., 1930), 5–6.

35. "Cash for Veterans," *Nation,* 132 (Feb. 4, 1931): 113; "Bonus Raid," 170; "Mercenaries of Patriotism," 30–31; Hoover to Reed Smoot, Feb. 18, 1931, PP 297, HHPL.

36. Summary of Proceedings, Twelfth Annual National Convention of the American

Legion, Boston, Mass., Oct. 6–9, 1930, pp. 8–11, American Legion Papers; Summary of Proceedings, Thirteenth Annual National Convention of the American Legion, Detroit, Mich., Sept. 21–24, 1931, pp. 9–10.

37. The best source on Wright Patman is his extensive collection of personal papers, which he allowed me to examine. See especially the Adjusted Service Certificate files.

38. "Needy Served First," *Time* 18 (Mar. 9, 1931): 11–12; "Resolution," American Legion National Executive Committee, Jan. 25, 1931, Adjusted Service Certificate file, ALP; Lisio, pp. 26–50.

39. *Historical Statistics of the United States,* p. 711.

40. For evidence of substantial aid see Senator James Couzens to Frederick Payne, June 23, 1932; Payne to John J. McSwain, June 25, 1932; Colonel H. N. Cootes to Adjutant General, War Department, June 13, 1932; Major General R. E. Callen, "Memorandum for Chief of Staff," Mar. 2, 1933, Office of the Adjutant General, RG 94, 240 (Bonus), Box 1180, NA. Callen discusses the canned meat, forks, spoons, knives, cups, and repair of 108 of the 1116 large pyramidal tents. War Department Militia Bureau to Adjutant General, Mar. 17, 1933. Also see French Strother to Arthur McKeogh, Strother papers, HHPL. Lisio, *The President and Protest,* pp. 72–86.

41. *New York Times,* June 17, 1932; "Approval of the Bonus Bill Defeat," *Literary Digest,* 114 (July 2, 1932): 9; U. S. Congress, Senate, *Congressional Record,* 72nd Cong., 1st sess., 1932, 75, pt. 12: 13255–60, 13268.

42. Theodore J. Joslin, *Hoover off the Record* (New York: Doubleday, Doran, 1934), p. 265; *New York Times,* June 29, July 7 and 9, 1932.

43. Donald J. Lisio, "A Blunder Becomes Catastrophe: Hoover, the Legion, and the Bonus Army," *Wisconsin Magazine of History,* 51 (autumn, 1967): 38–42.

44. Ibid., 42–43.

45. Ibid., 43–46.

46. Ibid., 46–49. For a more extensive analysis see Lisio, pp. 139–257.

47. Franklin D. Roosevelt, *The Public Papers and Addresses of Franklin D. Roosevelt,* ed. Samuel I. Rosenman (New York: Random House, 1938), VI, p. 809; FDR to R. D. Baker, Oct. 29, 1932, Democratic National Committee, Georgia, FDRL.

48. Veterans' Administration, Public Law No. 2, 73rd Cong., and executive orders (Washington, D.C.: Government Printing Office, 1933), in Republican National Committee file, correspondence, HHPL. For more infomration on Roosevelt's relations with the veterans, see Ross, pp. 25–29; Daniels, pp. 211–241; Lisio, *President and Protest,* pp. 279–99.

49. Ibid.; Stephen Early, memorandum to General Hines and enclosures, May 13, 1933; Early to Roy Roberts, May 12, 1933; L. S. Ray to Early, Mar. 13, 1933, OF 95; James E. Van Zandt to FDR, Sept. 22, 1933, PPF 87, FDRL.

50. Daniels, pp. 219–26. Also see recently discovered voluminous evidence in "Historical Studies, Adjusted Compensation," which is housed in the Veterans' Administration Building, Washington, D. C. Warren MacDonald, special assistant to the administrator of veteran affairs, helped me locate these materials.

51. FDR, Public Papers, IV, pp. 182–93, but especially p. 193. Also see FDR, Public Papers, V, pp. 67–69, and Adjusted Service Certificate File 1933–1936, Patman papers, as well as the numerous correspondence files at the national headquarters of the American Legion. For an excellent analysis of continuing veteran influence and major shifts in federal policy after 1940 see Ross. Another excellent account is Keith W. Olson, *The G. I. Bill, the Veterans, and the Colleges* (Lexington, Ky.: Univ. of Kentucky Press, 1973).

52. For the detailed, statistical report see H. Bruce Brougham to Wright Patman, Apr. 27, 1935, Patman papers.

FRANCE:
Veterans' Politics Between the Wars

Despite victory in 1918, France emerged from the First World War a divided nation. During the last half of the war, before the German military collapse, a war-weary army and a war-weary public had been ready for peace without victory. Only Premier Clemenceau's fierce determination and semidictatorial methods had held peace sentiment in check long enough to defeat the Germans. With peace, the *union sacrée*, the spirit of "sacred union" which led Frenchmen at the outset of the war to lay aside old ideological disputes in behalf of wartime consensus, was gradually replaced by *désunion normale*, a reversion to prewar doctrinal divisions and party politics. The war had united, the peace divided. Almost all adult Frenchmen, however, shared one sentiment: a strong desire to avoid a repetition of the bloodbath and suffering of 1914–18. This "pacifism" was strong among returning war veterans as well.

The various veterans' associations which were established after the war reflected not only the antiwar feeling but also the ideological divisions of the civilian populace—as one might expect from a citizens' army. French war veterans were distinguished from other Frenchmen by their deeper sense of the horrors of war, their nostalgia for the comradeship of the trenches, and their corporate interest in postwar veterans' benefits. But beyond that they were divided along traditional ideological lines on questions of domestic and foreign policy.

While most veterans came away sick of war in 1918, they disagreed as to the best way of avoiding another such conflict in the future. Three broad alternatives were proposed by different veterans' groups, alternatives which conformed closely to their civilian political affiliations. Socialist veterans argued that only a socialist society and Marxian internationalism could bring a permanent end to war; liberal veterans emphasized the need for reconciliation with Germany and liberal internationalism; and conservative veterans took a hard-line stand based on narrow nationalism and distrustful realpolitik.

On domestic political issues, veterans divided along equally ideological lines. Some veterans, it is true, came away feeling personally regenerated by the war and longed for an extension of military values to civilian life. This attitude was strongest in the French Right, especially the radical Right, and with veterans' associations allied with the Right. Domestically, the greatest danger to the Third Republic during the interwar years came not from the extreme Left but from the extreme Right—particularly with the onset of the depression and with the rise of fascism in neighboring countries. While the communists could count on only proletarians and poor peasants for mass support, the various fascist organizations could expect a much broader base in a revolutionary or civil-war situation. Conservative as well as radical rightists blamed the Republic for losing the peace, for parliamentary corruption, and for allowing socialism to threaten *la patrie* and property rights—with radical rightists openly flaunting paramilitary formations to give weight to their protests. The culmination of this backlash occurred on February 6, 1934, when a number of right-wing veterans' groups, in league with the Action Francaise, the Federation of Taxpayers, and a group of conservative Parisian municipal councilmen, marched on the Chamber of Deputies and as a result of massive and violent street action forced the Daladier government to resign.

However, if in 1934 it was veterans of the radical Right, not the radical Left, who dominated the headlines, in 1918 the opposite was often the case. Appealing to widespread antiwar sentiment, the Left worked hard to mobilize veterans for peace—and for their own domestic political ends. Most of the veterans' associations formed in the wake of the war took pains to underline their "apolitical" nature, presenting themselves as fraternal organizations dedicated simply to keeping alive the personal bonds established during the war, commemorating their dead comrades, providing mutual aid for members, and acting as watchdogs for veterans' benefits. An exception was the

ARAC, Association Républicaine des Anciens Combattants [Republican Association of War Veterans], founded by Henri Barbusse and a small group of left-wing pacifist intellectuals in 1917.

Barbusse, author of the famous antiwar novel *Le Feu* [*Under Fire*] (1917), had been a successful poet and literary critic before the war. In 1914, at the age of 40, he joined the army as an enlisted man, viewing the war at that time as a conflict between democratic, libertarian France and reactionary, militaristic Germany. Fighting at the front, he was disillusioned by what he saw and came to blame the conflict on war profiteers, callous statesmen, and mass chauvinism on both sides. In 1917 he published *Le Feu,* which created a sensation and won him the Goncourt prize (the novel was subsequently translated into more than fifty languages). Denouncing the "goldstriped caste" which sent thousands of young men to their deaths so that they, the perpetrators, "may write their princely names in history," *Le Feu* went on to analyze the larger psychological and intellectual bases of the war:[1]

There are those who admire the exchange of flashing blows, who hail like women the bright colors of uniforms; those whom military music and the martial ballads poured upon the public intoxicate as with brandy; the dizzy-brained, the feeble-minded, the superstitious, the savages.

There are those who bury themselves in the past, . . .the traditionalists for whom an injustice has legal force because it is perpetuated. . . .

With them are all the parsons, who seek to excite you and to lull you to sleep with the morphine of their Paradise, so that nothing may change. There are the lawyers, the economists, the historians—and how many more?—who befog you with the rigmarole of theory, who declare the interantagonism of nationalities at a time when the only unity possessed by each nation of today is in the arbitrary map-made lines of her frontiers, while she is inhabited by an artificial amalgam of races; there are the worm-eaten genealogists, who forge for the ambitious of conquest and plunder false certificates of philosophy and imaginary titles of nobility. The infirmity of human intelligence is short sight. In too many cases, the wiseacres are dunces of a sort, who lose sight of the simplicity of things, and stifle and obscure it with formulae and trivialities. It is the small things that one learns from books, not the great ones.

And even while they are saying that they do not wish for war, they are doing all they can to perpetuate it. They nourish national vanity and the love of supremacy by force. "We alone," they say, each behind his shelter, "we alone are the guardians of courage and loyalty, of ability and good taste!" Out of the greatness and richness of a country, they make something like a consuming disease. . . .

They pervert the most admirable of moral principles. How many are the crimes of which they have made virtues merely by dowering them with the word "national"? They distort even truth itself.

Barbusse's remedy? In 1917 it was still vague, although resounding: a cry for more participatory democracy, social equality, and internationalism. Barbusse was not yet the revolutionary socialist he would become later. In 1917 he was still more of a Kantian "idealist" than a Marxian "realist," a liberal-democratic humanist who believed that principles, not force, ideas, not economics, were, or could be, the prime mover of social change. Near the end of *Le Feu* Barbusse's philosophical idealism, as well as his strong egalitarianism, is expressed in a dialogue between soldiers at the front:[2]

Liberty and fraternity are words, while equality is a fact. Equality should be the great human formula. . . . That formula is of prodigious importance. The principle of the equal rights of every living being and the sacred will of the majority is infallible and must be invincible; all progress will be brought about by it, all, with a force truly divine.

Or, as Barbusse later declared: ". . .the most beautiful idea there is in the world: *All men are equal.*"[3] For Barbusse, the natural corollary to this idea was internationalism: all men deserved equal respect whatever their nationality. Internationalism was also a force for peace, counteracting the nationalistic passions which underlay modern war. Barbusse maintained that all peoples "are everywhere the same, everywhere have the same faults and the same great virtues, the same aspirations, the same chains, the same enemies."[4] In 1918 he supported Woodrow Wilson's Fourteen Points as a viable plan for peace—a judgment later described as naive by Barbusse's communist biographers Jacques Duclos and Jean Freville.

By 1918 Barbusse had decided to abandon art for politics, to dedicate himself to organizing veterans for pacifist and leftist ends. When he was chided by former friends for sacrificing his literary career, he replied that his previous existence now seemed "abstract" and socially irresponsible. He added: "We know that the social question is not the whole question of the race; but it is the one in which we can be most helpful, the one which most urgently demands immediate intellectual elucidation."[5] Declaring "It was the war that educated me," he turned his back on those who were not in contact "with reality."[6] Part of that "reality" was the masses, from whom, as a bourgeois intellectual, he had felt alienated before the war. The war had changed all that; it had brought him into contact with the masses. The sense of comradeship it produced was an important element in his political activism. The bond that had been forged between himself and other war veterans, particularly those of working-class background, eventually led him into socialism. He was later to write as a communist:[7]

Of all the families which I have found in life as part of an ideal community, it is with the war veterans that I have the closest ties. It is toward my brother war veterans that my heart and spirit turn most willingly. They are my oldest and dearest friends. I owe them a great deal. It was through contact with them that, [as] a bourgeois intellectual, I learned to abandon abstract idealism which is the intellectual trap par excellence; it is through them that I was put into direct contact with the working class. From them, I have learned much. They have never betrayed nor abandoned me.

It was in 1917, during the war itself, that Barbusse (who was recovering from pneumonia contracted at the front) was approached by two left-wing intellectuals, Paul Vaillant-Couturier and Raymond Lefebvre, who asked his help in founding a veterans' association which would work for peace. Together they launched the ARAC, largely financed at first by Barbusse's royalties from Le Feu. Vaillant-Couturier later recalled:[8]

Barbusse, Raymond Lefebvre, and I met in the early days of 1917, dressed in our army coats stiff with mud and blood. Barbusse had just written Le Feu. And Le Feu bespoke the feelings of the soldier. The spirit of the trenches was expressed in it. From our meeting, during an intermission in the murdering, was born the ARAC.

The first national convention of the ARAC was held in September, 1919, in Lyons. Like other veterans' organizations, it promised to defend veterans' benefits in the postwar period—with the difference that its principles on this issue, as on others, were more egalitarian. In his opening speech Barbusse demanded: ". . .for an equal wound, an equal pension, the leg of a general is not worth more than the leg of an enlisted man."[9]

But Barbusse and his colleagues saw the ARAC as more than just a special-interest group for veterans. From the beginning it was committed to broader political activity: to working for permanent peace ("to make war on war") and to keeping alive among veterans the "anger and disgust born on the field of battle." It was not enough just to secure financial compensation for war wounded and war widows and to defend veterans' retirement pensions, for, Barbusse declared at Lyons, "benefits of this sort would never be very large or even apparent without a social order that was truly democratic. . . ." Although Barbusse strongly suggested that the Russian Revolution had launched such a social order and noted that "the struggle against war" required "class struggle" as well, he maintained that the ARAC was independent of all political parties. Like the leaders of other veterans' associations, Barbusse hesitated to give his movement a clear-cut political identification, recognizing that the more doctrinaire the movement was the fewer fellow travelers it would attract. Officially, the ARAC welcomed veterans of all political parties and all religious persuasions, its motto being "Do nothing to divide, do everything to unite."[10] And yet, however broad-gauged its rhetoric, the ARAC was already closely allied with the communist cause. At Lyons Barbusse defended the Soviet Union against its critics and denounced the League of Nations as a facade for capitalist hypocrisy.

The ARAC's pro-Soviet stance was made quite clear at the first Congress of the International des Anciens Combattants (IAC), held at Geneva in 1920. Eager to internationalize the veterans-for-peace movement, Barbusse called for a European conference of veterans' organizations in 1920. The hope was expressed that men who had only two years before been trying to kill one another on the battlefield would, out of their common hatred of war, come together to insure the peace. The first meeting of the IAC heard Barbusse give the keynote speech:[11]

It is true that since man has inhabited the earth there has been war. But it is true also that in no previous wars has one ever

seen the "heroes" of each country uniting fraternally, and re-
pudiating their own "heroism," their own glory, all the false-
hoods which have driven them to destruction.

It is said that it is France which entertains the greatest hatred
against Germany. Well, it is from France that comes the initiative, the gesture of reconciliation between all those who yesterday were massacring one another.

To those who accused the veterans at Geneva of being bad patriots,
Barbusse replied:[12]

They speak to us of country. We speak of it also. But ours is
not, like theirs, a kind of ferocious citadel placed opposite
others with the money-chests inside. It is another country
which has only the horizon for its border—as with nature and
the human spirit—and which is too large for them to be capable of understanding.

True patriotism has a horror of that which disseminates
hatred and war. . . .

Attending this first meeting of the IAC were delegates from England, France, Germany, Italy, and Belgium, with Barbusse presiding.
The Italian delegation, backed by the ARAC, argued that the IAC
should affiliate itself with the communist Third International, but the
British, German, and some of the French organizations were opposed, insisting that the IAC should remain strictly an antiwar movement and not get involved in "political" propaganda—a view that
the majority of the conference accepted. The British delegation conceded that, although the economic roots of the war sprang from
capitalism, by working against the military-industrial complex—the
military, the armaments industry, and the foreign offices of
Europe—the chances of war could be diminished even if capitalism
continued. The British also proposed that all future IAC
correspondence be conducted in Esperanto! There was one tough resolution passed: that if a new war broke out in Europe the IAC would
call for a general strike.[13] Although Barbusse was elected general
secretary of the IAC, the conference was a setback for him. In 1920
the British withdrew from the movement, and although a second conference was held in Vienna in 1921, the IAC died soon after for lack
of broad-based support. The fact that from 1920 onward Barbusse
and the ARAC were clearly allied with the French Communist party
and the Third International was largely responsible for the demise of
the IAC.

Barbusse himself did not officially join the Communist party until 1923, believing (like Jean-Paul Sartre later) that he could be more useful to the party on the outside, serving as a bridge between the communist and noncommunist Left. But in 1923, when the entire Central Committee of the French Communist party was jailed, Barbusse took out a party card: "Since I embrace their ideas, I must embrace the risks that go with them."[14] From 1923 onward the ARAC was simply the veterans' auxiliary of the French Communist party. Any lingering ties with the noncommunist Left were thus severed. Barbusse's adherence to communism also destroyed another movement he had launched after the war, the Union of International Intellectuals. Its major organ was *Clarté*, a pacifist newspaper founded by Barbusse in 1919. Among its original contributors were some of the most renowned names in European letters: H. G. Wells, G. B. Shaw, Heinrich Mann, Jules Romains, Léon Blum, Stefan Zweig, and—from America—Upton Sinclair. Like the ARAC in the beginning, *Clarté* also declared itself "independent of political parties," but with Barbusse's all but formal commitment to communism after 1920 a split developed on the editorial board and, like the IAC, the Union of International Intellectuals folded.

Barbusse's efforts to organize veterans and intellectuals of the noncommunist Left for peace had failed. After 1920 he fell back on a more sectarian position, defending the communist Third International as the major agency of world peace. In 1929 he wrote: "Every international act of the Soviet Union is an expression of its peace aspirations and its unwavering efforts to win over and reinforce the position of peace."[15] He denounced capitalist imperialism in Morocco (1925), Abyssinia (1935), and elsewhere, and in 1927 wrote a book, *Jesus,* presenting Christ as a percursor of pacifism and communism. In 1932, with Romain Rolland, he helped found the World Committee for the Struggle against War and Fascism—an organization whose very title symbolized the dilemma of left-wing pacifist intellectuals during the appeasement era. How was one to truly fight fascist expansionism without risking war against Germany and Italy? Like many leftist intellectuals of the thirties, Barbusse evaded the dilemma with murky rhetoric. On his deathbed in a Moscow hospital in 1935, he criticized Mussolini's invasion of Abyssinia, only to caution: "Abyssinia can lead to a very big war and that can only be avoided if we do something large, very large. We have already enlarged a good deal, but that is not enough. We must even more enlarge, enlarge. . .enlarge. . .enlarge. . . ."[16]

Despite Barbusse's failures as an organizer for peace and despite his conversion to communism, he was less doctrinaire than some of his cohorts on the left. For all his belief in human equality and participatory democracy, he had no illusions about the ignorance that continued to plague the masses he loved. *Le Feu* had blamed the First World War not just on the privileged classes and the munitions makers but also on the "accumulation of. . .ignorance [and]. . .the immovable masses."[17] In 1921 he stated his credo with a singular lack of utopianism:[18]

I do not propose a new religion. I do not propose a terrestrial paradise, or anything else that savors of magic and of the supernatural. Our task is no longer to seek "the perfect happiness of mankind," or to discover some magic formula that will make love and fraternity blossom upon the earth. These terms relate to emotional ideals, to metaphysical entities, with which social science is not called upon to deal. They are matters which relate to the private life of the individual—and should remain there.

Many noble spirits insist upon confusing social and moral progress. They refuse to believe in material reforms except as an outcome, a result of spiritual and moral reforms modifying radically human nature. They say: "If you are going to reform society, you must first reform men."

By this enlarging and confusing the problem, we render it vague and impossible of accomplishment. Undoubtedly, if all men were good, society would immediately become perfect; but we have no grounds for believing that human goodness will ever become so universal as to supersede our social and political restraints. All history teaches the natural fallibility of man, and that, even though the masses may be stirred for a brief period, or even a whole generation, by some great moral or aesthetic ideal, the latter loses its force—and indeed degenerates into its very opposite—unless it is constantly corrected and reinforced by some stable criterion, by some positive knowledge.

Sentimental reform has but momentary value in social progress. As a reaction from an evil, it may be a wholesome, destructive force, to clear the air, but it is of brief utility. When faced by the task of construction, the emotional reformer is without a plan, and helpless. Let us cherish the pious hope in the future moral betterment of our race, but let us not overlook the futility of making that hope the basis of a practical social program.

However, if Barbusse was unmessianic about the ends of socialism, he was an avowed radical regarding the means that would be employed to achieve them: socialist revolution would require socialist violence, and there should be no shrinking from it when the time came. What Barbusse could not abide, in both the struggle for peace and the struggle for socialism, was the tactical moderate, the liberal humanist, who believed that socialism and permanent peace could be brought about through ideas and moral suasion alone. Hence his break with Romain Rolland: "Romain Rolland believes that we must not lay ourselves open to the reproach which we make against fascists and imperialists and that we must proscribe violence. . . . I do not agree."[19] Hence, too, Barbusse criticized Erich Maria Remarque's *All Quiet on the Western Front* for its "prudent and restrained" conclusions. Barbusse wrote of Remarque's novel: "The suffering of men, the horror of war are facile themes that readers, *today,* adopt immediately in arriving at the extreme limit of their good will in the domain of human solidarity. They have such a fear of revolution that they are already afraid of hearing it mentioned."[20]

His experience with the International Association of Ex-Soldiers and the Union of International Intellectuals had been that of defeats at the hands of moderates, and he blamed the failures of the peace movement on their shortsightedness: "There are those who believe that everything will work out: a small concession here, a capitulation and a cowardice there and little by little progress will take place. It is a lie: compromises only serve to consolidate the established order. Morality means not falling into traps."[21]

Most veterans in France during the interwar period, however, while having no love for war, were just such creatures: moderates. Indeed, of the many veterans' associations established in France after the war, the ARAC was one of the smallest, its affiliation with communism severely restricting its appeal. Even within the international veterans' movement, it and the IAC were of much less consequence than the less militant, nonsocialist FIDAC, the Fraternité Interalliée des Anciens Combattants [International Federation of Ex-Soldiers], founded in 1920. Compared to the IAC, the FIDAC was immense, representing as it did the major French, British, and Italian veterans' organizations, plus the American Legion, comprising an estimated three million French, two million Italian, two million English, and 750,000 American ex-servicemen.

Although the FIDAC sought better international understanding as a means of avoiding future wars, the nationalism of its respective delegations was often stronger than its internationalism. The Americans were wary of attempts to use the FIDAC to draw the United States into the League of Nations or to make their country "subservient to a world court," while the French, at the London congress of 1924, fought an English proposal to permit representatives of the former enemy countries, Germany and her allies, admission to the FIDAC. An American delegate took the opportunity to criticize the French for being "notoriously slow" in accepting the idea of reconciliation, pointing out that it was not until the fiasco of the Ruhr invasion of 1923 and the inauguration of the Dawes Plan of 1924 that they had relented at all.

In their "slowness" the French delegation differed little from its civilian counterparts at home. French veterans at the congress echoed French government policy and the mainstream of French public opinion rather than acting as an independent force—which was only natural inasmuch as the veterans' organizations they represented sprang from the broad center of French political life. The FIDAC was a moderate, middle-of-the-road affair, with the French delegation voicing the mistrustful nationalism of most of their countrymen. When it came to foreign policy, the leaders of the major French veterans' organizations (with the exception of the ARAC), like their counterparts in French electoral politics, usually took a hard line toward Germany in the early 1920s and a softer line in the late 1920s—in tune with French public opinion in general throughout. There were moments, of course, when veterans' opinion was more poignant—as at a joint congress of French veterans' associations in Oran in 1930 when a reporter commented upon the strong mood for peace and disarmament which gripped the delegates as they watched a ship bearing mutilated war veterans sail into the harbor. Typically however, at the congress itself the same veterans voted that along with disarmament must go a guaranteed mutual security pact among nations; i.e., without such a safeguard France must be prepared to fight another war.[22]

The two largest veterans' associations in France during the interwar period were the Union National des Combattants (UNC) and the Union Fédérale des Combattants, each in 1934 with approximately 950,000 members. Politically, the UNC was right-wing, more conservative than radical right—although its vice president at the time of

the February 6, 1934, riots, Jean Goy, was to join the fascist Ras-
semblement National Populaire in 1942. The Union Fédérale was
more centrist, ideologically attuned to the French Radical and
Radical-Socialist parties. The influence of the French Socialist party
(SFIO) was seen in the Fédération Ouvrière et Paysanne (about
100,000 veterans), that of the French Communist party in the ARAC
(about 5000), the smallest of all. There was also the Catholic-
oriented Semaine du Combattant and various specialized veterans'
groupings: the associations of war wounded (100,000 members), of
chest wounded (50,000 members), of soldiers blinded in the war, of
officers, of war decorated, etc. Englobing all these formations (with
the exception of the ARAC, which was excluded on grounds of insufficient membership) was the Confédération Nationale des Combattants [the National Confederation of War Veterans]. The Confédération
Nationale was administered by a council of fifty members elected by
an assembly of some five hundred delegates designated by the various veterans' associations according to the size of their membership.
Altogether some eighty-five associations were represented, with the
UNC and the Union Fédérale being the two largest. In 1934 the secretary general of the Confédération was Georges Rivollet, who was
also a member of the French cabinet, appropriately minister of pensions. Thus the Confédération had a representative of its own within
the government itself.

Despite ritualistic declarations by almost all the veterans' associations that they were "apolitical," it was nevertheless true that most
veterans joined associations which accorded with "their affinities,
their personal convictions, their social origins, their military rank,
etc."[23] Whereas in the United States there were only two veterans'
associations, the American Legion and the Veterans of Foreign
Wars, in France there were several, allowing a much wider ideological choice, even if, ultimately, the UNC and the Union Fédérale
tended to dominate the scene. An important aspect of this ideological
diversity was that the French Right, although strongly present in the
UNC, was not the sole spokesman for veterans and was never able to
monopolize veterans' politics. Moreover, the UNC shrank from being
overtly "political" in the 1920s, limiting itself to lobbying for veterans' benefits (i.e., pensions for ex-servicemen and war widows, and
government aid to war orphans) and commemorating their dead. The
same was true for the Union Fédérale and the Confédération
Nationale as well as for most of the subassociations. However political their members were as private citizens, as veterans they remained

theoretically "apolitical"—the official statutes of the Confédération Nationale expressly forbidding any involvement in "political" activity.

With the coming of the depression to France, however, the UNC and the Union Fédérale became more actively political—although even then the change was more in degree than in kind, the primary goal remaining the protection of veterans' benefits. Faced with the prospect of a government austerity budget which would reduce these benefits, the UNC and the Union Fédérale sought to exert direct pressure on the government to stem such cuts. The right-wing UNC was the more militant of the two, participating actively in the February 6, 1934, demonstration which toppled the Daladier government and brought the more conservative Doumergue to power. The president of the UNC in 1934 was George Lebecq, a Parisian municipal councilman who, along with fifteen other right-wing municipal councilmen, signed a proclamation on the eve of February 6 protesting the formation of a more left-wing government and calling for its overthrow by street action. The vice president of the UNC was Jean Goy, in 1934 a right-wing member of the Chamber of Deputies, in 1942 a Nazi collaborator.

In 1934 Lebecq and Goy were anxious to go beyond simply defending veterans' benefits to enlisting the UNC in action against the Third Republic itself. In this, they met considerable resistance, or apathy, from the rank and file of the organization. In January, 1934, Lebecq sent out a circular to UNC members in the Paris region asking for volunteers to act as squad leaders in case the UNC leadership should decide "to launch an action of some sort." Lebecq later testified before the parliamentary commission that investigated the background and nature of the February 6 riots:[24]

> We needed 500 energetic commissioners, resolute, determined to exert authority over their comrades, and to themselves obey orders transmitted to them. Five hundred squad leaders, out of 70,000 members in the Paris region—we should have been able to find that many easily. Do you know how many responses we got from the 95 sections which received our circular? Eleven only, and those 11 presidents offered us a total of 50 commissioners.

The provinces were even more apathetic. Police reports indicate that on February 6 it was only UNC units of the Paris region that demonstrated—none from the provinces. Nor was the Union Fédérale

or the Confédération Nationale willing to lend support to staging
the demonstration.[25] Lebecq and Goy were finally able to mobilize
some ten thousand UNC veterans on February 6, but only after qual-
ifying their antisocialist and antiparliamentary proclamation of February 5 with assurances that "in saving the country, we are defending the regime of liberty to which we are profoundly attached."[26]
Support was also forthcoming from the National Association of Officer Veterans (whose one thousand members were led by Colonel
Ferrandi, another Parisian municipal councilman) and from two other
small veterans' groups, the Union of Cosican Veterans and the Decorated for Peril to Their Lives.

The driving force behind the February 6, 1934, riots, however,
was not the UNC but the fascist leagues: the Jeunesses Patriotes, the
Solidarité Francaise, the Croix de Feu, the Francistes, and the Action
Francaise. All but the Action Francaise (the royalist league of
Charles Maurras founded during the Dreyfus affair) were products of
the First World War and the veterans' mystique; most of their original members were veterans. Although these movements were much
smaller than the UNC, they were more ideological, more eager to engage in direct political action, and much more militaristically organized. Although unrepresentative of French veterans as a whole,
during the political-economic crisis of February, 1934, their discipline, activism, and alliance with the Action Francaise and other rightist groups allowed them to extert a momentary influence far exceed-
ing their numbers. They were to the radical Right what the ARAC was
to the radical Left, with the important difference that their membership was much larger and their social-economic views more in tune
with those of the middle classes and most of the peasantry. For all
their talk of national "socialism," it was clear that they were far
more nationalist than socialist and that their main enemy was the
Marxist Left.[27]

Denouncing class struggle and Marxist internationalism, the fascist
leagues stood for class "reconciliation," "patriotism" (i.e., right-
wing nationalism), property rights, low taxes, company unions, and
the suppression of the CGT and other socialist organizations. It was
their politics, not their economics, that separated them from most
Frenchmen: they were enemies of political liberalism as well as of
socialism, condemning parliamentary democracy as hopelessly corrupt and divisive and calling for "strong" government and national
"unity." They were set off from the UNC and the Union Fédérale, as
well as from France's major political parties, by their paramilitary

organization and preparations for political violence. Eschewing electoral politics (at which they knew they could not win), they sought to mobilize public opinion against the communist menace. Should the communists attempt a coup d'état, they would be in the streets against them; should circumstances become propitious for a coup of their own, they would be ready to seize the opportunity (if their leaders publicly denied the latter, police reports did not).

There were two other important differences between the leagues and the major veterans' organizations: the leagues were subsidized by wealthy financial backers with special economic interests to defend, and by 1934 the leagues had opened their ranks to nonveterans, especially the young, in an attempt to increase their political power. The effect of the latter was not to civilianize the veterans in these movements but to militarize the civilians who joined them. Military morality was the hallmark of these organizations, both in style and thought. Not only was the official garb of the movements semimilitary, but so too was their organizational structure, each with a supreme commander at the top of a hierarchical order of command, with the troops divided into divisions, brigades, sections, and squads, ready to be mobilized on short notice and to act, if need be, in an equally military manner. The Croix de Feu's famous "maneuvers" in which thousands of young men were periodically alerted and, within a few hours, transported from one part of France to another in the movement's cars and trucks made the Croix de Feu a political force to be reckoned with—a *military*-political force. The *Freikorps* and Ernst Roehm's SA might have been German inventions, but the French radical Right was happy to emulate them.

The paramilitary character of the French fascist leagues was noted by the parliamentary commission which, following the February 6 riots, held hearings at which the league chieftains were questioned. Although Colonel de La Rocque of the Croix de Feu and the other league leaders quibbled about the "military" nature of their formations (La Rocque arguing that such charges were inaccurate since the Croix de Feu did not train its members for foreign wars and since they did not carry arms), they conceded that their members executed the orders given them without prior democratic agreement—a blind military obedience which La Rocque preferred to describe as "a freely consented discipline." The parliamentary commission concluded, however, that such formations, "comprising dozens of thousands of members who obey the will of a single person or a small number of leaders," posed a grave danger to the republic. It was on the commission's recommendation that the leagues, in their paramilitary form, were eventually banned in 1935.[28]

Nor was the commission moved by the argument that the leagues were "apolitical." As one commission member pointed out, "behind the expression 'no politics' was generally understood 'no party politics.' "[29] The leagues were antiparliamentary but hardly antipolitical: their politics were simply more authoritarian than democratic. The leagues tried to exploit the veterans' mystique to cover their political designs—soldiers being, theoretically, apolitical—but the fact that almost all the league leaders and their lieutenants were war veterans made them no less political—as was true of French veterans in general. Moreover, the fact that some of the league leaders were members of the Municipal Council of Paris and a few even members of the Chamber of Deputies made their "apoliticality" all the more dubious.

In 1934 the largest of the French fascist leagues was the Solidarité Française with 180,000 members, 80,000 in Paris. Its major financial backer was Francois Coty, the perfume and newspaper magnate.[30] In the wake of the February 6 riots, it also received a subsidy of two million francs from Georges Vautier, a member of the Redressement Francais. The Redressement Francais was a business lobby officially committed to "leading an energetic propaganda campaign against the extreme Left." Vautier himself was the director of some fifteen hydroelectric and gas companies.[31] Coty, who described himself politically as a "plebiscitary Bonapartist Republican," assigned Jean Renaud, an ex-colonial officer, to organize the movement along military lines. Its member wore the SF uniform—blue shirt and beret, gray trousers, and military boots—and stood ready to resist any communist uprising, particularly the SF's elite battalion of fifteen hundred "shock troops." Ideologically, the Solidarité Française was antisocialist, antiparliamentary, anti-Masonic and anti-semitic. It was also theoretically pro-Arab, recruiting one squad of its shock troops from unemployed North Africans in Paris. At the same time, however, it was an ardent defender of the French empire.

Colonel de La Rocque's Croix de Feu had some 50,000 regular members in 1934, 18,000 in Paris. Originally restricted to war veterans who had won the prestigious Croix de Feu on the battlefield, its membership was later extended to all comers. Together with the "Sons of the Croix de Feu" and the Volontaires Nationaux, its youth movements, it counted 130,000 in France, including 25,000 in Paris. It also, like some of the other leagues, had its own women's auxiliary (the morality here was Catholic, traditionalist, and unemancipated—the ladies being informed that the women's emancipation movement was based on the same assumptions as socialist class struggle and that "conciliation," not conflict, was the proper path—conciliation on male terms).[32] The male units of the Croix de Feu, like those of the Solidarité Francaise, were organized and trained for potential combat against a communist insurrection, although, as the French minister of information later noted, not all members of the Croix de Feu, especially its older members, were willing "to descend into the street with a helmet on their head." But the Croix de Feu did have some fifteen hundred "dispos" who could be mobilized on short notice for just this purpose. It even had its own small "air force," a rickety collection of civilian aircraft whose existence nevertheless added to the notoriety of the movement. As the February 6 riots were to demonstrate, the Croix de Feu was perhaps the most highly disciplined of all the leagues.

Like the other leagues, the Croix de Feu was subsidized by certain big-business groups, mainly banks, utility companies, and the steel trust (Comité des Forges). La Rocque himself was on the board of directors of a major hydroelectric company, the Compagnie Générale d'Electricité, which, like other French utility companies, feared the coming to power of a left-wing government which might lower electricity rates and even nationalize the industry. The head of the Compagnie Générale d'Electricité was Ernest Mercier, who in 1934 was also head of the Redressment Français, the same right-wing propaganda organization and business lobby whose political slush fund helped subsidize the Solidarité Française. The Banque de France was also probably an early financial backer: the treasurer of the Croix de Feu was one of the bank's lawyers, the assistant treasurer one of its cashiers. Francois Coty also chipped in when the Croix de Feu was founded in 1927. Another early financial backer was Pozzo di Borgo, a former French air force pilot, a wealthy landowner—and vice president of the Croix de Feu.[33] In 1937 it was discovered that the Croix de Feu had even benefited from government subsidies between 1930 and 1932 when the conservative André Tardieu had been a government minister. Tardieu later testified that on the recommendation of a "high military personality" he had provided La Roque with secret funds to help him expand his antisocialist movement. As Tardieu characterized his part in the transaction, "I thought that it would be interesting to help in organizing the forces of order against the forces of disorder."[34]

Following the Croix de Feu's display of disciplined force during the February 6 riots, its membership numbers soared and new money flowed into its treasury. Police reports indicate that it was able to launch its own daily newspaper—a sure sign of financial prosperity—due to the backing of Francois de Wendel (industrialist and president of the Comité des Forges), Ernest Mallet and Pierre Miraband (bankers), Schwob d'Hericourt (industrialist), Jacques de Neuflize (banker and railroad director), and Otto de la Havraise (a major electrical-industry stockholder).[35] Police reports also reveal that by 1936 La Rocque's movement was receiving large sums from the Banque de Paris et des Pays Bas and the Banque Mallet Fréres—the latter acting as a go-between for some of France's richest nobility, particularly the Guise and Luynes families and the Duchess of Uzès.[36] Why was so much money forthcoming? According to a police report in 1935, "The principal cause of [the Croix de Feu's] success is obviously its fundamental antiparliamentarianism."[37]

In an effort to legitimize its subversive goals, however, and to exploit the veterans' mystique, Colonel de La Rocque repeatedly insisted that the Croix de Feu was "not political," that it was "above parties." But the official program of the movement in 1933 was political enough, calling as it did for lower taxes, higher tariffs, the "elimination of government intervention in areas belonging to free enterprise [monopolies, services, confiscations, more or less disguised]," and the protection of family property and "legitimate profits" from savings.[38] Heavily Catholic in membership, highly nationalistic, culturally traditionalist, the Croix de Feu took as its motto "Fatherland, Family, Work"—the same motto which the Vichy regime later adopted. Presenting itself as a "moral" force in French political life and as a force for class conciliation, the Croix de Feu denounced the communists and the socialists for stirring up class conflict and serving not the patriotic French tricolor but the red flag of international revolution.

La Rocque emphasized that his movement was "republican," not royalist, but its "republicanism" was strongly antiparliamentarian in 1934, more authoritarian than democratic. Recognizing that its mass base was narrow and that its chances of overthrowing the Third Republic by force were slim, it underscored its paramilitary usefulness in the event of a socialist uprising. According to its official statutes, it stood ready to intervene "if need be, alongside the government or in response to public opinion" to help crush a socialist revolution. Despite such declarations, the tone and membership of the Croix de

Feu was more respectable and upper class than some of the leagues. This was seen in the support it received from students at the Grandes Écoles of the École Polytechnique, Saint-Cyr, and the Naval Academy—the prestigious schools which trained scions of the *haute bourgeoisie* for top positions in the civil service and the military. Some 350 such students, members of the Volontaires Nationaux, paraded in their school uniforms with other Croix de Feu units up the Champs Elysées to the Arc de Triomphe on Armistice Day, 1933. The link with the military establishment was particularly noticeable. Although officers on active duty were discouraged from joining such organizations, many reserve officers belonged. More importantly, many young cadets who were being groomed for high positions in the army already belonged.

After the Croix de Feu the next largest league in 1934 was the Jeunesses Patriotes, with some 90,000 members, 6,400 in Paris. Its chief was Pierre Taittinger, the champagne and real estate millionaire. Like the Croix de Feu's, its membership was more upper middle class than that of the Solidarité Francaise and paid higher dues, but it was Taittinger who financed such of the league's activities. It appears that important funds were also provided by Henri de Kerillis, head of the Centre de Propagande des Républicains Nationaux, another right-wing propaganda organization subsidized by businessmen.[39] The official purpose of the Jeunesses Patriotes was[40]

to impede the action of the parties of anarchy by the diffusion of a doctrine uniquely inspired by the national interest and to constitute an organized force ready to oppose communist activities by all means necessary and prepared, if need be, to put itself at the disposition of an energetic national government which, in the event of revolutionary troubles, has decided to maintain order.

The Jeunesses Patriotes also had its own paramilitary uniform and emblems and its own hard-core "shock troops," some 1,900 of the latter, 400 of whom were university students, "Phalangeards" from the Latin Quarter. The Jeunesses Patriotes specialized in military-nationalistic ceremonies (including annual parades up the Champs Élysées to the Tomb of the Unknown Soldiers and processions to the statue of Joan of Arc), fascist salutes, and antisocialist, antiparliamentary, procolonialist oratory. Its chain of command was military, its central committee all war veterans.

The least important but most openly fascist of all the leagues was

Marcel Bucard's Francistes, which numbered only 1,500 followers, a mere 300 in Paris. Bucard, a highly decorated war hero, played the military mystique for all it was worth. According to Bucard, there were only two Frances, "that of the front and that of the rear."[41] He made no effort to conceal the fascist goals of his movement, a movement appropriately founded in 1933, and called for the overthrow of the Third Republic and the creation of a totalitarian state which would put an end to socialist class struggle and liberal party politics. Poorly subsidized (even though some funds were forthcoming from Italy), lower middle class to lumpenproletariat in membership, and too blatantly modeled upon the German brand of fascism for French taste, the Francistes remained the weakest of the leagues.

Why in 1934 did an estimated 370,000 men belong to the Solidarité Francaise, the Croix de Feu, the Jeunesses Patriotes, and the Francistes, over 100,000 in Paris? For a variety of reasons: hatred of socialism, liberalism, and parliamentarianism, opposition to secularized public education (a high percentage of members were Catholic), subsidization of some members during a period of economic depression, nostalgia for the spirit of the trenches of the First World War, a desire on the part of younger members to emulate the deeds of their elders in domestic combat, sheer love of excitement and camaraderie (police reports on the February 6 riots noted that the most combative rioters were "in general rather young"[42]), and even, possibly, because the wearing of paramilitary uniforms had its sexual uses.[43] A recurring theme in French radical Right propaganda was that only a restoration of military morality could overcome the "decadence" which plagued French society, a decadence that was due to Marxist materialism, internationalism, and class conflict and to liberal hedonism, individualism, and parliamentary corruption. Both Marxism and liberalism, it was argued, lacked the "spiritual" values necessary to regenerate the nation and make it strong, vital, and noble again—as it had been during the war.

An early exponent of this philosophy was Georges Valois. In 1925 Valois founded the Faisceau, a French fascist movement modeled upon Mussolini's blackshirts, which flourished briefly during the backlash to the Cartel des Gauches [Left coalition government] of 1924. Valois called for a "dictatorship of war veterans" to restore "morality," i.e., military morality, to French life.[44] A leading writer for the Faisceau, Philippe Barrès (son of the anti-Dreyfusard Maurice Barrès), sounded the keynote of the movement in the first issue of the party newspaper, published symbolically on November 11, 1925,

in memory of the "day of victory" of the First World War, a day
which Philippe Barrès described as "the highest moment of our
lives." Since then, he said, France had grown decadent.[45]

We are filled with the certitude that it is because [France] has
abandoned the teachings of war that. . .she has declined. And
we are sure that in returning to the lessons of war France will
rediscover grandeur and each Frenchman the joy of living.

What are. . .the lessons of war for present political action?
What does the spirit of war provide for the conduct of the
country in peacetime?

[It reminds us of] the union, of the *faisceau,* that the war
formed for our salvation, between the masses and the elite who
knew how to join together for the defense of a. . .sacred cause
indispensable to their life in common: the Fatherland.

Ah! then there was no question of class hatred. . .although,
God knows, many suffered. . .and the outcome of the struggle
was uncertain. But there we were, a people who have been
called the most divided in the world, no longer at odds, who
had found a goal worthy of themselves, for once. . . .

However, you will say, all was still not well. Behind the
army, behind that young France unanimously defending and
ennobling itself, there continued to exist certain incorrigibles
obstinately pursuing their old parliamentary quarrels. . . .

Yes, true! But it is precisely here that the lessons of the war
attain their final conclusion. . . . We soldiers saw well. . .how
the politicians continued to play their miserable game, . . .how
a parliament withdrawn into itself remained absorbed in selfish
concerns. . . .

We soldiers would have gladly allowed politicians and Parliament to be abolished during the war. . . .

[After the war, France returned to] the reign of old politicians, to their incompetence. . . .

The remedy: penetrate the State with the spirit of victory.

But this time we must be careful: it is no longer a question,
for the victors, of simply pleading the cause of the State with
the people, nor of dealing with a government personnel whom
it is henceforth impossible to defend. It is rather a question of
penetrating the State itself with the spirit of victory. . . . It is
necessary that this spirit of victory. . .shine at the very summit
of the national edifice.

Although the Faisceau collapsed after the conservative Poincaré returned to power in 1926 and undercut its appeal, the ideas of the Faisceau did not die.

The public proclamations issued before the February 6, 1934, riots by the Solidarité Francaise, the Croix de Feu, the Jeunesses Patriotes, the UNC, and other right-wing organizations spoke in much the same terms as the Faisceau of 1925. The Solidarité Francaise newspaper *L'Ami du Peuple* berated the Third Republic: "Your parliament is rotten. Your politicians are compromised. . . . The police mobilized because persons in high places want to aid the revolutionary socialists. All this in order to protect corrupt politicians against the honest man, who is fed up."[46] A Jeunesses Patriotes tract denounced the "decadence of Parliament" and spoke of *"insurrection as the most sacred of duties."*[47] Colonel de La Rocque telegraphed Croix de Feu section commanders throughout France on the eve of February 6: "The end we pursue is to put an end to the dictatorship of the socialist influence and to call to power a clean government, free of politicians of whatever kind. . . ."[48] The UNC's newspaper *Le Petit Bleu* predicted that war veterans "would *without warning* undertake the *work of cleaning out* [the political trenches] which the UNC had only deferred."[49]

There were other parallels between Valois's Faisceau of 1925 and the rightist leagues of 1934. The Faisceau had risen during a national financial crisis, following a shift to the Left in the French government, and emulated Mussolini's blackshirts abroad. The leagues grew rapidly with the onset of the Great Depression of the 1930s, capitalizing in 1934 on another shift to the Left in the French government, and were not unaware of the similarity between their blueshirts and Hitler's brownshirts (the fascist salute being utilized at some meetings). Hitler had come to power in Germany only a year before. As one French politician later recalled, ". . .the idea of dictatorship was in the air."[50] It was a time in French history when the official newspaper of the UNC was not averse to publishing a cartoon on its front page picturing the Chamber of Deputies in flames and some of the deputies hanging by their necks from lampposts on the Concorde bridge—and the UNC was one of the *least* radical of the veteran's groups which participated in the February 6 riots.

Circumstances were ripe in February, 1934, for a right-wing backlash. The depression was taking its toll: business was hard hit, bankruptcies were multiplying, unemployment was accelerating, university students could not find jobs, and yet the cost of living remained

high.[51] Business groups were disturbed by possible socialist or re-
formist moves against them. A police report of November, 1933,
noted that "in banking circles the establishment of a Cartelist cabinet
with the participation of the Neo-Socialists was feared."[52] At the
same time the French Right was eager to use the budget crisis facing
the new Chautemps cabinet to exert pressure of its own. It found the
Stavisky scandal an excellent opportunity to increase this pressure.

In January, 1934, it was revealed that Serge Stavisky, a confidence man with a lengthy criminal record who had defrauded hundreds of investors in municipal bonds in Bayonne, had benefited for
years from the protection of friends in high places. Several prominent
French politicians and judges were implicated in the scandal. When
Stavisky committed suicide (some claimed he was killed by the
police to prevent him from testifying), the rightist press called for the
political hide of his protectors and seized the occasion to blame such
corruption on parliamentary democracy (even though similar scandals
had occurred under previous undemocratic regimes). When the Action Francaise and other right-wing newspapers called for the establishment of a parliamentary commission to investigate the scandal
and expose the wrongdoers, Premier Chautemps refused to consent
and won a 367 to 201 vote of confidence in the Chamber of Deputies
on the issue. This only added fuel to the fire.

The right-wing press now intensified its charges that the whole
parliamentary system was corrupt, the most extreme critics demanding not only "throw the rascals out" but the creation of a new political order based on the fascist model. As a result of the press campaign against Chautemps, plus several nights of street rioting by
young radical rightists in the Latin Quarter protesting the Stavisky
scandal, the Chautemps government resigned. This was on January
27, 1934. Shortly afterwards Daladier assumed the premiership.

In forming his new Cabinet Daladier sought to go beyond his own
Radical-Socialist support and broaden his base in the Chamber by
appointing two conservative deputies to the posts of minister of finance and minister of war. However, the parliamentary Right, led by
André Tardieu, sought to sabotage the new government and intensify
the crisis by withholding its support. As a result, Daladier turned to
the Left, to Léon Blum and the Socialist party deputies in the
Chamber, for support—which was forthcoming. On February 2
Daladier made a tactical error which was to arouse the full fury of
the Right against him. In an attempt to get at the heart of the
Stavisky scandal, in which both the French police and judiciary were

implicated, and to firm up lax police response to increasingly violent street demonstrations by radical rightist youths, Daladier fired three prominent officials: the heads of the French judiciary, the national police, and the Paris police. Rather than reducing public pressure on the government, however, this act led to a new uproar.

The prefect of police, Jean Chiappe, bitterly protested that he was a victim of the machinations of the Left, that he had been fired as a result of a deal that Daladier had made with the Socialists to get their support. Chiappe, who had been indulgent toward rightist youths rioting nightly in the Latin Quarter, was now pictured in the right-wing press as a martyr, a defender of law and order who was being sacrificed to the Left. Tardieu wrote in *Le Soir* on February 3 that Daladier had wooed the Socialists by "offering the head of the prefect." Daladier's appointment of Eugen Frot, a Socialist deputy, to the vital position of minister of interior acerbated rightist sentiment even more. Conservatives in the Chamber argued that "the head of the army of order had been sacrificed to the elements of disorder."[53] Stavisky was submerged by Chiappe; the Right had a new pretext for street action.

This street action had been snowballing since January when Action Francaise youths began roaming the Latin Quarter at night, turning over newsstands, wrecking café terraces, breaking store windows, and clashing with the police. The tolerance of police and judicial authorities (there were few arrests, and those who were arrested were given small fines) only offered encouragement to the rioters. By late January militants of the Solidarité Francaise and the Jeunesses Patriotes, some in their league uniforms, had become involved. The greatest incitement to riot, however, had come with Chautemps's resignation itself. Extraparliamentary action had shown its political efficacy: a government chosen by a democratically elected Chamber had been overthrown by street violence. The rightist minority was elated. It was at this point that the UNC, the French Taxpayers' Federation, the fascist leagues, and other rightist groups decided to hold a mass demonstration on February 6 to exert further pressure on the Chamber of Deputies—a demonstration that was to escalate into the greatest outbreak of public violence France had seen since the Paris Commune of 1871. Had the street gangs of January been dealt with more firmly and had Chautemps not rewarded them for their actions by resigning, the February 6 riots might never have taken place. But Chiappe had not applied the same procedures of mass arrests that he had applied against communist demonstrators on previous occasions.

Some police grumbled about Chiappe's practicing a "benevolence toward the demonstrators of the Boulevard Saint-German [right-wing students of the Latin Quarter]" which he did not practice "toward the demonstrators of the Place de la République [a left-wing neighborhood]."[54]

Encouraged by Chautemps's resignation and by what some took to be the sympathy of police authorities for their cause, the Right moved in for the kill. For some rightists this simply meant preventing the formation of a new Cartel des Gauches; others dreamed of overthrowing the Third Republic itself; while for many UNC demonstrators the main goal remained the preservation of veterans' benefits. However much they may have differed on ends (which were not necessarily incompatible), they agreed on the use of radical means to achieve them. None respected the right of a freely elected Parliament to decide the course of the nation: the streets of Paris, not the grassroots, would decide.

Prior to February 6 the Paris mass-circulation newspapers, most politically conservative and subsidized by big-business interests (*Le Temps,* for example, by the Comité des Forges, *Le Figaro* and *L'Ami du Peuple* by Francois Coty), launched a press campaign against Daladier and an alleged leftist takeover. As the parliamentary commission which later investigated the background to the February 6 riots pointed out, "almost the whole of the press indicated to the public that [Daladier's firing of Chiappe] was a political maneuver."[55] *Le Temps, Le Figaro, Le Jour, Le Petit Parisien, L'Echo de Paris, L'Ami du Peuple, L'Intransigeant,* and *La Liberté* joined the fascist newspapers in accusing Daladier of selling out to the Socialists and alluded sympathetically to the possibility of a violent overthrow of the government by "the nation." On February 4 *Le Temps* declared that "the worn decor of our electoral and parliamentary theater risks being thrown out overnight by a national uprising." On February 7, the day after the riots, *Le Figaro* endorsed the protest and, seemingly, any further violence that might be necessary to bring down the hated government: ". . .the first Cartel led us to ruin. This one brought us yesterday to the brink of civil war. . . . Tomorrow? One had the impression yesterday at the Chamber that this regime, tomorrow, will be near its end."[56] A month before, *La Victoire* had hoped that a "providential leader" would emerge in France "as he emerged in Italy and Germany."[57] On February 5 a Jeunesses Patriotes proclamation designated General Weygand for such a role. On February 7 *L'Echo de Paris* sounded a similar note when it reported that should veterans decide to march again against the government, Marshal Lyautey would be at their head. On February 5 the leadership of the UNC had gone beyond simply the issue of veterans' benefits, publishing a proclamation which not only denounced Daladier for delivering Chiappe "to the vengeance of the Socialist Party" but called upon its members to demonstrate against the "vote merchants."[58]

Typical of the radical Right press on the morning of February 6 was the thinly veiled appeal of *L'Ami du Peuple* for a right-wing revolution: "The country is in danger! Daladier is leading you like sheep to be butchered by Léon Blum. That is the dictatorship which awaits you, people of France."[59] On February 5 Colonel de La Rocque had addressed a public letter to the president of the Republic explaining why he intended to mobilize his followers the next day: "Conscious of my heavy responsibilities, I have decided to send into the streets, for a visible demonstration, the irreproachable veterans [of the Croix de Feu] against the quasi-dictatorial *coup de force* that has been carried out under socialist influence."[60] On the morning of February 6 a number of Paris newspapers published a Croix de Feu appeal that had been posted on walls throughout Paris. The language was now bolder, the suggestion that a coup d'état was afoot less guarded. Addressed to the "nation" in general and to "former comrades in arms" in particular, the proclamation read:[61]

> A government at the service of the red flag is attempting to reduce us to slavery. . . . A dictatorship of sectarianism wants to implant itself. Do not submit to this, follow the Croix de Feu: it stands above parties, all of which are discredited. . . . It will impose a government of decent Frenchmen free of any abject political combinations. . . . With order reestablished, it will know how to maintain it without delivering you to anyone. . . .

The demonstration was set for the evening of February 6, after working hours—to increase the turnout. Some of the participants hoped that the police, angered by the firing of their chief, would join them in the showdown—hence their shouts at the outset of "Long live Chiappe, the police with us!" The leaders of the major organizations involved were playing it by ear, ready to push the Chamber of Deputies as far right as events allowed, yet hesitant to engage in full-scale revolutionary action in case the police, the government, and the army stood firm. Few of the demonstrators were armed with guns—and these were mostly pistols. The "weapons" used were primarily canes and paving stones. Despite the revolutionary rhetoric that preceded the demonstration, there was little serious planning to make a revolution. Indeed, as it turned out, both the organizers and the Daladier government were surprised by the success of the riots. Police estimates on the eve of February 6 predicted a much smaller demonstration than actually developed, and neither the police nor the government were prepared for the amount of violence which erupted against them. Also, compared to police tactics today, French police tactics in 1934 were still in a primitive stage. Surprised by the size and fury of an event which had begun as a peaceful demonstration and exploded into a near insurrection, the government was handicapped by its reluctance to employ maximum force (it had cautioned the police not to fire on the demonstrators) or military troops to quell the riot.

This reluctance was partly due to the presence of so many veterans in the demonstration. Public respect for war veterans was high in France, less because of admiration for military values than because of recognition of the sacrifice these men had made for their country. (At one point during the riots, firemen, in the midst of putting out a fire started by the rioters at a government building, stopped to doff their hats as a column of the UNC marched by.) The government was anxious to treat veterans with kid gloves on Febrary 6. Eugen Frot, the Socialist minister of the interior, later described the attitude of the government toward members of the UNC and the Croix de Feu during the riots as one of "maximum benevolence."[62] Although the government sought to draw a distinction between veterans demonstrating solely for veterans' benefits and veterans involved in "political formations," it was clear that, on February 6, the distinction was largely academic and that the veterans' mystique posed a severe problem for the government.

It was against this background, with the government on the defensive on several fronts, that the French Right mobilized for a massive street demonstration on February 6, the day the new Daladier Cabinet was to present itself to the Chamber of Deputies for confirmation. Although, according to police reports the next day, there was no unified command coordinating all the movements of the various leagues and associations involved, separate agreements had been reached beforehand assigning each group a rendezvous point so that that evening they could march upon the Chamber of Deputies from several directions. The rendezvous points, which formed a wide circle around the Chamber, were conveniently announced in many Paris newspapers.

There was even a contingent of the communist ARAC who—not to be outdone by the Right as protesters against parliamentary corruption ("Chiappe-Stavisky to prison," they shouted) and as defenders of veterans' rights ("Long live the integrity of the rights acquired by war veterans," proclaimed *Humanité* on February 6)—met near the Champs Élysées and later fought alongside rightist demonstrators at the Place de la Concorde. The ARAC formation was small, some four hundred communists led by the young Jacques Duclos, the radical Left having not yet formed paramilitary units comparable in size to those of the radical Right. When the demonstration turned out to be more of a success than the ARAC counted on, a right-wing success, the French Communist party called for independent demonstrations of its own on February 9 and 12 to counteract the "fascist menace." (The police response to February 9 and 12 was much more brutal and efficient than its response to February 6.)

If, on February 6, the ARAC had no intention of bringing the fascist leagues to power, these leagues and the other rightist groups that participated in the riots were themselves only loosely allied. The leagues, especially, were divided by sharp rivalries, no league chieftain wishing to lose his troops to another league chieftain. They were willing to ally on February 6 but not to merge—and even this temporary alliance was a mutually suspicious affair, with no central command in charge once the demonstration was underway. But if the demonstration lacked cohesion once the marchers left their rendezvous points, the intent of the marchers was nevertheless clear: to exert massive political pressure on the government through street action. February 6 may not have been, strictly speaking, a "fascist plot," but it was no exercise in parliamentary democracy either.

All in all, there were some forty thousand demonstrators involved, many of whom were war veterans. At the Place de la Concorde, separated from the Chamber of Deputies by the Seine River, ten thousand of these clashed with police defending the bridge. It was here that the bloodiest fighting took place, although there were clashes at other approaches to the Chamber as well. Casualties on both sides were heavy. William L. Shirer has summarized the police statistics:[63]

> Among the estimated 40,000 rioters, fourteen were killed by bullets and two died later from their wounds; some 655 were injured, of whom 236 were hospitalized and the rest treated at first-aid stations. The police and guards lost one killed and 1,664 injured, of whom 884 were able to resume service after

having their wounds dressed. The guardians fired 527 revolver bullets; the number of shots fired by the rioters was never ascertained. It was the bloodiest encounter in the streets of Paris since the Commune of 1871.

At the Place de la Concorde the first clashes took place around 6 P.M. when the first contingent of marchers began throwing stones at the police who refused to let them pass over the bridge. Several police charges were made to drive the mob back, but after briefly retreating the demonstrators would return to pelt them again. At 6:40 a bus crossing the Place de la Concorde was overturned and set afire by some five hundred demonstrators, many of whom "were respectably dressed, several decorated with the Legion of Honor."[64] Police reinforcements were brought in, mounted Gardes Républicains, whose horses during the fighting were slashed with razors which the demonstrators attached to their canes. At the other end of the square, the Naval Ministry building was set afire. The police began to receive isolated gunfire, as well as the firemen who arrived to deal with the flames at the Naval Ministry. As time passed and more marchers arrived, the mob grew more powerful and more violent —while the police were becoming more harried and more exhausted. By 9 P.M. half the police at the bridge had been put out of action, many being taken to the Chamber of Deputies to be treated for their wounds (a scene which did not fail to make an impression on the deputies who were engaged in a heated debate on whether to confirm the Daladier government; the tension mounted with the sound of gunfire from across the Seine). Although the rioters at the Place de la Concorde fought spontaneously, in isolated groups, without commanders, their action was taking a heavy toll. Even when the police finally opened fire on the rioters (news of this raised a howl from right-wing deputies in the Chamber), the rioters did not desist. Instead, the fighting increased in fury and the police grew increasingly exhausted. Had it not been for a Colonel Simon, an enterprising gendarmerie officer, the mob might well have broken through the police barricade, crossed the bridge, and stormed the Chamber. Colonel Simon, officially off duty that evening, observing the fighting at the bridge and judging that the police could not hold out much longer, persuaded the mounted guard to launch one more attack followed by the rest of the police on foot in an attempt to clear the square for good—an operation which was successfully accomplished shortly after 11:30. This broke the back of the mob, and the fighting came to an end at the Place de la Concorde.

The other major threat to the Chamber of Deputies came from the opposite direction, from the left bank, from some three thousand Croix de Feu approaching the Chamber from the rear by way of the rue de Bourgogne. Some wore military helmets, others berets, but they were not armed. In contrast to rowdy Action Francaise youths and some of the other demonstrators that evening, the Croix de Feu column was orderly, disciplined, and relatively calm. La Rocque himself was not with them, choosing to direct the movements of this and another Croix de Feu column from a secret "headquarters," using messengers and telephone calls to members stationed at cafés along the way to maintain "military" communications. Shortly after 7:30 a Garde Républicain squadron established a barrage on the rue de Bourgogne to block the advancing Croix de Feu column. The column came to a halt, and a parley ensued between the officer in charge of the government unit, Sergeant Dumorat, and the leader of the Croix de Feu column, a M. de Puymaigre, a Paris municipal councilman and a former army lieutenant colonel. Both men appealed to a code of military honor and wartime comradeship to dissuade the other. Puymaigre informed the police officer: "I am a former colonel, we wish to go to the Chamber," while other Croix de Feu at the head of the column declared: "We are former officers, let us pass, join with us." Dumorat replied: "Messieurs, I have my orders. I am a soldier. Since you are officers, what would you do in my place?" Noticing that some of the Croix de Feu rank and file were becoming increasingly angry, Dumorat called for calm and told their leaders that he would hold them responsible if they failed to control their troops. Impressed by Dumorat's "appeal to the spirit of military discipline," Puymaigre finally ordered his column to withdraw —which they did, singing the Marseillaise to pick up their spirits.[65]

Soon afterward they tried to approach the Chamber from the nearby rue Saint-Dominique, where they encountered another police barrage. This time about a hundred Croix de Feu broke through the barrage, which quickly closed behind them, and made it to the very gates of the Chamber—where they were met by police reserves who beat them back with clubs. When at 9 P.M. La Rocque learned that the Chamber of Deputies had adjourned and that the deputies were leaving, he employed a face-saving tactic. He telephoned instructions for the column to split up and surround the Chamber, without, however, ordering his troops to launch an assault. This tactic allowed him to achieve a public-relations coup but not a coup d'état. The next day he claimed (quite erroneously) that "the Croix de Feu surrounded the Chamber and forced the Deputies to flee."[66]

Had La Rocque truly intended his troops to storm the Chamber from the left bank by way of the rue de Bourgogne, he doubtless would not have assigned the remainder of his troops that evening to the right bank—the latter a column three thousand strong whose destination was the Place de la Concorde. The gap between Croix de Feu rhetoric and Croix de Feu reality was underlined the next morning when police authorities ordered La Rocque to cease 'all further demonstrations. He complied. However, because Daladier resigned the same day, February 7, in favor of the more conservative Gaston Doumergue, La Rocque was able to claim a major victory. A communiqué went out to all Croix de Feu sections: "The government [has] resigned, first objective attained, suspension of all maneuvers. Until further notice, maintain state of alert. Will send instructions."[67]

And yet, although La Rocque could indeed take credit for helping to block a new Cartel des Gauches, his troops had not overthrown the Third Republic itself. The Croix de Feu and the other leagues had come amazingly close to accomplishing just this, much closer than they had expected, but, when the smoke cleared, they had still fallen short of their revolutionary proclamations of the day before. On February 7 La Rocque lamely announced that he had decided to suspend "maneuvers" in behalf of "national mourning" for the rioters who had been killed the previous evening. At the same time, he continued to talk tough—much tougher than he acted. In a statement to the press, he declared:[68]

> The new [Doumergue] government represents—alas!—only a palliative without a future, a union of parties, without a "sacred" character. The most highly respectable personages elbow those left for the sake of politics and the neo-socialist servants of the red flag. It is a temporary bandage for gangrene. Let us not tear off the bandage, but let us remain on guard. Let us remain disposed to clean out the gangrene which will not be long in advancing further.

Two months later, testifying before the parliamentary commission which investigated the riots, La Rocque spoke quite differently, denying that the military language he had used in his dispatches to his troops had been significant and describing the "objective" he had referred to in his communiqué of February 7 as being merely the constitution of "a cabinet of national truce, of public well-being."[69] Denying allegations that he had tried to overthrow the republic by force, he pointed out that had that been his intention he would have

armed his men with guns and tear-gas grenades—which he had not.[70]
On the last point, at least, he was telling the truth. Clearly, neither
La Rocque nor the other league chieftains had anticipated their
strength (or the government's weakness) on February 6 and had been
unprepared to exploit the situation fully. Moreover, the effect of
Daladier's resignation and Doumergue's accession to power was to
pacify the conservative Right and deprive the radical Right of sufficient mass support. For French conservatives, enough had been
gained to forestall any need for a fascist revolution.

The UNC and other veterans' groups, however, were to be bitterly
disappointed by the outcome of events. On the night of February 6
the actions of the UNC had been less violent than those of the Jeunesses Patriotes, the Solidarité Francaise, the Action Francaise, or the
Croix de Feu. Their procession had been on the whole orderly, and if
some of their marchers had later abandoned the column to join in the
fighting at the Place de la Concorde, most did not. The majority of
UNC veterans felt that with Daladier's resignation their major purpose
had been achieved: to prevent the coming to power of a government
which might reduce veterans' benefits. While they had feared that
Daladier, unopposed, might make such cuts, they counted on the
Doumergue government to defend their interests staunchly: had they
not helped bring him to power, after all? When Daladier's resignation was announced, they ceased all further street action.

From the beginning the UNC had been much less militant than the
paramilitary fascist leagues. Unlike the leagues, they had not engaged in street demonstrations before February 6. Georges Lebecq,
the president of the UNC, later testified that there had been considerable opposition within the UNC to engaging in political activity of any
kind—and little support was forthcoming from related veterans'
groups such as the Union Fédérale: "We were not followed by most
of the associations resembling ours. Even among our comrades, it
was said that it could be dangerous for our association. And the decision of the Congress of Vichy was not immediately accepted."[71]

Nevertheless, on February 6 the UNC managed to form a column
of some ten thousand marchers on the right bank and, together with a
column of three thousand Croix de Feu, march to the Place de la
Concorde. Preceded by its flags (which several police along the way
saluted) and by a large banner ("The Union Nationale des Combattants of Paris demonstrates so that France May Live in Honor and
Cleanness"), it reached its destination singing the Marseillaise. Although some members of the column clashed with the police during

the march (Lebecq later claimed that the column was trying to avoid police barricades when it ran into one), there was no concerted attempt to assault the bridge leading to the Chamber of Deputies. Instead, after entering the Place de la Concorde and making a tour of the square, the UNC column was directed by its leaders back to the rue Royale from whence it came. Compared to casualties suffered by members of the fascist leagues, UNC casualties were few. For the most part, UNC behavior was fairly respectable—as riots go. Still, by lending its name and numbers to the demonstration and by enhancing the notion that it was a veterans' protest, the UNC played an important role in toppling the Daladier government.

February 6, 1934, revealed the vulnerability of a democratically elected government to right-wing street action and the veterans' mystique. This was seen in the consultation within the government which led to Daladier's resignation on the morning of February 7. At the outset of the rioting and throughout the night of February 6, Daladier had held firm despite a stormy session in the Chamber of Deputies (where he was twice shouted down by right-wing deputies) and despite the fear of some that the mob might indeed break through the police barricades and make true their slogan to "throw the rascals out." Daladier capitulated the next morning, however, along with the majority of his Cabinet, when he was told by Frot, the minister of interior, that the police would not be able to hold out another day without army troops being brought in to back them up. Stunned by this news, and worried that leftists throughout France would counter further rightist demonstrations with demonstrations of their own, taking France to the brink of civil war and deepening the government's financial crisis, Daladier chose to resign. As an ex-serviceman himself and as a politician who knew that it would be tantamount to political suicide to order army troops to fire on war veterans, he preferred to turn the reins of government over to the more conservative Doumergue. He later said that the "determining factor" in his decision had been his realization "that to maintain order, he would have perhaps had to resort to machine guns and to sending [army] troops against the crowd."[72] Loath to do this, he capitulated.

Had Daladier decided to call upon the army to crush a right-wing insurrection, would army leaders have obeyed? Or would the army have sided with the veterans, with their former "comrades-in-arms"? Frot later insisted that he had supported proclaiming a state of siege "which would have had the effect of turning over the powers of the police to the military governor of Paris." But Daladier rejected this

proposal, partly because he was unsure of the legality of such an action, perhaps also because he was not absolutely sure the army was
reliable. Frot himself later testified that some army units were slow
in responding to government orders to send tanks to Paris. Two army
regiments received telephone calls during the afternoon of February 6
asking them to take a "pacifistic attitude" if the government asked
them to attack veterans. The callers identified themselves as Croix de
Feu. That night some army units did not respond at first to Frot's
instructions that they be alerted for action, claiming that they had not
received an official requisition order. When Frot learned of this, he
exploded: "It's inadmissible!" Earlier that evening Colonel Barthe,
the army liaison officer between the minister of interior and the
minister of war, had pointed out to Frot that "until now army troops
have not been used against any kind of demonstrations, at least not
since the war."[73] There is no record that the minister of war was
consulted on February 6, nor was he asked to testify later on his action (or inaction) that night. Nevertheless, tanks and troops were finally mobilized (after the riots had ended), and they were available
to the government on February 7. There is little evidence that the
army was prepared to violate its professional code of political
neutrality—although, clearly, many officers harbored right-wing sentiments and would have found it repugnant to fire on war veterans.
Then, too, like other "power elites" on February 6, they were
caught off guard.

Unlike the situation in Germany prior to the Nazi takeover, this
one showed little collusion between the regular army and the fascist
movements. Although the political sympathies of the French officer
corps were often Action Francaise or Croix de Feu, officers were
discouraged from joining the leagues or other political movements by
the knowledge that to do so would jeopardize their careers. There
was a strong tradition in the French army, an army which had served
several different regimes since the French Revolution, of political
"neutrality," a tradition reinforced by Republican retaliation against
anti-Dreyfusard officers in 1901. In the face of a possible right-wing
revolution on February 7, however, "neutrality" could work both
ways. While army leaders may not have been willing actively to
support such a revolution, they had little stomach for suppressing it
either.

There were attempts during the interwar period by French fascist
groups to rally army leaders to their side. In 1934 the Solidarité
Francaise and the Jeunesses Patriotes touted the retired army marsh-

als Lyautey and Weygand as men who represented the kind of leadership France needed. In 1936 Taittinger noted that millions of Frenchmen were calling for one man: "Pétain! Pétain!"[74] Between 1936 and 1937 contacts were established between the "Cagoule," the underground anticommunist terrorist organization headed by Eugene Deloncle, and a secret army organization of anticommunist officers called "the Corvignolles." Like the Cagoule, the Corvignolles were dedicated to countering a communist putsch. Both groups were also hostile to the Third Republic. Although there were Corvignolles on Pétain's own military staff, the marshal, like most army officers, preferred not to compromise himself by direct involvement.[75]

On balance, direct liaison between the army and French fascist movements was weak to nonexistent. And yet, although they remained organizationally apart, the French officer corps and French fascism shared many sentiments in common: a hatred of communism and socialism, dislike for the Third Republic, a taste for authoritarian leadership, and the military mystique itself. Daladier's decision on February 7, 1934, to avoid using the army against right-wing rioters left the question of the army's ultimate loyalty to the regime unresolved. Doubtless, had Daladier used the army to shoot down veterans, he would have severely alienated both army and veterans. His unwillingness to pay that price was a major factor in the French Right's undemocratic victory of February 7.

As it turned out, that victory, the coming of Doumergue to power, was, as far as many veterans were concerned, eventually disappointing. Not only did communist and socialist counterdemonstrations the following week largely negate rightist and veterans' pressure, but Doumergue himself, resolved to meet the government's financial crisis with a tough austerity program, proved much less bending to veterans' wishes than had been expected. The blow fell the following month. On March 23, 24, and 25, the Confédération Nationale des Anciens Combattants, representing three and a half million veterans, held a congress in Paris to decide what demands it would make of the new government. Georges Rivollet, secretary general of the confederation and also the minister of pensions, was strongly applauded for his speech describing his efforts to defend veterans' interests within the government. Buoyed by the events of February, the confederation went so far as to instruct Rivollet to resign from the government should it fail to respect veterans' rights.

That these veterans had badly overestimated their influence became clear during the congress itself when an official delegation was sent

to speak with Doumergue. An earlier delegation of the central council of the confederation had gone to see Doumergue shortly after he
became premier and, without an official mandate from the confederation as a whole, had urged him to purge the government of "corrupt" elements and to appoint a cabinet of "new men" chosen
largely from war veterans. Doumergue had replied that the crisis facing the French state was so urgent that it did not permit him to appoint a cabinet "composed of persons inexperienced in the practice
of affairs of state."[76] But the major blow came during the March
congress. Instead of being intimidated by the confederation's ultimatum, Doumergue responded with an ultimatum of his own: if
veterans were unwilling to make the necessary "sacrifices" that
would be demanded of them in the new budget, he would resign.
The delegation reported back to the congress what he had told
them:[77]

> When the government has completed all its additions and has
> compared the debit column with the credit column and if the
> difference is too great, it will say to you, "Messieurs, do you
> want to do something?" If you reply: "There is nothing to be
> done," I will have no other choice than to resign.

This was not what most veterans wanted, especially rightist veterans,
for Doumergue's resignation might return a more leftist government
to power, or one even less sympathetic to veterans' demands, and
they would be back to the pre–February 6 situation.

The debate which followed in the congress was mainly concerned
with the question of just how far the confederation should go in
abandoning its previously "apolitical" stance for more direct political involvement. Several motions were passed which indeed comprised a political program which extended well beyond veterans' issues. It called for the dissolution of the Chamber of Deputies and
new elections based on proportional representation, and for women's
suffrage, reduced public spending (but not on veterans' benefits), tax
"reform" through an expanded sales tax (i.e., a regressive tax), and
tax reduction elsewhere—plus government control over credit, "severe moral control" over the press, and, finally, government measures (unspecified) to fight inflation and unemployment, to encourage
agriculture and industry, and to keep women at home and off the job
market. It was a cleverly ambiguous program, often vague, with
something in it for liberals as well as conservatives. The congress
split, however, when Jean Goy of the UNC proposed that the confed-

eration engage directly in electoral politics by entering a list of its own candidates in the next election. A member of the Union Fédérale, Micheau, countered with a motion calling upon the confederation to reject such a course for the present and to work instead to get candidates of all parties to accept their ideas. The Micheau motion finally passed, against the "large opposition" of the UNC bloc. At the same time, partly as a face-saving device and partly to maintain its pressure on the government, the confederation went on record that it intended "to defend ferociously acquired [veterans'] rights."[78]

But Doumergue refused to relent. Two weeks later he proposed a budget which included sharp cutbacks in veterans' pensions and other benefits—all at the expense of the "acquired rights." On April 21 the confederation met again to decide how it would respond to this development. One faction argued that the confederation should abide by its previous resolution and not compromise its acquired rights, that it should refuse even to discuss the new government program. But an overwhelming majority of the delegates (the vote was 560 to 105) decided for compromise. The confederation finally agreed to approve most of the government cuts with certain minor revisions. Even Jean Goy of the UNC backed down, although he continued to talk loudly while carrying a small stick. A reporter later summarized the majority position:[79]

> What can we do in this situation? Refuse to support the government? We could—but what would we put in its place? Are we ready ourselves, the veterans, to take power? On this issue, all the speakers loyally replied: "Not yet!" "In this situation," they concluded, "let us accept those government proposals we can accept. . .while reserving the right, if in six months or a year [the government] has not succeeded, to intervene and assume. . .the responsibilities of power."

A month later, at Metz, the UNC held its own congress and voted to engage more actively in electoral politics, recognizing that "the economic preoccupations which, for sixteen years, have played a legitimate but perhaps too prominent role in congresses of this type, seem today to be less important and more secondary."[80] The UNC also called for dissolution of the Chamber, proportional representation, and a revision of the constitution.

On the second of the following month, the more liberal Union Fédérale held a congress at Vichy, presided over by Rivollet, the

minister of pensions. Although the Union Fédérale still refused to
engage in electoral politics as a corporate body, it no longer made a
pretense of being "apolitical." It also called for constitutional revision, proposing an increase in executive power so that the premier
could dissolve the Chamber without the consent of the Senate, and
insisted, too, that the Chamber's right to interpellation be sharply
curtailed. On social-economic issues, however, the Union Fédérale
was clearly to the left of the UNC, condemning free-enterprise
capitalism as a failure and advocating stiff government regulation of
industry, the banks, corporations, and the press—the latter notorious
for its venality and subservience to big-business interests. The Union
Fédérale also solicited the collaboration of moderate elements within
France's major trade union, the socialist Confédération Générale du
Travail, and of left-wing peasant and civil-servant unions. Finally it
emphasized that, although it supported constitutional revision, it desired "neither a totalitarian State, nor a corporate State." Its solutions, it insisted, were "French solutions." "Collective discipline
must not destroy individual personality. In a word, no 'political
militarism.' "[81] For all its anger at government cutbacks of veterans'
benefits, the Union Fédérale remained more Radical-Socialist than
military-fascist in its basic political outlook.

As for the less civilian-minded of the veterans' leaders—including
the chieftains of the fascist leagues—they recognized that their
chance of overthrowing the government by force was, for the time
being at least, nil. Doumergue had cooled the Right by taming the
Left. A renewal of the February 6 riots was unlikely, a veterans'
coup d'état even less likely. A few days after the Union Fédérale
ended its congress at Vichy, Henri Lévêque, president of the General
Association of Wounded War Veterans, candidly declared that
French veterans were not yet able to take power and that the best
policy for the present was for veterans' associations to work at the
political education of their members so that one day they might be
worthy of governing.[82]

On July 7 and 8 the Confédération Nationale assembled once
again. A motion condemning the government for not protecting the
acquired rights of veterans passed nearly unanimously. Another motion calling upon the government to move more swiftly toward re-
forming the constitution also passed easily. A real fight developed,
however, when it was moved that Georges Rivollet resign as minister
of pensions to protest government policy vis-à-vis veterans. The congress split largely along ideological lines, rightist delegates viewing

the motion as an attack upon Doumergue, who was, for them, better at least than a more left-wing premier, leftist (and left-center) delegates supporting the motion for the opposite reason. For once, the Right (and right-center) edged out the Left (and left-center) at the congress. The motion lost by a vote of 292 to 288: Rivollet was to remain in the Doumergue government.

In effect, the Confédération Nationale admitted defeat. Not only was it unwilling to engage in revolutionary action to overthrow or revise the Third Republic, or even to vote as an electoral bloc for the same ends, but it also hesitated to protest Doumergue's budget cuts too loudly lest he resign in favor of a less conservative premier. It would seem that the political attitudes of the great majority of veterans were conditioned more by the Third Republic than by the First World War. Fundamentally, these attitudes were more democratic than militaristic. For all their demands for constitutional revision, the last thing most of them wanted was a military dictatorship. As one reporter noted, there was indeed a certain irony in "an assembly which, on the whole, claimed to be antiparliamentary and which paradoxically adopted for itself purely parliamentary procedures and methods."[83]

But the democratic sentiments of most of the confederation membership went beyond simply an attachment to parliamentary forms. This was made clear in 1937 when, following the establishment of Léon Blum's left-wing Popular Front government in France, the president and former president of the UNC, Jean Goy and Georges Lebecq, made a trip to Franco Spain in order to drum up opposition to the Popular Front at home. Upon their return, at a joint meeting of five Paris sections of the UNC, they praised Franco, denounced the Popular Front, accused the communists and socialists of plotting civil war in France, and called upon UNC members "to be ready to resist." Shortly afterwards they were off on another voyage, this time to Nazi Germany—and accompanied this time by Henri Pichot, president of the Union Fédérale. News of the trip raised a storm of protest from the rank and file of the UNC, the Union Fédérale, and the Confédération Nationale. A police report of February 16, 1937 describes the general reaction:[84]

> The voyage of the delegation of French veterans to Berlin has aroused an outcry.
> At the Confédération Nationale, people were astonished to have no official knowledge of this initiative. . . . They say that the French delegates—Messieurs Goy, Pichot, Desbons, Lé-

vêque—have no mandate, nor does the Confédération or its respective associations, to so speak in the name of French veterans.

Among the members of the national veterans' associations, opinion is unanimous: for a meeting in Berlin, only the directors of the Confédération Nationale, who during the course of various national councils have defended the doctrine of pacifistic veterans' action, should be mandated to represent and speak in the name of French war veterans.

The most acerbic criticisms are raised against this delegation whose departure has been the subject of such publicity in the Paris press.

At the Paris branch of the Union Fédérale, members speak angrily of the presence of Henri Pichot, president general of the Union Fédérale, in the delegation, and they underline that the latter. . .has not received a mandate to participate at a meeting alongside Messieurs Jean Goy and Desbons, who are both politically "marked."

In sum, this trip to Berlin is viewed very unfavorably by the majority of French veterans, and it is probable that a very serious explanation will be demanded of the delegates upon their return from the capital of the Reich.

A similar breach between leadership and rank and file occurred again in October, 1938, when Henri Pichot called a press conference and announced (again, without the approval of the Union Fédérale as a whole) that the Union Fédérale, dismayed by the failure of various French cabinets to solve the same pressing problems ("an increasingly unbalanced budget, an intolerable fiscal surcharge, continued rise in the cost of living, a blocked economy, a growing menace of social opposition, all in the face of foreign threats which increase as a result of domestic difficulties"), demanded that parliamentary procedures be suspended for a minimum of one year so that a government with "full powers" could deal with such problems without interference.[85] Pichot's declaration was couched in terms of an ultimatum, with the suggestion that veterans were prepared to rebel militarily if their demands were not met. But there was little evidence that this was actually the case. *L'Illustration,* a conservative magazine which often reported on veterans' affairs, was more in tune with reality. What, it asked, should be the response of French war veterans to Pichot's call to descend into the streets and "impose a solution by force"?[86]

To that, we can only respond: never. Veterans have too much respect for their country to tear it apart. They do not want to take on the role of rebels. Formerly loyal soldiers, today they act as faithful servants of the nation as of the regime. And that will not be up to Henri Pichot to belie.

French radical rightists deeply lamented the failure of French veterans to overthrow the Third Republic during the interwar period. In 1918 a budding young author, Pierre Drieu La Rochelle, who had fought in the war and who would turn fascist in 1934, had high hopes that his comrades returning from the front might oust "decadent" civilians from political power and replace parliamentary democracy with a more "virile" form of leadership: veterans' rule. In 1921 he declared his preference for all writers of the war generation over any of the previous generation, "Peguy because he was of an age to be mobilized and was willing to destroy his genius without precaution, D'Annunzio who was a beautiful soldier."[87] By 1939, however, Drieu could only express bitterness at the outcome of events: "The war veterans let themselves be totally frustrated."[88]

But in depicting all war veterans as radical rightists, Drieu was indulging in a form of myth making deliberately cultivated by the French Right. For, as the behavior of the major French veterans' associations as well as their membership figures demonstrated, veterans' politics was hardly synonymous with right-wing politics. Even if one discounts the communist ARAC as politically inconsequential, nearly half of French war veterans were represented by the Union Fédérale, whose politics were liberal to Radical-Socialist. The UNC, to be sure, was also a major force, as well as more conservative politically, but even the UNC—or at least the bulk of its membership—shrank from truly revolutionary action, censuring their leaders when they flirted openly with fascism. Only the highly politicized fascist leagues, financed by special business interests, were willing to engage in truly authoritarian politics—and they were not representative of French veterans in general.

The French army during the First World War had been mainly a civilian army, and when French war veterans returned home in 1918 most of them returned to their civilian political attitudes as well, joining veterans' associations which conformed to those attitudes. The veterans' "movement," like the Chamber of Deputies, was divided into Right, Left, and Center. In terms of the vast spectrum of French veterans' politics, February 6 was a limited affair—the bulk of the rioters representing only its right wing, many of these being as concerned with veterans' benefits as with parliamentary corruption. The rioters also lacked veterans' support outside of Paris. The provinces were singularly quiet on February 6, Paris being more rightist than the countryside on this occasion. If the fascist leagues succeeded in mobilizing the military mystique for their own ends on February 6, they did so without the active support of most French war veterans.

Furthermore, that mystique, for all the nostalgic appeal it held for many ex-servicemen, was largely negated as a major factor in French political life by countervailing pacifist sentiment—a sentiment that was strong also among war veterans. The war values, the military moralism, which the fascist leagues constantly extolled conflicted sharply with the horror most veterans felt at the idea of repeating the bloodbath of the First World War. Indeed, French fascist journalists, perceiving this, and put on the defensive by it, took pains to argue that fascism was a program for peace, not war, that only a French fascist state could make France strong enough to deter her enemies from attacking her. Eugen Weber and David Sumler have shown the weakness of prowar sentiment in France on the eve of the First World War.[89] As a result of the carnage that ensued from that conflict, antiwar sentiment was even stronger after the war. Pétain's popularity in 1940 was due less to his being a military man than to his having been an *unaggressive* military man, a saver of lives, during the First World War.

At the same time Frenchmen respected their war veterans, men who had sacrificed so much for their country. No French government, including the Daladier government in 1934, was anxious to use police or military force against a ''veterans' '' demonstration, however unrepresentative it might be of veterans in general. This was helpful to radical rightists who wished to exploit the veterans' mystique to cloak their own special aims and interests.[90] But during the interwar years, in France, that mystique was not enough to bring them to power. For most Frenchmen, like most veterans, remained more civilian than military at heart.

NOTES

1. Henri Barbusse, *Under Fire* (New York: Dutton, 1917), pp. 354–56.
2. Ibid., pp. 349–50.
3. Barbusse, quoted in André Lang, ''Henri Barbusse,'' *Les Annales politiques et littéraires* (November 1, 1929), 405.

4. Vladimir Brett, *Henri Barbusse* (Prague: Editions de l'Academie Tchecoslovaque des Sciences, 1963), p. 138.

5. Barbusse, "The Duty of the Intellectuals," *Living Age* (September 17, 1921), 733.

6. Anette Vidal, *Henri Barbusse: Soldat de la paix* (Paris: Les Editeurs Francais Réunis, 1953), p. 71.

7. Ibid., pp. 81–82.

8. Vaillant-Courturier, quoted in Jacques Duclos and Jean Freville, *Henri Barbusse* (Paris: Editions Sociales, 1946), p. 12.

9. Vidal, p. 75.

10. Ibid., p. 79.

11. *Daily Herald* (December 16, 1919).

12. Barbusse, quoted in Vidal, p. 77.

13. *Daily Herald* (May 6, 1920); British Cabinet paper, "The Labour Situation," Ministry of Labour Report, C.P. 1398, June 2, 1920 (Cab. 24/106).

14. Duclos and Freville, p. 15.

15. Henri Barbusse, Introduction to *The Soviet Union and Peace* (London: Martin Lawrence, 1929), p. 19.

16. Barbusse, quoted in Duclos and Freville, p. 22.

17. Barbusse, *Under Fire*, p. 352.

18. Barbusse, "The Duty of the Intellectuals," 732–34.

19. Barbusse, quoted in Lang, 404.

20. Ibid.

21. Barbusse, quoted in Vidal, p. 80.

22. Paul-Émile Cadilhac, "Le Congrès de l'Union Fédérale des Anciens Combattants en Algérie," *L'Illustration* (May 3, 1930), 6–7; Rex Harlow, "FIDAC and Nationalism," *Nation* (January 28, 1925), 94; Willard Cooper, "The FIDAC: Defining the Brotherhood of Man," *Independent* (May 30, 1925), 614–15.

23. R. Chenevier, "Pour une France nouvelle: L'Appel des Combattants," *L'Illustration* (October 29, 1938), 268.

24. Chambre des Deputés, *Rapport général fait au nom de la commission d'enquête chargée de rechercher les causes et les origines des événements du 6 février 1934 et les jours suivants ainsi que toutes les responsibilités encourues*. 15ieme legislature, session de 1934. Bibliothèque Nationale, Paris, France. No. 3387, p. 44.

25. Ibid., p. 173.

26. Ibid., no. 3385, p. 122.

27. See Robert Soucy, "The Nature of Fascism in France," in Laqueur and Mosse (eds.), *International Fascism, 1920–45* (New York, Harper and Row 1966), pp. 27–55; and Soucy, "French Fascism as Class Conciliation and Moral Regeneration," *Societas—A Review of Social History* (autumn, 1971), 287–97.

28. Chambre des Deputés, *Rapport général au nom de la commission d'enquête*, no. 3385, pp. 25, 27.

29. Ibid., no. 3383, p. 46.

30. Ibid., no. 3385, pp. 31–32.

31. Archives Nationales, F⁷ 13238, police report, April 12, 1934.

32. Charles Vallin, *Aux Femmes du Parti Social Francaise* (Paris: Société d'Editions et d'Abonnements, 1937), pp. 1–2. See also Soucy, "French Fascism," 293–95.

33. Chambre des Deputés, *Rapport général au nom de la commission d'enquête*, no. 3385, pp. 17, 28, 34, 35.

34. *Le Jour* (October 27, 1937).

35. Archives Nationales, F⁷ 13241, police report, June 29, 1935.

36. Ibid., July 6, 1935, and F⁷ 12965, police report, March 30, 1936.

37. Archives Nationales, F⁷ 13241, police report, June 29, 1935.

38. Chambre des Deputés, *Rapport général au nom de la commission d'enquête*, no. 3387, p. 120.

39. Ibid., no. 3383 1², p. 138; and Henri Coston, *Dictionnaire de la politique francaise* (Paris: Librairie Française, 1967), p. 225.

40. Chambre des Deputés, *Rapport général au nom de la commission d'enquête*, No. 3385, p. 11.

41. Archives Nationales, F⁷ 12959, police report, May 16, 1935 on Francistes meeting, Salle Wagram, May 15, 1935.

42. Archives Nationales, F⁷ 13309, police report, February 7, 1934.

43. Note the lament of one French journalist in 1934: "Napoleon was not unaware that the prestigious uniform of his soldiers served many purposes, for women loved those handsome soldiers, with their irresistible panache. We should recognize that we no longer do anything to develop our *sex appeal*. . . . In the animal world, the male excites the female with his more highly colored plumage or his more abundant hair. The uniform replaces these natural advantages; it facilitates first contacts and, when the victim surrenders to her conqueror [the proof is clear]. . . . Our puritanical democrats have suppressed all that. . . ." Henri Valentino, "Commisssions Internationales," *Mercure de France* (September 15, 1934), 485.

44. Georges Valois, *Le Fascisme* (Paris: Nouvelle Librairie Nationale, 1927), pp. 139, 142, 143–144.

45. Philippe Barrès, "Le sentiment de la victoire," *Le Nouveau siècle* (November 11, 1925), 3.

46. *L'Ami du peuple* (February 6, 1934).

47. Chambre des Deputés, *Rapport général au nom de la commission d'enquête*, no. 3385, p. 124.

48. Ibid., p. 151.

49. *Le Petit Bleu* (February 4, 1934).

50. Laurent Bonnevay, *Les journées sanglantes de février 1934* (Paris: Flammarion, 1935), p. 20.

51. Ibid., pp. 15–20.

52. Archives Nationales, F⁷ 12962, police report, November 24, 1933.

53. Bonnevay, p. 72.

54. Ibid., p. 56.

55. Chambre des Deputés, *Rapport général au nom de la commission d'enquête*, no. 3385, p. 107.

56. *Le Figaro* (February 7, 1934).

57. *La Victoire* (January 10, 1934).

58. Chambre des Deputés, *Rapport général au nom de la commission d'enquête*, no. 3385, p. 122.

61. Ibid., no. 3387, p. 134.

62. Ibid., p. 20.

63. William L. Shirer, *The Collapse of the Third Republic* (New York: Simon and Schuster, Pocket Book ed., 1969), p. 200.

64. Bonnevay, p. 89.

65. Chambre des Deputés, *Rapport général au nom de la commission d'enquête*, no. 3387, pp. 139–140.

66. Bonnevay, p. 144.

67. Chambre des Deputés, *Rapport général au nom de la commission d'enquête*, no. 3385, p. 151.

68. Ibid., p. 152.

69. Ibid., no. 3383, p. 1584.

70. Ibid., no. 3387. p. 134.

71. Ibid., p. 8.

72. Ibid., no. 3385 (2–3), p. 2764.

73. Ibid., no. 3383 (2–3), p. 2362.

74. *Le National* (March 14, 1936).

75. Philippe Bourdrel, *La Cagoule* (Paris: Editions Albin Michel, 1970), pp. 125–27.

76. Bonnevay, pp. 241–42.

77. *L'Illustration* (March 31, 1934), 357.

78. Ibid. (April 21, 1934), 443.

79. Ibid.

80. Ibid. (May 19, 1934), 70.

81. Ibid. (June 2, 1934), 184.

82. Ibid. (July 14, 1934), 344.

83. Ibid.

84. Archives Nationales, F[7] 12966, police report, February 12 and 16, 1937.

85. *L'Illustration* (October 29, 1938), 268.

86. Ibid.

87. Maurice Martin du Gard, "Drieu La Rochelle," *Ecrits de Paris* (December 1950), 66.

88. Pierre Drieu La Rochelle, *Sur les écrivains* (Paris: Gallimard, 1964), p. 177.

89. See Eugen Weber, *The Nationalist Revival in France, 1905–1914* (Berkeley and Los Angeles: University of California Press, 1959) and David E. Sumler, "Domestic Influences on the Nationalist Revival in France, 1909–1914," *French Historical Studies* (fall, 1970), 517–537.

90. For further analysis of the veterans' mystique, see René Remond, "Les anciens combattants et la politique," *Revue francaise de science politique* (April-June 1955), 267–90.

ITALY:
War as a Style of Life

The question of the role of veterans of the Great War in Italian politics leads us into an area at once fascinating and frustrating. The fas-
cination, as we shall see in due course, derives from the variegated
activities of ex-soldiers and officers, ranging from participation in
anarchist plots to overthrow the national government to the organization of Fascist squads. The frustration is due to the paucity of information available on veterans' organizations per se, and hence much
of what follows here must be considered only a first approximation.
We simply do not know enough about Italian veterans to permit anything resembling a final synthesis.

The participation of many veterans in the rise of Fascism, and in
particular their involvement in the violent sorties of the *squadristi,*
has made it difficult for historians to appreciate the diversity of veterans' groups following the war. Much of this easy identification of
Fascism with elements involved, first, in intervention, then in the
war itself, was fostered by the Fascist regime. One of the leading
Fascist intellectuals, Giuseppe Bottai, wrote in 1939: "If I had to
draw a line between the 'arditismo' of the war, of the assault battalions, and the civil 'arditismo' of the Fascist squads, I would not
know where to put it. . . ."[1]

The creation of paramilitary groups within Fascism, first in the
form of the squads, then the National Militia, helped to sustain this
notion of Fascism as a continuation of the struggle of the Great War.
Much of Mussolini's rhetoric was devoted to this theme, especially

in the thirties, when Italy was mobilized for one war effort after another.

Yet many veterans, by far the great majority, were not simply raw material for Fascism. They were involved in all kinds of activities, much of which placed them in conflict with the Fascists. As we shall see, it was not unusual, even after the march on Rome, to find Fascists and veterans' organizations involved in hand-to-hand combat in the streets of Italy. It is on these other, non-Fascist organizations, that this essay is concentrated because the role of veterans in the creation of Fascism is relatively well known to the English-speaking public, while the other part of the veterans' story has been largely ignored. A temporal boundary has also been set at 1925, the year of Mussolini's consolidation of power. After that time veterans were not as free to organize as during the period 1918–25.

For a country which had devoted its energies and passions to the cause of victory for three long years, the euphoria surrounding the outbreak of peace was remarkably short-lived. In its original incarnation, peace came wrapped in the mantle of victory, and hence seemed to represent the vindication of those hundreds of thousands of dead and wounded Italians who had fought against the Hapsburgs. Furthermore, the triumphant conclusion of the war drew the sting of the humiliation at Caporetto, and veterans of the successful battles of the last year of the war could expect to return home with all the glory and satisfaction which the interventionists had promised at the outset of the conflict.[2]

But from the very beginning there was another side to the sudden and dramatic peace which "exploded" in 1918. The Italian press clamored for the rapid return of the war veterans to their families and jobs—only to discover that the transformation of soldiers to citizens was a most formidable undertaking. The end of the war found the Italian General Staff largely unprepared for this new task, and the problems were serious indeed. The sheer weight of numbers posed enormous logistical difficulties for a country with limited transportation abilities. This situation was particularly acute in the Veneto, which had seen massive destruction of roads, bridges, and railroad lines during the course of hostilities. There were other problems as well: the strained national economy might not be able to absorb the heavy influx of veterans into the labor force, and the generals, as always, wished to retain a solid military nucleus for the future. Finally, a monumental bureaucratic chaos permeated the entire undertaking—a chaos which Italian journalists exposed and condemned with tireless enthusiasm.

Thus, the very fact of peace posed numerous problems to a government and a people which wished desperately to savor the joys of victory. All these problems contained elements which concerned both the political and military forces of the country, and Italy's long tradition of separation of civil and military powers made the resolution of these problems doubly difficult. The Italian victory was, then, somewhat tainted even before the cries of "mutilated victory" came to be directed at the negotiators around the Versailles conference tables.

The immediate question before the government was that of the demobilization of the armed forces and the disposition of the discharged veterans. Roughly 3,760,000 men were in uniform at the end of the war (excluding the officers), and nearly a million and a half of these were discharged in the first two months following the armistice. These veterans represented the eleven oldest "classes" as well as some of those in "needy" categories and others whose labor was considered essential for the recovery of the economy: civil servants, mayors, and other local officials, working-class leaders, and so forth. The initial demobilization program, if that is the word for it, made no provision for any assistance whatsoever for nonofficers; they were simply sent home with the thanks of the nation and left to fend for themselves. Indeed, it was not until January that veterans began to get some sort of financial reward upon discharge, and this was largely the result of a nationwide campaign by all sectors of the national press.[3]

The outcry against the government's treatment of Italy's war heroes lasted for the first two months of 1919, a period which saw the institution of various programs on behalf of Italian veterans. By February all discharged soldiers were receiving some sort of stipend, even though the sums involved were hardly of heroic proportions. One hundred lire were awarded for the first year of service, and an additional fifty lire were given for each additional year. To put these figures in perspective, a noncommissioned officer who had fought during the entire war received less upon discharge from active service than the salary for a single month of a newly commissioned second lieutenant.[4] In short, the foot soldiers and noncommissioned officers got token rewards from the army, while officers were treated considerably better.

There were other privileged categories. A member of a profession could request transfer to his native city where he could pursue his own affairs, dressed in civilian clothes, and continue to draw his full salary! In addition, a professional could refuse discharge and delay it until after that of the rest of his "class." By the middle of February there were more than five thousand of these fortunate souls.

Students enjoyed similar good fortune. The press had demanded the discharge of all students in order that they could renew their studies, a policy which was opposed by the military. However, under the pressure of a virtually unanimous outburst in the press, the army relented and permitted students (in uniform) to attend special classes at the universities, while still retaining their military privileges and drawing their salaries. Further, no attendance was taken at these special classes, which made the situation idyllic for those involved in the program. While no figures are available on the number of such soldiers who actually attended classes, by the summer of 1919 some 23,000 had availed themselves of leave from their units in order to attend the universities.[5]

Such gross inequities were well known, yet after the initial outburst in the winter of 1919 the press by and large stopped its attacks upon the demobilization policies of the Orlando government. Significantly, this coincided with a virtual standstill in the pace of demobilization itself. Rather than accelerate the tempo of discharging veterans, the government first slowed, then stopped the process altogether. Between January and March an additional half million soldiers were discharged, and in March the government suspended all discharges for three months. Indeed, the project of demobilizing the army would not be renewed until the advent of the Nitti government in the summer. Further, despite the reduced number of men under arms, the cost of the military apparatus underwent a Parkinsonian expansion: from 1.4 billion lire per month at the end of the war to 2 billion in March of 1919.[6] Why the sudden termination of the demobilization program? Why the newfound quiescence throughout the press? And why the increased cost of a smaller army?

The answers to all these questions lie in the sphere of politics, and perhaps the easiest and most dramatic way to answer them is to take a look at the actual deployment of Italy's military forces in the summer of 1919, some eight months after the armistice. As of the first of July there were some 1,578,000 men in the army. Slightly more than half of them, 876,000, were under the Supreme Command, and of these some 737,000 were in the war zone. These troops served to defend Italian frontiers, and represented a form of insurance against a new outbreak of fighting. Of the remainder, one-half (315,000 of the 630,000 men not under the Supreme Command) were used to guarantee "public order." They were deployed domestically, and represented a new departure in the history of the Italian army. Whereas prewar troops had been employed in a wide variety of tasks, the so-called three hundred men of Orlando had only police chores. They were, then, a new sort of National Guard, used to safeguard the government against potential internal enemies.[7]

The maintenance of so many men in the armed forces testifies to the uncertainties surrounding the Orlando regime, and the fears of domestic insurgency which were widespread in the government. It must be pointed out, although it is by now a commonplace in the literature,[8] that these fears were not restricted to the political parties of the peninsula. There was considerable preoccupation about many of the troops themselves. Such fears extended even to the most celebrated and honored members of the army: the Arditi, or shock troops. General Enrico Caviglia, who became minister of war in February, 1919, voiced these attitudes with typical clarity:[9]

> . . .As commander of the army, I had expressed my opinion in favor of dissolving the Arditi. . . . But as minister of war I saw the necessity of maintaining them.
>
> In moments of political disorder, which were sweeping Italy, [the Arditi] constituted a useful force in the hands of the government, because they were greatly feared for their inclination for swift and violent action. If they were dissolved, they would pass to the reinforcement of the revolutionary parties.

We shall return to this problem at much greater length, but for the moment it is sufficient to stress the highly ambivalent attitude toward Italy's war heroes by their leaders. While such attitudes endured, the policy of maintaining a private army for domestic purposes did not. With the advent of Nitti to the head of the government, a rapid and thorough demobilization was initiated. By December the number of men in arms was down to roughly half a million, less than a third the number when he came to power. For Nitti, the demobilization was intended to tranquilize an agitated country: ". . .The foreign policy of the entire nation will be calmer and more conscious; domestic policies will be more moderate and serene. . . . We want to give the country the sense that the war is finished. . . ."[10]

As it turned out, however, Caviglia's fears proved to be more realistic than Nitti's desires. The Great War had produced a profound change in the attitudes of the soldiers, and their return from the front meant that a new political element had been introduced into the political life of the country.

If war is the pursuit of politics by other means, in the case of post-war Italy the converse proved true: domestic politics rapidly took on the characteristics of the Great War. In two recent works on the political consequences of the war, Piero Melograni and Roberto Vivarelli concur in both the nature and the profundity of the change in the essence of the political process.[11] "In reality," Vivarelli writes, "an entire world fell with the war,"[12] a world of traditional political behavior. With the arrival of peace, he suggests, Italian politics existed in a kind of moral vacuum, deprived of all fixed guidelines; the traditional ideological premises had been reduced to a tabula rasa.

The new element in Italian political life which the veterans brought with them from the front was, ironically enough, a set of democratic attitudes, a demand for the participation of the masses in the political arena. "No ruling group could exercise stable power without establishing ties with the great masses of people." This new reality was, in large part, the result of a psychological transformation of the troops:[13]

> In 1915–1917 the dominant psychology of the conscript was resignation, but later—after the propagandistic campaigns of 1918—the dominant psychology of the soldier became impatience. Those soldiers who, a few at a time, returned home with the desire to see a new society arise, did not constitute a "class," but they were numerous enough to produce anxiety in all classes.

What sort of new society was desired by these veterans? What demands did the soldiers bring back with them from the trenches? The first point to be made is that although there was certainly a desire for something new, this desire was rarely stipulated with sufficient precision to permit it to be "captured" by one or another of the traditional political parties. Veterans, as such, were not inclined to pass *en bloc* into the ranks of existing organizations; rather, they at first attempted to form their own: the Associazione Nazionale Combattenti. The Associazione was first proposed in January, 1919, and held its first congress in Rome in June. There the veterans' group expounded a highly democratic program, calling for the convocation of a constituent assembly to draft a new constitution, the abolition of

the Senate and its replacement by a series of councils elected by the
various categories of workers and management, and the reduction of
military service to three months. Furthermore, they demanded that
unused land be distributed among returning veterans, a promise
which had been made to the troops ever since 1915. Finally, the Associazione enunciated a notion of the *patria* which called for Italy to
be "integrated with humanity, and different from national
egotism."[14]

Such a manifesto clearly placed the veterans quite close to the position of the Socialist party, both in its demand for a new governmental structure, and in its rejection of traditional nationalism. The
judgment of Emilio Lussu was quite close to the mark when he wrote
that the veterans' program seemed to be written in order to permit
collaboration with the Socialists: "The veterans were, in
essence. . .philosocialists, not because they were familiar with the
classics of socialism, but because of their profound sense of internationalism, achieved in the reality of war, and because of their desire for land. . . ."[15]

Yet active collaboration between veterans and Socialists was, on a
formal level at least, out of the question, for the Socialists' opposition to the war itself made an alliance with the veterans impossible.
As a mass political party, however, the Socialists could ill afford to
alienate this large body of suddenly active citizens, and hence the
Socialist press wavered often on the subject of veterans throughout
1919. On some occasions they were portrayed as defenders of the
patria, on others they were described as barely human creatures, carrying out acts of terrible atrocity. Similarly, the Socialist position on
deserters oscillated between characterizing them as people who abandoned their units in a moment of weakness, and hailing them as men
who had given up acts of war in order to participate in more important struggles elsewhere.

Although veterans' social aspirations might often coincide with
those of the Socialists, the Socialist condemnation of the war inevitably divided the two groups. And if there was a single issue which
can be said to unify the majority of veterans of the Great War, it was
the belief that the war itself held a profound human meaning for
Italy, and contained important lessons for the future of the country.
In the last stages of the war, and the early days of the peace, the old
contrast between *paese reale* and *paese legale,* between the "real
Italy" and the Italian government, came to be heard again. But
whereas in the prewar period such a contrast was necessarily abstract

(the "real Italy" not having manifested itself as yet), the victory in the Great War made it possible for critics of the government to point to the heroism of the trenches as evidence of the vitality and discipline of the *paese reale*.

It is important to stress that such a development was quite different from a bellicose nationalism of the traditional sort, for the demand that the "real Italy" be recognized in the centers of national power was subversive of the existing order. Indeed, there was a widespread belief in the last days of the war that the fundamental conflict within Italy was not one of class, but rather a division between government on the one hand and the army, the embodiment of the nation's vitality, on the other. There is a considerable body of documentation which suggests that in the end the war itself came to be the one unifying concept of the latter phase of the conflict. The human qualities war produced, and the sensation of unity which emerged from the trenches, contrasted dramatically with the artificial unity represented by the parliamentarians who debated endlessly in Rome. As Mario Isnenghi has argued, it was the myth of the war, not the myth of the nation, which became the most potent ideological weapon of the period following 1918.[16]

Following the armistice, the notion that the war had served to unify the people in a new way, and had produced new qualities of heroism, became a commonplace in all sectors of the press. Most often it took the form of the contention that the war had been won by "the people," as opposed to the old institutions, governmental or military, of the prewar period. General Capello expressed this view in 1920: "The war was not won by the standing army. The nucleus of the permanent army was exhausted in the first few months of war. . .it was not only the permanent officers who led the Italian soldiers to victory."[17]

In other words, had it not been for the newly mobilized energies of "the people," the standing army would have proven inadequate to the great task. Thus, there was a virtually unanimous demand for a reorganization of the army following the end of the war, and the form of this demand was inevitably the same: a new, more democratic army was proposed, involving an extremely brief universal military service. All would serve in this new force, and all would be ready if the nation required them. At the same time the elimination of the old bureaucracy and the rigid lines of demarcation between ranks would guarantee a degree of enthusiasm and unity which no professional standing army could hope to possess. This call for a new army was couched in the slogans of the *nazione armata,* the country in arms. Once again a question which was ostensibly restricted to the military sphere became transformed into a broader political issue, for the demand for the *nazione armata* simultaneously subverted the old military order, and entailed the participation of the entire population in a national enterprise.

Here again General Caviglia's preoccupations were justified, for the theme of the nation in arms was one which many European socialists had voiced throughout the period following the French Revolution, from which the slogan had emerged. Yet this slogan transcended the traditional party divisions of the Italian political scene, and was part of the program of virtually every political group in the country, with the notable exception of the extreme Left. The Combattenti demanded it, as did the Fascists and the most colorful of the veterans' organizations, the Arditi.[18]

The Arditi were the most celebrated Italian troops of the Great War. In contrast to the foot soldier who awaited his death in a muddy trench, the Ardito died a "beautiful death," participating in desperate assaults on enemy positions, leading charges up exposed hillsides, singing, according to the legends of the epoch, his own songs. These assault units lived in their own barracks, conserving their energies for those moments of intense struggle and derring-do for which they were reserved. The end of the war was particularly difficult for these men, trained as they were for lives of violence and combat, and even before the formal declaration of peace one can find the melancholy musings of the Arditi as they speculated on the life which awaited them outside active service. Ferruccio Vecchi, one of the most literate of the Arditi, put it this way in the fall of 1918:[19]

> At the end of the war those who have no direction any more, those surrounded by the abyss, those without bread, are precisely us. Every one of us, having interrupted our studies, our jobs, or our professions for four consecutive years, is obliged to exclude the possibility of picking up our lives at the point at which they were interrupted in 1915. . . . The war by now has become our second nature. . . . I was used to it! Now another one begins, perhaps the more difficult: that for existence. . . . Where shall I go? What shall I do? I don't know. . . .

For such personalities as these, peacetime pursuits could not possibly offer the drama of the lives they had lived during the war. As the elite corps of the armed forces, the Arditi had become accustomed to both excitement and glory, neither of which was offered by a return to civilian life.

In December, 1918, rumors began to spread about the impending discharge of various Arditi units, and one of their members, the noted Futurist Mario Carli, took it upon himself to call to his comrades to continue their ardent labors for Italy outside the armed forces. "There is much to be done down here," he had told the readers of *Roma Futurista* in September, and two months later he elaborated upon the glorious future which awaited his fellow Arditi after the war: "For you the future can only be a continuation of the glory conquered on bloody fields, and a recognition by the nation of your immense *human* value, which must be used and channeled in the best possible way in the works of peace. . . ."[20]

Here, again, Carli was voicing the widespread belief that veterans of the war possessed certain qualities of spirit which set them apart from the grand mass of the citizenry. In keeping with this view, he organized the Associazione fra gli Arditi d'Italia in January of the following year. The constitution of the association is a fascinating document,[21] and warrants a fairly detailed analysis. Article 3 stated the "spiritual" quality of the Arditi:

> The association promises to sustain that flame of idealism and that spirit of ardor which made the *Arditi* the finest soldiers in our army and of all the armies in the war, conserving in the country the atmosphere of "Arditismo" [Italian pride, the spirit of adventure, interventionism, physical and moral courage, worship of energy, and solidarity].

Despite such grandiose claims, the association (article 2) had "no political goals"! Their goals, rather, consisted in creating others like themselves. To this end the Arditi proposed a vast program of physical education, promising to create gymnastic clubs, boxing and fencing schools, athletic competitions, and "all those things which can keep the youth in good condition. . . ."

Further, the association naturally promised to provide for the material well-being of its members, attempting to find jobs for all, and organizing public demonstrations and "spectaculars" on behalf of impoverished Arditi.

In brief, then, the association was both an organization of mutual aid and the base from which the Arditi hoped to launch their program for the revivification of the country. Within a few months there were offices throughout the country (Rome, Milan, Turin, Florence, Ancona, Bologna, Genoa, Palermo, Messina, and Naples), and by the middle of the summer they had enlisted approximately ten thousand members.

Later Arditi proclamations contained some remarkably colorful language ("We will love, with frenzy, both speed and beautiful women. Given the choice, we will speedily love beautiful women. But, at the opportune moment, speedily flee from beautiful women"), and also some paragraphs which suggested that the Arditi were quite interested in political intervention: "Take apart, clean, lubricate, and modernize all the parts of the complicated political-bureaucratic-judicial Italian machine, or, finding it out of service, hurl it into the melting-pot of revolution. . . ."[22]

The Arditi made it clear from the outset that they intended to pursue their domestic opponents with the same determination—and much the same violent techniques—that they had demonstrated during the war. Their domestic enemies were those who had opposed the war, had failed to grant veterans their just due following the war, and those who were viewed as sabotaging the greatness of the nation. In other words: Socialists, Popolari, and anything smacking of parliamentary government. These were viewed as the blackguards who were preventing Italy from realizing the greatness she had achieved in the Great War, and the Arditi took to the streets to protect that grandeur.

There had been sporadic violence in Italy for some time, much of its originating on the left of the political realm. But the emergence of the Arditi marked a new kind of conflict in Italian history, and the uniqueness of the moment has been fairly and succinctly characterized by Renzo De Felice: "Political conflict in Italy had always been a 'family affair,' of orators, manifestos, newspapers, demonstrations, and mass meetings, which, while often raucous, were also peaceful. . . . But now the Arditi put political conflict on a new plane, organizing it according to military criteria."[23]

Passionate outbursts, then, had existed throughout the history of united Italy, but violence organized with meticulous ruthlessness was something brand-new. The Arditi undertook their campaigns as if they were attacking enemy positions on the Piave. The most celebrated of these assaults was the sack of the offices of *Avanti* in Milan on the fifteenth of April, 1919. This event is a most revealing one, not only for what it demonstrated about the ferocity of the Arditi, but also for the startling lack of governmental reprisals.

During the assault itself there was a singular lack of intervention on behalf of the local forces of law and order, and when General Caviglia was asked to investigate the matter, his attitude was one of patient toleration. If one can believe the testimony of Ferruccio Vecchi, the general privately expressed his satisfaction at the "lesson" which the veterans had given the Socialists in the streets of Milan.[24] But even his own testimony shows that Caviglia was not shocked by this outbreak of political violence. Instead of reprimanding the Arditi, Caviglia warned the Socialists that they would do well, in the future, to avoid such tests of strength:[25]

> I warned the Socialists not to resort to violence, because they would undoubtedly get the worst of it. I said, "Do not delude yourselves. . . . You are up against men who for four years risked their lives every day, a thousand times a day. . . . They know how to fight. It will do you no good to resort to violence. Stay within the framework of the law, and behave moderately."

It seems, then, that at least some elements of the government were pleased to see the Arditi performing acts of violence against left-wing groups. After all, this was the function which had necessitated the maintenance of the "three hundred men of Orlando" in the months following the armistice. But if we look more closely at the treatment of the Arditi leadership, the picture becomes far more complicated. Already, before the Avanti incident, there had been voices in the government calling for the dissolution of the Arditi units, cries which had been opposed, by and large, by the military. But, as we have seen, the desire to keep the shock-troops under arms was not the same thing as favoring their political activities, and Caviglia himself acted to restrict the actions of the Arditi leadership.[26]

In March, Mario Carli, the founder of the Associazione, had been subjected to lengthy questioning and had been warned by the police that he was not to indulge in political activities among the troops so long as he wore the uniform of the army. Furthermore, he had already violated regulations by issuing his *Appeal to the Flames,* and was sentenced to a ten days house arrest, a sentence which does not appear to have been carried out. Arditi leaders in other cities were subjected to constant harassment and interrogation by agents of the Ministry of the Interior, and their activities were under close observation. Indeed, by the time of the *Avanti* incident, the general director of public security was able to report on numerous incidents involving Arditi during the same month, in Rome, Novara, Piacenza, and Palermo.[27] Such reports testify both to the diffusion of the Arditi throughout the country and to the seriousness with which their activities were considered in Rome.

There was a constant fear that the Arditi would inevitably pass into the hands of the Left, a fear that was nourished by some of the boisterous public statements of the Arditi leadership. This is hardly surprising, considering the nature of the leadership, much of which participated simultaneously in the Futurist movement. The case of Carli may be taken as symptomatic. Born in 1889, he was one of the founders of the Futurist movement (along with Marinetti and Vecchi). After the war he participated in various Futurist enterprises, including the so-called Futurist synthetic theater, and, in addition to the Associazione degli Arditi he organized the Fascio di Combattimento in Rome, and was one of the editors of *Roma Futurista*.

At the same time that they were attacking Socialists in the streets, then, many of the leaders of the Arditi were calling for the overthrow of the Senate, and for the "devaticanization" (the phrase is Marinetti's)[28] of Italy. Furthermore, although the Arditi's anti-Socialist incursions might bring pleasure to some members of the government, many of their rhetorical attacks were reserved for the government itself. Above all, the Arditi resisted any attempt by the government to "capture" their association for acts of national defense. This was the thrust of a notorious article written by Carli in May, entitled "Arditi, not police." The diatribe, which appeared in the second issue of *L'Ardito*, responded to reports that the government was planning to reorganize the assault battalions in order to use the Arditi as a National Guard:[29]

> Now that you have (finally!) understood our function of disciplinarians and precursors of the march of our people to the future, now that you have realized that only we are capable of bursting the anti-Italian bubble, you want to capture us again. . .you want to make us loyal and obedient pretorians.
>
> Once again you are wrong. . . . *We are volunteers who want to intervene if and when we want to,* and in a manner which pleases us.
>
> But to confuse us with the police. . .good heavens!

This outburst cost Carli three months confinement, this time in a military prison in Cremona. It also cost the Associazione whatever coherence it had possessed. Escaping from confinement, Carli joined D'Annunzio in Fiume, where he hoped to participate in the government of the "city of holocaust." For the remainder of the year the Associazione, torn between the radicalism of its rhetoric and the reactionary nature of its armed assaults, floundered without direction and without a solid base of support. It is not surprising that for a time they were wooed, with considerable success, by wealthy northern industrialists,[30] who hoped to tame the violence of the Arditi for their own purposes. In the late spring and early summer of 1919 it appeared as if the Arditi would become the pretorian guard of Italian capitalism. Vecchi himself sounded the keynote of this interlude: "The Arditi are too practical not to see the splendid future of their country in Italian industry. . . . Industrialists are Arditi, too: the fortunes of Italy are entrusted to them; they will find their strongest allies in the veterans and the Arditi."[31]

But whatever the goals of the Arditi might be on the political scene, their devotion to the cause of "trenchism," to the support and mobilization of the veterans of the Great War, remained undisturbed. In this context it is easy to understand their place in the forefront of the newly founded Fasci di Combattimento in the spring, for these were largely the creation of Arditi and other veterans. One need go no further than the first declaration at the famous initial rally of San Sepolcro on the twenty-third of March, 1919:[32]

> This rally directs its first salute. . .to the sons of Italy who fell for the greatness of the nation and the liberty of the world, to the injured and the crippled, to all veterans and to all the ex-prisoners. . .and declares itself ready to vigorously support the moral and material demands of the veterans' organizations.

From the moment of the founding of the Fasci di Combattimento, a significant part of the Arditi membership passed under the control of this new group, and, ultimately, into the hands of Mussolini. The evolution of the Fasci is a story both too complicated and too well known to occupy us here at any great length. What is of importance in our study is the recognition of a split in the ranks of the Arditi: one element would move progressively toward the right, following the convoluted path which saw Mussolini move from a socialist interventionist to the *Duce* of Fascism; the other part of the Arditi would move toward the left, some passing into the ranks of D'Annunzio's Legionnaires, others attempting a more formal union with openly subversive organizations.

The first moment of rupture between Arditi and Mussolini came with the disastrous elections of the fall of 1920. The so-called *blocco delle teste di ferro,* consisting largely of Mussolini and his allies, the Futurists and the Arditi, managed to win only 4,657 of the 270,000-odd votes cast in Milan. The electoral debacle was closely followed by the breakup of the coalition. The first to go were the Futurists, and their exit from the coalition was paralleled by their move away from political involvement per se. In short order *Roma Futurista* became a weekly review of the arts, rather than a political journal.

The Arditi suffered a similar decline throughout the Italian peninsula. In Milan things reached bottom in early January, 1920, when the membership rolls listed no more than fourteen active members, of whom three were imprisoned! They were in debt for more than three thousand lire, and, faced with the prospect of death by exhaustion, they were compelled to open their membership ranks to new recruits. Instead of restricting membership to those who had actually served in the assault battalions, the Arditi now recruited fifteen-to-twenty-year-old youths for participation in schools of *arditismo civile* which would train such youngsters militarily and spiritually for the battles ahead. These would possess "such intellectual and moral merits, and such singular personalities, that they would merit the name of Ardito." Much the same process was under way in Rome, under the leadership of Giuseppe Bottai, who launched his membership drive with the slogan "Not a closed caste of veterans, but a free organization of energies."[33]

In Milan the Arditi were forced to turn to Mussolini for financial aid, but such aid was obtained at the cost of the loss of the "left wing." By May of 1920, at the Fascist Congress of Milan, Mussolini had finally turned toward the right, and by June, Marinetti and Carli had resigned from the Fasci di Combattimento. Ferrucio Vecchi was driven from the ranks of both the Arditi and the Fasci for his left-wing tendencies, and he was replaced in the editor's chair of *L'Ardito* by Piero Bolzon, a close friend of Mussolini. Through this process of attrition and internal conflict, the Arditi had virtually ceased to exist as an independent organization by the end of 1920. For the most part they had passed to Mussolini, assimilated in the ranks of the Fascist squads.

Yet they reemerged, both in Milan and in Rome. In the north their recovery was closely tied to the reappearance of Gabriele D'Annunzio and his Legionnaires following their expulsion from the

city of Fiume. In the south, however, there was a series of actions
by an Arditi group quite different from any we have discussed thus
far. Rome was the setting for one of the most fascinating episodes in
the history of veterans' organizations: the grouping of anarchist Arditi
around the incredible figure of Lieutenant Argo Secondari.

In the summer of 1919 the Roman police had uncovered a bizarre
plot to overthrow the national government. According to the police
informants, Argo Secondari, a lieutenant in the Arditi, had organized
a group of anarchists and fellow Arditi to seize various centers of
power in Rome and proclaim a constituent assembly.[34] On the night
of July 6 the forces of the Roman Questura arrested a group of conspirators in a *trattoria* around midnight, and then seized some twenty
other revolutionaries who had gathered outside the fortress of Pietralata to urge the soldiers there to join the revolt. The entire conspiracy was crushed in routine fashion and its members were incarcer-
ated. Secondari himself, who escaped the original wave of arrests,
was tracked down and imprisoned until he was amnestied in March
of the following year. It appears that most of the leaders of the Arditi
were informed of the maneuvers of Secondari and his accomplices,
even though the conspiracy was a small one.

The next we hear of Secondari is in a power struggle with Bottai for
control of the Roman section of the Associazione in the early summer of 1920.[35] Interestingly enough, both of them attempted to in-
stall General Giuseppe Garibaldi as honorary president of the Associazione, even though they held widely divergent views on the role
of the Arditi in the future. Bottai wished to transform the organization into a viable national political party, while Secondari wanted to
use the shock troops as the spearhead of a communist revolution.
Garibaldi's involvement with both these groups is quite in keeping
with the myriad rumors which swept the country at that time, purporting to involve him in projects ranging from participation in a coalition government to a joint march on Rome with D'Annunzio and the
Fiuman Legions. In any event, by early June the Questura considered
the Roman section defunct. Such, however, was not the case, for in
the following summer Secondari reappeared at the head of an organization which—for a period of a couple of months—threatened to
pose a genuine proletarian counterforce to the Fascist squads, a counterforce under the direction of radical Arditi. This organization,
known as the Arditi del Popolo, organized for the defense of the
working class against the violence of the Fascisti.

The Arditi del Popolo represented the culmination of two years of intensive organizational efforts by Argo Secondari, and immediately attracted considerable support from workers who had been terrorized by Fascist squads. Secondari made no secret of his opposition to the Fascists: "Until the Fascists stop assassinating our brother workers, until they cease their fratricidal war, the Arditi of Italy can have nothing in common with them."[36]

The scope of the Arditi del Popolo was twofold. First of all, as an organ of proletarian defense it undertook to defend the socialists, anarchists and communists against Fascist aggression, and promised to respond to such initiatives with equal violence. Secondly, as Secondari made clear on several occasions, the ultimate goal of the organization was the leadership of a revolutionary movement which would overthrow the existing institutions of Italy and seize power.

Such a program shared in the fantasies of the Pietralata plot of two years before, yet, given the atmosphere of the times, it is not surprising that the Arditi del Popolo acquired a sensational following in a remarkably brief period. On the sixth of July some two thousand members marched through the botanical gardens of Rome to the enthusiastic applause of a large crowd of supporters. The minister of the interior received reports of similar organizations throughout the country, from Milan to Inglesias, from Catania to Genoa, and the membership numbered several thousand.[37] Such was the enthusiasm which surrounded this organization that some amazing alliances developed, such as the group of Arditi in Mantova which, under the leadership of the Popolari, promised to defend *all* manifestations of "faith and ideas" from attack.[38]

In Rome, Secondari established headquarters in the Palazzo Venezia, in that section of the building which had been occupied by the Associazione Nazionale Combattenti. This fusion produced considerable consternation among members of the government, who viewed the entire situation with alarm.

Yet no proletarian alliance seemed possible in the summer of 1921. The newly created PCI was willing to join any organization which was not under its own total control, and thus Bordiga and Grieco, offering a variety of rumors and suspicions as excuses for their nonparticipation, ordered their followers to remain outside the ranks of the Arditi del Popolo. Surprisingly enough, they took this course despite the rather positive attitude toward the new organization adopted by the International.[39] The Socialists, for their part, withdrew from participation early in August.

As if this were not enough, the leadership of the Arditi del Popolo was soon torn apart by internal struggles, and by the middle of August the final blow was delivered by the defenders of public order: a wave of arrests throughout the country signaled the elimination of the Arditi del Popolo. From this moment on, the police forces waged a relentless campaign until, in October, the prefect of Rome advised the minister of the interior that the Arditi del Popolo had been formally dissolved. Here and there, in the years that followed, independent groups of the organization surfaced in armed conflicts with the Fascists. But under the double onslaught of Fascist squads and governmental repression, the organization vanished as a national force. Secondari, seized by mental disorders, was institutionalized in the summer of 1924 and died in a mental hospital in the spring of 1942, a forgotten man.

Organizations such as the Arditi were approaching low ebb in the winter of 1920–21, the moment when D'Annunzio was driven from Fiume along with his Legionnaires (many of whom were Arditi). His return to Italy could not have come at a more auspicious moment for other veterans' organizations, especially those who viewed Fascism as a betrayal of the ideals of the war. No figure commanded more respect in military circles than D'Annunzio, and no figure was capable of generating more enthusiastic passions than the "Comandante." Thus, both as a dynamic leader in the newly expanded political life of the country, and as a figure with proven appeal to the armed forces, the poet was a phenomenon of enormous potential power. One need only read the journals of the period to become convinced of this, for hardly a week passed without the circulation of some rumor involving D'Annunzio's involvement in a plot to take over the government. Much of Italian public opinion (and by no means the worst-informed segment!) was convinced that D'Annunzio was desstined for the leadership of the country, whether it be by parliamentary means or a march on Rome.[40]

Many of the poet's public statements and early actions following his Fiume adventure seemed to bear out these suspicions. D'Annunzio expressed his firm desire to keep his Legions intact, and he therefore organized the Federazione Nazionale dei Legionari Fiumani in January, 1921, to "sustain the flame of the ideal sacrificed with blood, for which [the Legionnaires] fought and suffered in Fiume for sixteen months." In keeping with the Fiuman antecedent, the federation was solely under his command although there were provisions for the creation of a directoral committee. Here, too, the Legionnaires seemed to be an exceedingly potent force, for they were blessed with outstanding leadership: Alceste De Ambris, Eno Mecheri, Tom Antongini, Eugenio Coselschi, and Ugo Foscanelli constituted D'Annunzio's "shadow cabinet." As ever, the poet quickly expanded the journalistic activities of his movement, and in short order the country was presented with ten D'Annunzian newspapers. The most important of these were *La Vigilia* in Milan, and *La Riscossa dei Legionarii Fiumani* in Bologna.

Yet with all this, the most crucial element for an effective national organization was lacking: the will of the poet himself. In a state of profound depression, D'Annunzio confided to his closest associates that he had lost faith in everything and everybody. Determined to remain pure in an impure world, he returned to his literary and amorous enterprises, holding himself "above the parties" in a state of readiness. Like many a would-be national leader, he had decided that all his potential opponents on the political scene were worthless, that it was simply a matter of time before the people recognized this fact, and that he had only to wait until his country called him to service. Thus he withdrew to his "fantasms" in his palace, Villa Carnacco on the shores of Lake Garda, to await the fulfillment of his destiny.[41]

Lacking the personal participation of the Comandante, the Federazione Legionari could undertake no decisive action, but the most resolute veterans of Fiume nonetheless attempted to hold their forces intact, and sought to strengthen their ranks pending the return of D'Annunzio to action. Their success, though limited, testifies to the appeal of the myth of the Legions and of their leader. By May, 1921, they had managed to generate a substantial following among the Arditi, who felt themselves closer to D'Annunzio than to an increasingly reactionary Fascism. In the summer of 1921 the conflict for the support of the Arditi became manifest at the meeting of their national council at the end of June. The key speech at that meeting came from De Ambris, who had arrived from the Comandante's retreat at Gardone Riviera. Attacking Fascist violence, De Ambris called for fusion of the Arditi and the Legionnaires. If the Arditi wished to remain loyal to D'Annunzio, De Ambris proclaimed, no compromise with the leader of Fascism was possible. "No one is forced to be with us," he said, "but whosoever wishes to follow the Comandante must obey." He then continued by contrasting the goals of the Charter of the Carnaro with Mussolini's recent proclerical statements:[42]

In the Charter of the Carnaro life is limpidly examined in its social, political and religious aspects.

The institutional ideal is republican.

The religious ideal is laical.

The leader of Fascism has, with his recent speech, embraced a clerical concept. . . .

He also refers to some unjustified Fascist excesses in Parma, where they even attacked the Camere del Lavoro Sindacali, composed of interventionists and D'Annunzians.

Can Arditi and Legionnaires join with such people?

De Ambris's speech carried the day, and the leadership of the association voted to accept the constitution of the Carnaro as its program, and to proclaim D'Annunzio as its only leader. Further, it asked its members to resign from the Fasci de Combattimento with all due speed, "in order not to damage the discipline of the association."

This order of the day produced an irreparable rift within association ranks, and in short order such leading figures among the Arditi as Bottai, De Vecchi, and Bolzon were either forced out or resigned voluntarily. By the fall of 1921 the association had thus come full circle in its political meanderings. Once again pledged to vague ideals of political revivification of the country, once again under the leadership of those who felt that the experience of war, of struggle, of derring-do was indispensable for the Italy of the future, the Arditi joined forces with the Legionnaires. Those Arditi who instead had been captured by Fascism split from the main organization to found their own group, the Federazione Nazionale Arditi d'Italia in late October, 1922, the moment of the Fascist march on Rome.

The conflict between Fascism and D'Annunzianism was a complex contrast which had its roots in the most intense beliefs of both movements, as well as in the history of the Legionnaires. D'Annunzio and his followers could not forget the "betrayal" of the Fascists, who had not lifted a finger during the so-called Bloody Christmas of 1920, which had seen the Legionnaires driven from Fiume by Italian troops.[43] Moreover, the very nature of the membership of the Legionnaires' federation pointed to a deep ideological division between the two movements. Many of the leaders of the federation had come from the ranks of Italian anarchosyndicalism, and such figures as De Ambris, Foscanelli, and Mecheri could not but view with dismay the savagery of Fascist attacks upon workers' organizations. Finally, this background of anarchosyndicalism led the Legionnaires to a traditional radical disregard for the maneuvers of parliamentary politics, and Mussolini, by 1921, was firmly embarked upon the road of parliamentary tactics in his quest for national power.

At the same time that the Legonnaires moved to a position of the defense of the proletariat—producing many street conflicts between Legionnaires and Fascists—they nonetheless had much of the paternalism which intellectuals traditionally adopted toward the working class. It was not sufficient for the heirs of the "Free State of Fiume" simply to enlist the support of the proletariat; they had to provide for the spiritual uplift and education of the workers as well. This position is clearly reflected in an editorial in *La Riscossa* which appeared in March, 1921:[44]

> We recognize and support the contention that the proletariat has the most absolute right to improvement, but we are also convinced that this rise must not be merely material. Only if the improvement of material conditions corresponds to a spiritual elevation, only then will the working class be able to say that it has won its struggle.

D'Annunzio, then, appeared as the prophet of a "third way" in Italian politics, supporting the elevation of the proletariat and defending it against its class enemies, yet simultaneously providing for the creation of a new kind of society, and for the transformation of the members of the working class into a spiritually superior element of the modern world.

The ideology of the federation cut across many of the categories of Italian political life, and held out the possibility of a movement which would truly be "above the parties," as the poet wished. The traditions established by the short-lived "league of Fiume," which was to have been a kind of league of the oppressed nations of the earth,[45] made the Legionnaires' movement attractive to many who were repulsed by the hypernationalistic outbursts of the right-wing parties, and yet D'Annunzio's credentials with the nationalists were gilt-edged. The presence of the Arditi made the federation attractive to the military, while the syndicalist rhetoric made even such a figure as Gramsci contemplate cooperation with D'Annunzio.[46]

D'Annunzio's withdrawal to Gardone Riviera made all these projects credible, but as time wore on his followers became increasingly frustrated. As Fascism grew ever stronger, and the decisive moment of the fall of 1922 approached, such figures as De Ambris warned the poet of the importance of his active intervention, and begged him to hurl himself into the chaos. These appeals produced one act of considerable importance—the pact between the federation and Giuseppe Giulietti's maritime union, the Federazione Italiana dei Lavoratori del Mare, in April, 1922.

The maritime federation (the FILM) was one of the most successful and best-organized trade unions in Italy, and Giulietti had achieved an international reputation both for his forceful leadership of the federation and for his effective participation in the government during the Great War.[47] When, therefore, not only the FILM but also the Arditi association joined with the Legionnaires' federation in Genoa in a declaration of mutual solidarity on April twenty-fifth, it appeared that the long-awaited D'Annunzian movement had finally begun to form. The union of the three groups represented, at least in principle, a decisive step to the left for a great number of veterans, for there could be no question of the radical nature of the FILM, nor, for that matter, of the intentions of the leadership (with the exception, as always, of the poet himself) of the Legionnaires. This period witnessed the creation of the so-called Labor Alliance (L'Alleanza del Lavoro) involving the railroad workers, FILM, Legionnaires, and anarchosyndicalists. The Labor Alliance, like many of the organizations we have examined, came into being largely in response to Fascist violence, and was yet another attempt to organize workers into a coherent body capable of defending themselves against the *squadristi*. As in the case of the Arditi del Popolo, the Alleanza del Lavoro aroused considerable mass support, and the usual mixed reaction from the socialists and communists.[48]

Once again, a word from the poet would have sufficed to give these projects an enormous impetus, and once again the word was not forthcoming from Gardone Riviera. D'Annunzio was involved in a frenetic series of negotiations with all factions of Italian politics, attempting to put together the pieces of a monumental grand design which would have placed him at the center of an imposing union of movements and parties.[49] But in his quest for this union of all potent forces of the nation, D'Annunzio remained unable, or unwilling for the moment, to take any decisive step in any given political direction. Despite the calls of the Legionnaires for a national congress in the spring and summer of 1922, D'Annunzio procrastinated, awaiting some sign that his moment had come.

While he waited, the forces of Italian politics swirled around him, seemingly offering endless opportunities to strike out in a variety of directions. There were offers of collaboration from some of the leading Fascists, themselves disgusted or disenchanted with Mussolini's increasingly reactionary leadership of the movement. There were "feelers" from leaders of socialist organizations, both in Italy and from abroad. There were reports that Lenin himself had called the poet the only figure in Italy capable of leading a genuine revolution, and there were the usual rumors of collaboration with the army in a coup d'etat. In the meantime, while D'Annunzio considered this vast constellation of forces, the Labor Alliance launched an abortive call for a "legal" general strike at the end of July. The raucous failure of this attempt, which collapsed in the face of a Fascist ultimatum that either the strike be called off within forty-eight hours or the *squadristi* would take matters in their own hands, was later termed the Caporetto of the proletariat, and for the moment sealed the doom of the projected alliance.

The last in this formidable series of missed opportunities came in August, when it appeared that D'Annunzio had finally decided that he could no longer await his moment of triumph. Having by now spoken with representatives from every sector of Italian political life, he resolved to enter a tripartite governmental coalition with Nitti and Mussolini, evidently hoping to emerge as the dominant member of the *troika*. The plans for this arrangement were quite far advanced, and a final meeting among the three conspirators was planned, in Tuscany, for the fifteenth of August, Nitti had obtained a guarantee of safe passage from Mussolini, for the province had become a veritable war zone, and D'Annunzio had already made his plans for the journey from the north.[50]

These negotiations are still shrouded in mystery, and it may well be that we may never know all the details of the maneuvers around the poet in this period. But there are some reliable reports that D'Annunzio was contemplating the mobilization of the forces of the war to support him in his attempt to enter the government, in whatever form.[51] One hears of D'Annunzio speaking of rallying "all the veterans" of the Great War to him, and to that end he called a meeting of veterans' representatives at Gardone. There he spoke of "imposing their will of unification and peace" upon the country, and asked the veterans to maintain their forces in a state of constant readiness.

These plans, melodramatic as they were, fell with the poet in one of the most curious episodes in his singularly novel life. On the night of the thirteenth of August, D'Annunzio fell from a high window at Gardone, and remained in critical condition for several days. He never revealed the cause of his precipitous fall, and spoke of it in the most oblique terms, calling it the "flight of the archangel." Speculation, at the time and ever since, has been rife, for the accident had enormous political repercussions. Was the Comandante pushed, and if so, by whom? Some suspect that a jealous woman was responsible for the fall, others suspect the involvement of Fascist agents. Whatever the explanation, the archangel's crash landing terminated, for at least a month, any hopes for D'Annunzio's participation in an Italian government, and when he had recovered his strength the Fascists were involved in the plans for their march on Rome.

Those veterans who had pledged their loyalty to the spirit of the Charter of the Carnaro were soon confronted with a highly threatening situation, both because of the now total absence of leadership from the poet, and soon thereafter because of the installation of Mussolini in power in Rome. With the Fascists moving toward complete control of the country, the syndicalist leaders of the Arditi and the Legionnaires resolved to act on their own initiative, without waiting for the approval of D'Annunzio. Already in September De Ambris had organized the Comitado Nazionale di Azione Sindacale Dannunziana, which had gained the support of several of the largest and most important labor organizations. In October the Associazione Arditi moved an order of the day which allied them with the syndicalist Legionnaires, and reinforced their break with Fascism:[52]

> The Arditi of Italy were the true founders of Fascism. . . . But now they have nothing in common with the Fascist party. We now intend to guarantee the liberty of association to all the unions. We don't want war with Fascism, but we consider ourselves equidistant from the Fascists, who are now a degeneration of Fascism, just as communism is an aberration of the socialist idea. Our position is one of a middle term in the midst of the present chaos. . . .

In the spring of 1923 the Legionnaires' federation changed its name to the D'Annunzian Spiritual Union (Unione Spirituale Dannunziana), into which the Comitato Nazionale di Azione Sindacale Dannunziana and the Arditi flowed as well. Hence, by April, the veterans of Fiume had joined forces with the most distinguished veterans of the Great War, and with several workers' groups, in a potentially powerful movement which attracted support from all regions of the nation. But the time had passed, at least for the moment, when such an organization could effectively combat a Fascism now firmly installed in power. The secretary general of the Spiritual Union, Umberto Calosci, issued a call for the long-awaited syndicalist constituent assembly to be held within the month of April, and the Fascists were quick to act. The headquarters of the Spiritual Union were constantly searched and harassed by Fascist squads and by police functionaries; the leader of the Spiritual Union in Pistoia, the marchese Carlo Matteucci, charged with organizing Legionnaires' groups in the city, was put in prison for several days; in Prato, the Arditist and Legionnaire Ponticelli was similarly arrested, and these were relatively fortunate figures. In Alessandria, Pia Paelini Zuccotti was assassinated by the Fascists because of his attempts to organize an agricultural cooperative association among the veterans of three towns. Finally, with the danger of a constituent assembly effectively quashed, the government moved against Calosci himself. In September the minister of the interior advised Calosci that he could not leave the city of Florence, could not make speeches or lead political demonstrations, could not undertake any political action himself, nor encourage others to do anything which might create embarrassment for the government.[53]

The leadership of the Spiritual Union was thus effectively repressed. De Ambris, convinced that the cause was now irremediably lost, went into French exile, from which he never returned. The attitude of the Fascist government toward the Legionnaires could hardly be more explicitly defined than in this circular from General De Bono to the prefects of the kingdom in December, 1922:[54]

It is the firm intention of the government to put an immediate end in a total and absolute manner to the activities of the anarchists and subversives in general who, exploiting the name of D'Annunzio, try. . .to give life to a disruptive movement. . .and to stimulate agitation which can not fail to have serious and negative repercussions for our nation. . . .

As if this were not enough to submerge the Legionnaires and the Spiritual Union in a sea of troubles, the poet finally disassociated himself entirely from the enterprises of his followers. Proclaiming his disgust with the attempt to "adjectivize" him ("I hated the name 'D'Annunzian' in literature. It is totally repulsive to me in politics. When will I have peace?"), the Comandante made it clear that the Spiritual Union was not under his leadership, nor did it retain his blessings. This final withdrawal into his artistic vocation saw D'Annunzio accept even the presence of an official spy in his own household. Giovanni Rizzo, commissioner of police, served the dual role of guarding the poet and advising Mussolini of the activities at Gardone. In time the Comandante was finally convinced to abandon his "protection" of the maritime workers, and thus even this one act of solidarity with the proletariat came to naught.[55]

But while Mussolini had drawn the sting of the poet, the Legionnaires represented a different sort of menace. It was clearly necessary to eliminate the Spiritual Union, permitting D'Annunzio to live out his life in the glorious tranquility of the "Vittoriale" at Gardone without any further temptations to indulge in political heroism. To this end, Mussolini arranged with D'Annunzio to stage a final national congress of the Legionnaires in the city of Ronchi in January, 1924. The original plan was to have one final dramatic meeting and then announce the dissolution of the union. Yet it soon became evident that the membership of the Spiritual Union was anything but resigned to their assimilation into a Fascist state. Calosci opened the proceedings at Ronchi with a vigorously anti-Fascist speech, calling upon those who treasured the "human religion" and the idea of liberty to join with the Legionnaires in a period of intense struggle. And when the message arrived from Gardone in the hands of Eugenio Coselschi, the Legionnaires discovered that the poet had asked them to cancel their meeting, not to dissolve the union itself.[56] D'Annunzio could not bring himself to destroy his own creation.

Thus the Spiritual Union was still in existence when the Fascist state entered its moment of crisis in the summer of 1924, following the assassination of Giacomo Matteotti. Inspired by the purported phrase of D'Annunzio, "I am very sad in this fetid ruin,"[57] the Legionnaires prepared to undertake a final battle against the Fascists. In the months that followed, Calosci and his associates crisscrossed the country, talking to veterans' organizations and ex-Legionnaires, attempting to form a nationwide anti-Fascist organization which could wage civil war.[58]

While no attempt to overthrow Fascism could expect to have an easy victory, Calosci's efforts represented a substantial initial success. In Rome, for example, veterans founded a group called Free Italy (Italia Libera), which claimed some twenty thousand members. In July the Spiritual Union held a national congress in Florence, at which some twenty-eight delegates spoke, representing elements of Free Italy and the Aventine Opposition. In September the national council of the Spiritual Union met in Milan and took four important steps: they dissociated the union entirely from the person of D'Annunzio, while holding themselves loyal to his *ideas;* they proclaimed themselves unalterably opposed to Fascism, and dedicated their struggle to the defense of liberty; and they proclaimed themselves opposed to Fascist "corporativism," citing a letter from De Ambris in which he reminded the Legionnaires of the acts of destruction which Fascism had wrought upon the organizations and the bodies of the working classes. Finally the Spiritual Union and the Arditi association pledged to fuse their organizations throughout the country in order to present a united front in the struggle against Mussolini and his allies.[59]

These various groups of veterans were ideally suited to an underground struggle with the Fascists. Thus, when the government moved formally against the Spiritual Union in January, 1925, they found that the records of the union had vanished from Florence, and Calosci had similarly disappeared. Orders came only from the secretariat, and were sent only to regional secretaries. Each member was given a postcard with the seal of the union on it, to use as identification.

Ironically enough, the Legionnaires thus entered the political life of the country at the very moment that meaningful political activity was being snuffed out by the Fascist terror. As one might expect, the clandestine struggle of the Spiritual Union was eventually crushed by the government. In early November the prefect of Lucca uncovered a secret circular of the union, which contained the names and addresses of the provincial secretaries. The police were not slow to act, and by the end of the month there were no further traces of this last desperate attempt of Arditi and Legionnaires to impose their wills upon the nation.[60] There is some testimony claiming that Legionnaires continued to act in small groups here and there, but obviously the war had been lost, even if some minor skirmishes remained to be fought.

The final judgment on Italian veterans of the Great War remains to be written, and I do not propose to attempt that here. But there are several points which need to be stressed, if only to indicate the incompleteness of what has been said above, and at the same time to encourage others to delve more deeply into the matter. The most important consequence of the trench warfare would seem to have been the kindling of new passions in the body politic, passions which had no outlet in the traditional framework of Italian institutions and organizations. Furthermore, these passions were extremely difficult to "channel," both because peacetime existence is very different from the drama of warfare, and because many of these passions had been kindled by governmental promises (the most important of which was the promise of free land for veterans) which were subsequently broken.

The second major point, closely related to the first, is that veterans remained largely outside the framework of traditional politics, and did so by choice. Despite their ideological closeness to the Socialist party, most veterans were not attracted to the goal of proletarian revolution, unless it was associated with the kind of "enthusiasm" that surrounded, to take the most dramatic example, D'Annunzio's capture of Fiume. The war, it would seem, had produced a restlessness, a search for drama and meaning, which could not be satisfied in the framework of traditional political organizations. Thus, while many have criticized the Socialists for their failure to unify with the veterans, such union was hardly possible with a group such as that which returned from the Great War. The Arditi symbolized these men, and Emilio Lussu has described them very well indeed:[61]

> Discharged from service, [the Arditi] found themselves most uncomfortable in the new atmosphere of work and peace. It was not their climate. They were precious in wartime, detestable in time of peace. In war they ridiculed the footsoldiers, that is to say, discipline, the life of the trenches: in peace they detested democracy, that is to say, government by majority, the bureaucracy, the life of the law. If land had been offered them, they would not have known what to do with it. They were nomads, not sedentary, and they continued, restlessly, to search for action.

Yet what is so important about such men is that their attitudes came, in the end, to define successful political behavior in Italy. Is the triumph of Fascism not the triumph of such attitudes? In the end it was Mussolini, not D'Annunzio, who captured this dynamism and put it to his own use. But this should not be permitted to obscure the main issue: that Italian politics became the politics of war, and that the country, in the fall of 1922, had to choose between several armed camps, each with its own legions.

Therefore, the most legitimate criticism of the traditional parties is that they failed to recognize that the nature of politics had been vitally transformed by the war, and that the forces which had destroyed the Hapsburg empire could prove equally fatal to the state of Cavour. The revolutionary parties of the Left and the conservative parties of the Right proved equally myopic in the new atmosphere which followed the armistice of 1918. It is one of the lessons of the period that perhaps the last organization capable of resisting the Fascists was one which had enormous potential appeal to both extreme Left and Right: the legions of the poet-warrior, Gabriele D'Annunzio.

NOTES

This essay is based on the works of Italian scholars, and is intended to present the English-speaking public with an overview of the literature on this period of Italian history. By bringing the reader up to date, I hope to have indicated the areas in which further work is needed, and to have suggested the major problems which remain to be solved.

Where possible, I have checked the accuracy of the secondary sources. When I have been able to do this, I have simply cited the appropriate reference. When this has not been possible, I have used the form, "cited in. . . ."

1. Asvero Gravelli (ed.), *Squadrismo* (Rome, Antieuropa 1939), p. 53. This little-known work is a real goldmine of information on Fascist attitudes toward veterans.

2. Pietro Nenni, *Storia di quattro anni* (Turin, Einaudi 1946), p. 7.

3. Giorgio Rochat, *L'esercito italiano da Vittorio Veneto a Mussolini* (Bari, Laterza 1967), pp. 13ff.

4. Cf. "La mancata smobilitazione degli alti gradi dell'esercito," *Il Secolo* (March 27, 1919).

5. Rochat, p. 31.

6. Cf. "I ministri militari fanno il loro dovere per la ricostruzione economica del paese?" *Il Corriere della sera* (August 9, 1919).

7. For the details on the deployment of these forces, cf. Rochat, pp. 47ff. The document from which this analysis derives is *Ministero della Guerra, Ufficio smobilitazione e ordinamento del R. Esercito,* "Dati e notizie sulla smobilitazione dell'esercito al 1 luglio 1919," cited in Rochat.

8. The literature is voluminous. By way of example, cf. two of the most recent (and best-researched) studies of the period, Mario Isnenghi, *Il mito della grande guerra* (Bari, Laterza 1970), and Roberto Vivarelli, *Il dopoguerra in Italia e l'avvento del fascismo (1918–1922): I. Dalla fine della guerra all'impresa di Fiume* (Naples, Istituto italiano di studi storic: 1966).

9. E. Caviglia, *Il conflitto di Fiume* (Cernusco sul Naviglio, Garzanti 1948), p. 65.

10. *Atti parlamentari, Camera, Discussioni, 14-7-1919, Nitti,* 312–13.

11. Piero Melograni, *Storia politica della grande guerra* (Bari, Laterza 1969); Vivarelli.

12. Vivarelli, p. 14.

13. Melograni, p. 558.

14. Cited in Angelo Tasca, *Nascita e avvento del fascismo* (Florence, Le Monnier 1950), p. 19.

15. Emilio Lussu, *La marcia su Roma e dintorni* (Milan, Mondadori 1957), appendix 7.

16. Isnenghi, pp. 314–17.

17. L. Capello, *L'ordinamento dell'esercito* (Rome, 1920), pp. 9–10.

18. Rochat, pp. 196–203.

19. Ferruccio Vecchi, *La tragedia del mio ardire* (Milan, Arti Grafiche Italiane 1923), pp. 15–16.

20. Mario Carli, "Primo appelio alle Fiamme," *Roma Futurista* (September 20,

1918); "Secondo appello alle Fiamme—Fondazione dell'Associazione fra gli Arditi d'Italia," *Roma Futurista* (December 10, 1918). Both articles are reproduced in his *Arditismo* (Rome, Augustea 1919), but this book is virtually impossible to find.

21. Cf. Ferdinando Cordova, *Arditi e legionari dannunziani* (Padova, Marsiglio 1969), pp. 211–12.

22. From a manifesto entitled "L'Ardito Futurista" cited in Cordova, p. 214.

23. Renzo De Felice, *Mussolini il rivoluzionario* (Turin, Einaudi 1965), p. 484.

24. Ferruccio Vecchi, "La battaglia del 15 Aprile 1919," *L'Ardito d'Italia* (January 19, 1936).

25. Caviglia, p. 55.

26. Mario Carli, *Con D'Annunzio a Fiume* (Milan, Facchi 1920), pp. 5–23.

27. Archivio Centrale dello Stato (ACS), *Ministero dell'Interno—Direzione Generale della Publica Sicurezza—Div. aff. Gen. e Ris., 1919,* B. 49, cat. 1, fasc.: "Arditi (Militari)."

28. Cordova, pp. 51–53.

29. Quoted in Carli, *Con D'Annunzio a Fiume,* p. 27.

30. Cordova, pp. 28–29.

31. Ferruccio Vecchi, "Attorno alla casa dell'Ardito," *Il Popolo d'Italia* (February 1, 1919).

32. Quoted in Eno Mecheri, *Chi ha tradito?* (Milan, Libreria Lombarda 1947), pp. 29–30.

33. Cited in Cordova, p. 86.

34. ACS, *Min. Int.—Direz. Gen. PS.—Div. aff. Gen. e Ris., 1919,* B. 50, cat. C2, Fasc.: "Roma—Movimento Sovversivo."

35. ACS, *Min. Int.—Direz. Gen. PS.—Div. aff. Gen. e Ris., 1920,* B. 77, cat. G1, Fasc.: "Associazione fra gli Arditi d'Italia."

36. "La grande adunata degli arditi," *Il Paese* (June 29, 1921).

37. ACS, *Min. Int.—Direz. Gen. PS.—Div. aff. Gen. e Ris., 1922,* B. 59, Cat. G1, Fasc.: "Arditi del Popolo (Associazione)—Affari Generali."

38. " 'Arditi del popolo' popolari," *Il Paese* (August 25, 1921).

39. Cordova, pp. 97–100.

40. Introduction by Renzo De Felice to *Carteggio D'Annunzio-Mussolini (1919–1938),* ed. De Felice and Emilio Mariano (Vicenza, Mondadori 1971); cf. also F. Gerra, *L'Impresa di Fiume* (Milan, Longanesi 1966), pp. 258–64.

41. De Felice and Mariano, p. xxviii; also Nino Valeri, *D'Annunzio davanti al fascismo* (Florence, Le Monnier 1963), pp. 34ff.; and Renzo De Felice, *Sindacalismo rivoluzionario e fiumanesimo nel carteggio De Ambris-D'Annunzio (1919–1922)* (Brescia Morcelliana 1966), pp. 113ff.

42. "Il nostro Convegno Nazionale di Roma," *L'Ardito* (July 2–9, 1921).

43. Valeri, pp. 48–55; also Cordova, pp. 115–18; De Felice and Mariano, eds. pp. xxi–xxvi.

44. "Fiumanesimo e proletariato," *La Riscossa dei Legionarii fiumani* (March 5, 1921).

45. Valeri, pp. 27–28; De Felice and Mariano, pp. xii–xvi.

46. S. Caproglio, "Un mancato incontro Gramsci–D'Annunzio a Gardone nell'aprile 1921," *Rivista Storica del socialismo* (Jan.–Aug., 1962), pp. 263ff.

47. Giuseppe Giulietti, *Pax Mundi* (Naples, Rispoli n.d. [but 1945]), p. 64.

48. Cf. Pietro Nenni, *Il diciannovismo* (Milan, Avanti 1962), p. 227; De Felice, *Mussolini il fascista: I. La conquista del potere* (Turin, Einaudi 1966), p. 223.

49. Cf., for example, Valeri, pp. 57ff.; and De Felice and Mariano, pp. xxixff.

50. Valeri, p. 74.

51. Cf. the report of a conversation between Tom Antongini and Schiff Giorgini, representing D'Annunzio and Nitti in *La Voce Repubblicana* (January 2, 1923).

52. Cited in Cordova, p. 158.

53. Ibid., pp. 159–60.

54. Valeri, p. 101.
55. Ibid., p. 104.
56. Cordova, pp. 178–79.
57. Valeri, p. 117.
58. Cordova, pp. 181ff.
59. Ibid., p. 181.
60. Cf. Mecheri, pp. 10ff.
61. Lussu, p. 10.

FIVE   JAMES M. DIEHL

GERMANY:
Veterans' Politics under
Three Flags

Looking back on what he called the world crisis of 1914–18, the perceptive French historian Eli Halevy noted, "Certainly no responsible statesman would have said, at the beginning of 1914, that he felt safe against the perils of some kind of revolutionary outburst."[1] It is impossible to determine with certainty the extent to which some European statesmen and politicians may have welcomed, if not actually promoted, the international crisis in the hopes of overcoming or alleviating domestic tensions. One thing is certain, however: on the eve of the First World War all the major European states that were to become involved in the war were experiencing severe political and social crises. Broadly speaking, in each country a struggle for power was taking place between the "forces of movement," represented primarily by the rapidly growing socialist parties, which were pressing for political and social reform, and the "forces of order," composed of the traditional elites and their conservative allies, which were doggedly seeking to resist reform and to maintain the status quo.[2]

Initially the war had a unifying effect in all countries. In the enthusiasm accompanying the outbreak of the war, the political and social differences which divided the societies of the belligerents were either forgotten or voluntarily suppressed. In the face of the common external enemy, social and domestic truces were concluded between the conflicting domestic factions. Such truces naturally tended to consolidate the power of the incumbent forces of order. The fundamental causes of prewar social and political unrest were not removed, however, but only temporarily checked. The unprecedented length and scope of the war necessitated extraordinary sacrifices and imposed tremendous burdens, and under the strain of total mobilization the fragile foundations of the social truces eventually began to crumble in all the belligerent nations. By the end of 1916 prewar domestic conflicts were beginning to reemerge, exacerbated and compounded by the effects of mankind's first total war. One of the most significant of the new elements added by the war to the parallelograms of domestic political forces was the large mass of veterans produced by the conflict.

The voracious demands on manpower during the First World War had transformed the military structures of all the belligerent nations. Conscription, carried out on a massive scale, produced enormous citizen armies. The nonprofessional character of these armies, combined with the unprecedented carnage and horror of a mass war conducted in an industrial age, meant that the combatant nations had to cope with new, powerful, and potentially radical elements within their societies—the ex-servicemen, war-disabled, and next of kin of those who had died in the war. If either side in the domestic political and social struggles which began to reemerge during the winter of 1916–17 had previously been unaware of the importance of winning the allegiance of soldiers and veterans, this became impossible after March, 1917: the events in Russia dramatically demonstrated the political power of soldiers as well as the advantage, indeed the necessity, of winning the support of veterans.[3]

In Germany, the breakdown of the social truce, or *Burgfrieden,* began in the fall of 1916 and was accelerated by the hardship and suffering of the severe "turnip winter" which followed. In Germany, as elsewhere, the forces of movement, led by the socialists, began to reemerge in 1917. Spurred on by the general war-weariness of the German population and encouraged by revolutionary developments in Russia, they began to press the government for political reform and the adoption of liberal, nonannexationist war aims which it was hoped would facilitate a negotiated peace and bring a rapid end to the war. In response the government temporized, attempting to play down its annexationist war aims and trying to offset the desire for reform through minor concessions and promises of reform in the future. Meanwhile, the hard-core forces of order, represented by the

Supreme Command and its de facto leader General Erich von Ludendorff, continued to pursue a policy of all-out victory in the hope that a decisive victory and widespread annexations would consolidate their position and obviate the need for domestic reforms.

During the final years of the war there developed a continued and increasingly intense debate between the German forces of movement and forces of order. Although the public discussion focused on war aims, both sides were well aware that much more was at stake: the structure of postwar society. The debate over war aims unavoidably raised fundamental questions about the purpose and meaning of the war. As the war dragged on and its cost in blood and sacrifice increased, both sides worked to influence public opinion. In seeking to increase support for their political programs, foreign and domestic, both the forces of movement and the forces of order in Germany began to appeal to those who were most directly affected by the war, the veterans and the war-disabled.[4]

In the effort to mobilize veterans in support of their goals, the conservative forces had a powerful ally in the already existing veterans' organizations. Unlike most other European countries, Germany had a well-developed veterans' movement before World War I. At the outbreak of the war the veterans' associations, with nearly three million members, represented by far the largest of the many nationalist organizations which dotted the political landscape in Wilhelmine Germany. Veterans' groups had existed in Germany since the eighteenth century, but they became mass organizations only after the Franco-Prussian War of 1870–71. Whereas the earlier associations had limited membership to front-line soldiers and therefore had declined by the middle of the nineteenth century into little more than burial societies for former comrades in arms, the new veterans' organizations founded after the wars of unification opened their ranks to all men who had completed their military training. This created a massive, self-perpetuating base. In spite of the fact that they owed their origins to the wars which had united Germany, the new veterans' organizations themselves remained intensely particularistic. Although statewide organizations were formed during the 1870s and 1880s, no single nationwide organization existed until 1900 when, after much effort, the Kyffhäuser-Bund der Deutschen Landeskriegerverbände (Kyffhäuser League of German State Veterans' Organizations) was founded.[5]

The driving force behind the creation of the Kyffhäusser-Bund was Dr. Alfred Westphal. Westphal, a classic example of the "feudalized" reserve officer about which Eckart Kehr has written so brilliantly,[6] was a leading figure in both the Prussian state veterans' association and the Deutscher Kriegerbund (German Veterans' League), an organization which had been trying with only limited success to unite German veterans in a single organization since 1873. With the founding of the Kyffhäuser-Bund, which he also headed, Westphal became the dominant personality in the German veterans' movement, a position he was to retain until after the war.

Under Westphal's leadership the Kyffhäuser-Bund, and with it the entire veterans' movement, was converted into a tool for the "class struggle from above" that formed such an integral part of German politics before the war.[7] Originally the veterans' organizations had been spontaneous, without political objectives, and had accepted veterans from all walks of life. During the quarter century preceding the outbreak of the war, however, they became among the most active of the many nationalist organizations in Germany which through their mobilization of antisocialist resentment opposed political and social reform and fought for the status quo. According to Westphal, the primary objective of the veterans' organizations was to cultivate "monarchistic and patriotic feelings" and to counter "the revolutionary and traitorous Social Democratic movement with a monarchistic and nationalistic mass movement of former soldiers."[8] These goals were actively supported and encouraged by government officials, who saw the veterans' organizations as a useful means of continuing the fight against the Social Democrats after the antisocialist legislation of 1878 was allowed to lapse in 1890, as well as by military authorities who saw the veterans' associations as an effective means of propagating in the ranks of civilian society the "spirit of the army," i.e., intense nationalism, support of the existing system, and opposition to social democracy.

During the final decades of the empire, the German veterans' movement became highly politicized. Socialists were systematically purged from its ranks. Not only members of the Social Democratic party, but even those who voted for socialist candidates were excluded. Similarly, Social Democratic unions were attacked, and in 1909 measures were introduced which prohibited members of veterans' organizations from belonging to them. The opposition of the Kyffhäuser-Bund and its affiliated organizations to the Social Democrats also included an extensive program of antisocialist propaganda. In addition, the veterans' organizations, ostensibly "nonpartisan," campaigned vigorously against the Social Democrats during elections and actively supported the nonsocialist parties. In the view of the Kyffhäuser-Bund, being "nonpartisan" simply meant that political issues dividing the middle-class parties were to be avoided in the interest of building a firm front against the Social Democrats.[9] This practice, common among rightist organizations, was to be continued after the war.

Not surprisingly, the bitter hatred of the Kyffhäuser-Bund toward the socialists was returned in kind. The alleged "terrorism of the veterans' organizations" against Social Democrats was a constant headline in Social Democratic publications, and at times the party adopted the tactics of the enemy by denying membership in Social Democratic organizations to members of veterans' organizations. Thus, by the outbreak of the war in 1914, the Kyffhäuser-Bund and the Social Democratic party faced each other like two hostile armies across an unbridgeable social and political chasm.

This chasm, like other divisions in German society, was temporarily covered over by the *Burgfrieden,* which was concluded among the contending social and political forces in Germany at the outbreak of the war. As a result of the *Burgfrieden* as well as the fact that its own ranks had been thrown into disarray by the calling up of over one-half of its members, the Kyffhäuser-Bund largely discontinued its antisocialist activity during the early years of the war and instead limited itself to general patriotic support of the war effort. As the first year of the war came to a close, however, its leaders began to think about what the Bund's future policy should be.

Like other conservative elements in German society, the leaders of the Kyffhäuser-Bund were surprised by the Social Democrats' support of the war and the continued sacrifices made by the working class on behalf of the war effort. Never suffering from modesty when it came to evaluating the importance and efficacy of their organization, Westphal and his colleagues concluded that the unity of the German people and the patriotic action of the Social Democrats were in large part the result of their own activity during the prewar years. Impressed by the patriotism of the working class and what they felt was their own role in promoting it, they decided that they should open their ranks to Social Democrats. By doing this, it was hoped, the patriotism and loyalty to the monarchy evident among so many Social Democrats might be further strengthened and many workers won away from the pernicious influence of Social Democratic organizations.

Directives urging a reconsideration of the prewar attitude toward accepting Social Democrats began to be sent out in May, 1915, and in October the new policy was tentatively adopted by the executive council.[10] Although there was some opposition to the new course, it was ineffectual, and in September, 1916, when the Kyffhäuser-Bund held its first convention since the outbreak of the war, the executive council's policy was officially sanctioned. Thereafter, Social Democrats who were "patriotic" and "loyal to the monarchy" were to be considered eligible for membership. Following this, an extensive recruitment campaign was launched.

The reversal of the Kyffhäuser-Bund's previous policy came as a shock to many of its members as well as to outside observers; yet its volte-face should not have been as surprising as it was. By late 1916 the German people were becoming war-weary. The *Burgfrieden* was breaking down, and the objectives of the war were beginning to be questioned. In the following months the forces of movement began to reemerge after their temporary decline, and increasing pressure was put on the government to define its war aims and to fulfill its vague promises of a "new orientation," i.e., domestic reforms, which had been made during the early years of the war. The Kyffhäuser-Bund's new policy was only one aspect of the more general response by the conservative forces of order to resist change and to win support for their own policies of annexationist war aims and the maintenance of the political and social status quo. The new orientation of the Kyffhäuser-Bund, in short, was an attempt to mobilize veterans against the "new orientation" promised by the government and to prevent it from ever becoming a reality.

The Social Democrats were well aware of the implications of the renewed activity of the veterans' associations. Soon after the Kyffhäuser-Bund's official endorsement of its new policy toward Social Democrats, the problem of the postwar organization of veterans became a widespread topic of debate in Social Democratic publications. Because, among other things, the veterans' organizations before the war had attracted many whom the Social Democrats themselves had hoped to win over, they (in spite of official disclaimers) considered the veterans' organizations to be one of their more effective opponents.[11] That they would remain a threat after the war, especially if they were "modernized," seemed certain, and consequently a number of Social Democrats began to urge the creation of veterans' organizations of their own. In an article of November 9 entitled "The Organization of Veterans," *Vorwärts*, the leading Social Democratic newspaper, stated that it was certain that the veterans will consider the common representation of their interests after their return home. They will, especially if. . .disabled by the war, justly claim for themselves far-reaching welfare measures, and they will decisively oppose any attempt to reduce their political rights with respect to other segments of the population. Because of this obvious similarity of goals, they may find it necessary to join together.

In their present form the veterans' organizations are hardly organizations for the representation of social and political interests. Such an organization must be created from scratch. . . . It is only natural that the party and the unions follow such a movement. . .with great interest.

The reference to the need of "far-reaching welfare measures" for the war-disabled and the necessity for veterans "to oppose any attempt to reduce their political rights" pointed to the two issues that were to provide the basis for Social Democratic involvement in the problem of organizing veterans: social welfare and political reform.

In Germany, as in the other belligerent nations, two years of war fought with mass armies and modern weapons had produced an unprecedented number of casualties. This in turn had put an unbearable strain on the nineteenth-century institutions for the collection and distribution of funds for the war-disabled and next of kin of those killed. Before the war Germany had had one of the most effective systems for aiding war-disabled veterans, and German pensions were the highest in Europe.[12] Yet, although new measures were introduced during the war to provide medical care, pensions, and vocational rehabilitation, a comprehensive system of welfare for the war-disabled and their families was never developed. Instead, responsibility for this remained divided among a number of half-official and half-voluntary organizations. Many gaps existed and, more importantly, disabled veterans and their families had no legal claim on many of the services that did exist. In 1917, when war-weariness was already beginning to take its toll and civilian morale was declining, the inadequacies of Germany's programs for aiding the victims of the war became increasingly obvious.[13] The raising of mass citizen armies sounded the death knell of voluntarism. More and more disabled veterans and their families began to demand recompense from the state. The cry for "justice, not charity" became a strong impetus for the formation of new types of veterans' organizations not only in Germany but in all the belligerent nations.

The breakdown of the *Burgfrieden* and the reemergence of the forces of movement in late 1916 and early 1917 were also accompanied by renewed pressure for reform of the unjust suffrage system that existed in Prussia. Although elections to Germany's national parliamentary body, the Reichstag, were based on universal suffrage, those to the Prussian diet, the Landtag, were based on an antiquated and undemocratic three-class suffrage system that had been introduced during the wave of reaction which followed the abortive revolution of 1848. As a result, the Prussian Landtag continued to be dominated by Prussia's semifeudal and extremely conservative Junker class in alliance with wealthy industrial interests. Following the principle that representation should be proportional to the amount of direct taxes paid to the state, the Prussian three-class system gave enormous representation to the wealthy while virtually disenfranchising the poorer elements of society. In the 1898 elections to the Prussian Landtag, for example, two-thirds of the representatives were elected by less than 15 percent of the population. In 1913, although they polled nearly 30 percent of the vote, the Social Democrats won only 10 seats, while the Conservatives, who polled less than 15 percent, won 143. The manifest inequity of the three-class system was further compounded by indirect and public voting procedures as well as extensive gerrymandering. Since Prussia was the most populous and industrially advanced of the German states (comprising over two-thirds of the empire), it dominated Germany, and its hegemony was further reinforced by the peculiar structure of the Bismarckian constitution. Consequently, political reforms in Germany depended on a reform of the Prussian suffrage system.[14]

Needless to say, an important weapon in the arsenal of those advocating reform of the Prussian suffrage system was the argument that one could not deny an equal vote to soldiers who had fought and given their blood to defend the state. The moral weight of such arguments combined with the vast numbers of veterans and wardisabled provided a force of enormous potential power in the fight for suffrage reform. This gave impetus to those who urged that the Social Democrats should form their own veterans' organizations.

The driving force behind these efforts was Erich Kuttner, a fairly prominent personality in the Social Democratic party and himself a veteran. Kuttner had served at the front, been wounded, and then returned to Berlin in 1916 where he joined the staff of *Vorwärts*. His interest in veterans' affairs was a result of both humanitarian and political considerations. In a long article entitled "The Return

Home," for example, Kuttner discussed the difficulties which would face returning soldiers, especially the disabled. The problem of providing aid to the disabled, he argued, was enormous and could only be dealt with through active intervention of the state. It was the state's duty to insure that provisions be made for employing the disabled, that they be given a fair wage, and be provided with adequate pensions. Following this, Kuttner then turned to the broader question of political needs:[15]

> But the disabled will not only make economic demands, but also *political* demands on the state. Whoever has sacrificed an arm or a leg, been seriously inconvenienced or afflicted with sickness for the rest of his life as a result of defending the whole of the population, will not have the slightest understanding for a situation in which another person has more rights in the state because he pays a somewhat higher tax. . . .

Many, he continued, contended that existing organizations could handle the problems of the disabled, that their economic demands could be looked after by the unions, and that their political demands could be met by the party. In Kuttner's view this was unsatisfactory since it meant that the disabled were simply to stand by while others acted on their behalf. The war-disabled veteran, he concluded, wanted not only to be an "object but also a participant. . . . The fundamental fact that the disabled themselves must represent their cause. . .should be clear to everyone in the party."

Unfortunately for Kuttner and his supporters, however, the problem was not so clear-cut for many within the Social Democratic movement. In particular, the unions opposed the formation of separate veterans' organizations, claiming that they would be "superfluous" and that the unions themselves could best handle the needs of the war-disabled. Twice, in November, 1916, and in March, 1917, the question was raised at meetings of key union officials, and both times postponed. Kuttner in turn argued that the creation of veterans' organizations would not weaken the Social Democratic movement by fragmenting it, as the unions claimed, but would strengthen it by bringing in large numbers of new, previously unorganized elements.[16]

Kuttner's arguments, although initially unheeded, began to gain ground in the spring of 1917. By then the implications of the stepped-up activity of the Kyffhäuser-Bund were becoming more apparent and, in addition, there were indications that the forces of order were preparing to make a direct appeal to the war-disabled in the form of organizations modeled after the yellow (employer sponsored) unions.[17] Fearing that unless they acted soon their own members as well as potential new recruits might be lured into the ranks of their political opponents, Social Democratic leaders gave the go-ahead to Kuttner and his colleagues to found a veterans' organization. On April 29 an announcement in *Vorwärts* urged all those interested in the question to get in touch with Kuttner. On May 11, 1917, a preliminary meeting was held, followed twelve days later by the founding of the Bund der Kriegsbeschädigten und ehemaligen Kriegsteilnehmer (Confederation of War-Disabled and War Veterans). The new organization claimed to be nonpartisan and disavowed any connection with the Social Democratic party or its unions. Nonetheless, its program, which combined specific economic and social interests with general political demands, clearly reflected its origins. For the war-disabled the Confederation demanded a fundamental reorganization of the military pension system, a voice in the determination of public welfare benefits for the disabled, laws compelling employers to hire a certain percentage of war-disabled workers, and the prohibition of the practice of basing wages on pensions. In addition, it demanded in the "name and interest of all veterans" the removal of discriminatory political practices "which put the veteran in an unfair position with regard to other segments of the population," the transformation of the army into "a true people's army" (an old Social Democratic demand), and a foreign policy "which would prevent the outbreak of future wars."[18]

In the following months the new Confederation actively pursued its program. Petitions were presented to the war ministry protesting the calling up of war-disabled veterans for further war service and to the Reichstag demanding an immediate increase in pensions for victims of the war.[19] At the same time a vigorous campaign for political reform was launched. In a front-page article in *Vorwärts*, Kuttner criticized Prussia's unjust suffrage system, arguing that the best compensation the state could give veterans for their services would be reform:[20]

> Suffrage reform and a parliamentary system are not theoretical things without practical worth, as some would like to convince the veterans, for behind them stands the question of who shall bear the burdens of this war. Unless there is suffrage reform and the introduction of a parliamentary system, there will be crushing burdens for the working class and low pensions for the war-disabled, widows, and orphans. Equal suffrage and a parliamentary system, however, mean that the burdens will be

transferred to the shoulders of the rich, who can bear them, and that there will be far-reaching care for veterans and their next of kin. The soldiers who let themselves be persuaded that the questions of suffrage reform and a parliamentary system have nothing to do with them will later do bitter penance for their lack of interest.

Therefore, in the final analysis, the gratitude of the fatherland means nothing other than giving us the full political rights to which we are entitled! To refuse these rights is an injustice, a bitter injustice, which can never again be made good by talk. If full political rights are given now to the people who in the field and at home have accomplished the greatest deeds, then, within this, all possible rewards will be included. For then the people will have the power to transform every promised reward into fact.

Such editorial activity was backed by a number of meetings and demonstrations. At a meeting of the Confederation on January 20, 1918, for example, a resolution demanding equal suffrage in Prussia was passed and sent to the Prussian government.[21] These and similar measures became a constant feature of the Confederation's activity until the end of the war.

In addition to demands for social and political reform, the Confederation of War-Disabled and War Veterans also actively opposed the efforts of the conservatives to rally the German people to a policy of victory at all costs. In the debate over war aims which developed during 1917, the Confederation strongly backed the call for a negotiated "peace of understanding." The Reichstag resolution of July, 1917, calling for a "peace of understanding and the permanent reconciliation of nations," which marked the climax of the resurgence of the forces of movement, was heartily supported by the Confederation. When the forces of order responded by forming the Vaterlandspartei (Fatherland party) in order to rally support for their annexationist war aims policy,[22] the Confederation immediately denounced the new organization and its goals. In November, 1917, a meeting of the Confederation was called to demonstrate that those opposing the Fatherland party's policy of conquest were not shirkers or cowards, but men who had fought and made great sacrifices for their country. In a speech Kuttner rejected the attempts of annexationists to buy off veterans and the war-disabled with promises of booty and instead demanded a reformed social policy and equal rights. At the end of the meeting a resolution was unanimously adopted protesting against the Fatherland party's attempts to use the veterans for their annexationist policies and demanding instead that peace be concluded "as soon as it is possible to do so without injury to the Reich."[23]

During the final year of the war, an intense duel developed between the Confederation and the Fatherland party as each sought to rally the public to its program. Feelings eventually became so intense that in January 1918, there was a physical clash between members of the two organizations. In response to this incident and the continual accusations of the Fatherland party that the Confederation was an organization of cowards and deserters, Kuttner organized a protest in which members of the Confederation sent the ribbons of their Iron Crosses and other decorations to Admiral Tirpitz, the president of the Fatherland party. As a result, Kuttner, who had been elected president of the Confederation, was prohibited by military authorities from engaging in any further action on its behalf.[24]

In spite of this and other attempts of German authorities, both civil and military, to harass the Confederation, it continued to grow. By the end of 1917 it numbered five thousand, and by the time of its first convention, which was held in Weimar on Easter 1918, it claimed twenty-five thousand members.[25] At the Weimar convention a charter was adopted, and the general policy of the Confederation —called, after the convention, the National Confederation (Reichsbund) of War Disabled and War Veterans—was determined. In an effort to attract new members, as well as to obviate any further harassment by the authorities, the National Confederation officially claimed that it was completely neutral in political and religious matters. Proposals to include military reform, a pacifistic foreign policy, and the demand for equal suffrage among the organization's offical goals were consequently dropped, although it continued as before to work for these goals.[26] At the same time the National Confederation reiterated the demand that the state adequately recompense those who had suffered in its defense and proposed a thorough overhaul of the existing welfare system, including the creation of a special national agency for dealing with the problems of the war-disabled.

During the convention a serious debate developed over the question of whether the National Confederation should continue its policy of accepting nondisabled veterans. Some members felt that the interests of the war-disabled could be better represented if membership was limited to them. Since the leaders of the National Confederation wanted to use the organization for political as well as social ends, they adamantly refused to consider any changes that would limit its potential membership. They contended that there were no significant differences between the interests of the disabled and nondisabled veterans since both wanted economic and political justice. Moreover, they argued, by accepting nondisabled veterans the strength of the National Confederation would be increased, and this would allow it to represent the interests of its disabled members even more effectively. The main reason for accepting nondisabled veterans, of course, was to give the National Confederation a broader organizational base which would greatly aid it in its political goals of creating a counterbalance to the traditional veterans' associations and obtaining a reform of the Prussian suffrage system.

Meanwhile, the Kyffhäuser-Bund, supported by civil and military authorities, responded to the challenge of the Social Democrats by stepping up its own efforts to win over returning veterans. In early June, 1917, the executive council met to discuss the situation. In addition to initiating a more intensive recruitment program, the council decided that in the future the traditional veterans' associations should place more emphasis on providing aid for the war-disabled. The Social Democrats had adroitly capitalized on this issue, and the Kyffhäuser-Bund was an active supporter of the annexationist war-council members put it: ". . .Our organization has not kept up with the question of aid to the war-disabled. . . . We must exploit each opportunity to regain lost ground. . . . It is extremely desirable that we prevent ourselves from being pushed still further into the background." The government representatives who were present at the meeting heartily approved of the Kyffhäuser-Bund's new policy, agreeing that it should concentrate more on the material needs of veterans, and pledging their support.[27]

Significantly, the Kyffhäuser-Bund's social policy did not include the demand that the government must directly shoulder the burden of caring for the war-disabled. Instead, it promoted the idea of postwar land settlement for veterans—which tied into the annexationist war aims policy of the right—and the creation of a new source of aid for veterans, the Reichs-Krieger-Dank (National Combatants' Fund). The ostensible objective of the new fund, which was to receive moneys from both the public and the state, was to plug the holes in the existing welfare programs, but its real purpose was to attract new members to the Kyffhäuser-Bund, which was to have exclusive control over the administration of the fund. This, as a member of the executive council noted, would strengthen the position of the traditional veterans' associations in the state "as well as their recruiting potential." Following the June meeting of the executive council, Kyffhäuser-Bund publications were filled with articles proclaiming its concern with the social and economic needs of veterans and extolling the virtues of the Reichs-Krieger-Dank. At the same time local groups were urged to step up their recruitment of new members and to take measures which would promote the organization's new image.

The National Confederation responded with skepticism and scorn to the Kyffhäuser-Bund's attempts to fashion a new image. The decision to accept Social Democrats, it was declared, was simply a "confidence trick." The old veterans' associations would soon return to their previous practice of "political snooping" and would be up to their old tricks as soon as the first Reichstag elections were held after the war.[28] At the same time, the Social Democrats bitterly attacked the Reichs-Krieger-Dank. While they were not against new sources of aid for veterans, such funds must be administered by a completely nonpartisan body, not a "bodyguard for the activities of the conservative and reactionary parties" and an instrument of "political and economic reaction."[29] Ultimately, it was argued, all such programs were inadequate since they degraded the veteran by forcing him to accept charity when it was the state's obligation to compensate him for his sacrifice; administered by the Kyffhäuser-Bund, the Reichs-Krieger-Dank would be not only inadequate but dangerous, since it would become a source of corruption and a "tool of political combat."[30]

During the final eighteen months of the war, the struggle for the allegiance of German veterans intensified as political differences in Germany sharpened and both the National Confederation and the Kyffhäuser-Bund sought to mobilize veterans in support of their respective political programs. While the Social Democratic organization demanded social and political reform and urged a negotiated peace, the Kyffhäuser-Bund argued that domestic reforms had to wait until after the war and demanded a decisive victory. The Kyffhäuser-Bund was an active supporter of the annexationist war aims policy of the Pan-Germans, Fatherland party, and other diehard conservatives. A prominent feature of the propaganda of these groups was the promise that once German victory had been achieved, veterans would be given land for settlement. The land in question of course was to be provided by Germany's conquests in the east. In this regard, it is interesting to note that shortly before the end of the war Westphal and other leaders of the Kyffhäuser-Bund were taken on a conducted tour by the Supreme Command through recently conquered areas in the Baltic and the Ukraine.[31]

These plans, like so many others of the forces of order, were rudely upset by Germany's unexpected and precipitate military collapse. By the summer of 1918 the German army, which had virtually singlehandedly held off the combined armies of France, England, Russia, and Italy, finally began to crumble. On August 8, the Black Day of the German army, the troops broke completely under heavy Allied attack, and the initiative shifted to the Allies. By October, 1918, the German army was defeated, exhausted, and incapable of any further major offensives. As the army began to crack, so did the nerve of the Supreme Command. On September 29 General Ludendorff demanded that the government immediately seek an armistice and, in addition, agreed to constitutional reforms which it was hoped would facilitate negotiations with the Allies by giving the German government a more democratic appearance. The attempts to instigate a revolution from above were soon overtaken by a mass-based revolution from below. In early November Germany was swept by a wave of revolution that culminated in the proclamation of a republic on November 9. Two days later Germany signed an armistice with the Allies. In January, 1919, a newly elected National Assembly convened in the city of Weimar, where in the following summer it ended its deliberations with the promulgation of a new constitution. Germany had at last become a parliamentary democracy. Thus, under the cloud of defeat and revolution, was born the ill-fated Weimar Republic.

The revolution of 1918 and the subsequent emergence of the Weimar Republic completely changed the framework and nature of veterans' politics in Germany. With the founding of the National Confederation in 1917–18, the Left had seized the initiative and broken the previous monopoly of the Right over the veterans' movement. The National Confederation had become a powerful tool in winning support for the political and social demands of the forces of movement in general and the Social Democrats in particular. With the war's end and the introduction of parliamentary democracy, the basic political demands of the democratic Center and Left, veteran and nonveteran alike, were largely satisfied. Consequently, the need to mobilize veterans in support of political reforms disappeared, and the active interest and role of the democratic parties in veterans' affairs declined. During the Weimar Republic veterans of the democratic Left and Center, as veterans, were for the most part politicallly quiescent. After the war, as before, the political tone of the veterans' movement was set by the Right. As a result, the political profile of the major veterans' organizations during the republic was one of violent nationalism coupled with a virulent hatred of the republic and all those who supported it.

For its part, the republic seems to have been sympathetic to the needs of veterans, and German veterans were treated as well as or better than those in other countries.[32] In spite of the republic's good will and generosity, however, many veterans remained alienated from it, for although it might fulfill their immediate material needs, it was incapable of fulfilling their political, social, and psychological desires. Bewildered by defeat and faced with an uncertain civilian existence, many veterans were suspicious of the new republic and blamed it for Germany's and their own misfortunes. As a result of the stringent military provisions of the peace treaty, the republic was forced to demobilize many soldiers, especially young officers, who wanted nothing more than to continue their military careers. Defeat and revolution, with their attendant economic dislocation, meant limited opportunities for employment; this was especially true for young middle-class veterans who had no skills and who could not rely on the help of trade unions after the war as could their working-class counterparts. Social resentment combined with patriotic outrage turned many middle-class veterans against the republic and its new leaders. Humiliated by the Treaty of Versailles, and unwilling or unable to acknowledge the fact that Germany had lost the war, or that their sacrifice had been in vain, many veterans became prey to the infamous *Dolchstosslegende,* or stab-in-the-back legend, which attributed Germany's defeat to the betrayal of an undefeated army by a cowardly home front led by the Social Democrats.[33]

Rather than creating a consensus in German society, as many had hoped, the war and its aftermath only exacerbated old conflicts and opened new wounds. Not only was the earlier cleavage between the Left and the Right deepened and intensified, but new divisions arose within the two opposing camps as well. The lack of consensus and the political fragmentation of German society as a whole after the war were in turn reflected in the postwar German veterans' movement. Instead of a movement toward consolidation among veterans' organizations, such as that which took place, for example, in England, there was a proliferation of new groups.

The National Confederation, which had been founded by the Social Democrats and developed into a mass organization during the final years of the war, continued to exist and to grow after the war. As a result of the changes introduced by the revolution, however, its major political demands had been fulfilled, and consequently the need to mobilize veterans over political issues largely disappeared. Thus, while the National Confederation continued to accept nondisabled veterans—in order to keep them out of the grasp of the Kyffhäuser-Bund—the percentage of nondisabled veterans among its members remained low; after the war it devoted its attention almost exclusively to representing the interests of the war-disabled and next of kin of those killed during the war.[34] Whereas before the revolution its efforts in this area had encountered opposition from the government, afterwards, "with relatively few exceptions, the doors were suddenly, willingly opened."[35] In December, 1918, the National Confederation organized a demonstration in Berlin which led to a raise in pensions. In the following month the elections to the National Assembly produced a democratic majority dominated by Social Democrats, which assured it of a sympathetic hearing for its demands on behalf of the victims of war. During the next two years Germany's outdated system of aid for the war-disabled and their families was thoroughly overhauled and extended. Postwar care of the victims of war was made the responsibility of the national government, and the claim to benefits was made a legal right. The pension system was reformed, and provisions for medical care and vocational rehabilitation were systematically developed and expanded. In addition, a national committee to advise the government on questions dealing with the war-disabled and the next of kin of those killed in the war was created, which included representatives from the various organizations concerned.

While the National Confederation, with over half a million members by 1920, was by far the largest organization representing the interests of the war-disabled, it was not the only one. Like virtually every sphere of activity during the Weimar Republic, that of social welfare for war victims was divided along political and other lines. In addition to the National Confederation there were four other major organizations: the Einheitsverband der Kriegsbeschädigten und Kriegshinterbliebenen Deutschlands (United Association of German War-Disabled and Next of Kin); the Bund Deutscher Kriegsbeschädigten (League of German War-Disabled); the Zentralverband Deutscher Kriegsbeschädigten und Kriegshinterbliebenen (Central Association of German War-Disabled and Next of Kin); and, finally, the Internationaler Bund (International League). Although the National Confederation's relations with the first two were comparatively cordial, the only basic difference being over the question of accepting nondisabled veterans, its relations with the other two were far from harmonious.

The International League was a Communist organization which had broken off from the National Confederation in early 1919.[36] At the time of the revolution the National Confederation's leaders had quickly rallied to support the new government, and made it clear that they opposed any radicalization. A number of its members, especially in Berlin, were more radically inclined, however. In early 1919 these elements tried to gain control of the organization and put it on a more radical course. Failing this, the dissidents subsequently left the National Confederation and in February founded their own group, the International League. The International League followed the Communist line, arguing that the problems of disabled veterans could be settled only in the context of the general class war. In the following years relations between the International League and the National Confederation were marked by the peculiar animosity and suspicion which always seem to exist between competing Social Democratic and Communist organizations.

The National Confederation's relations with the Zentralverband, or Central Association, were, if anything, worse than those with the International League. The Central Association had been founded in late June, 1918, and in organization and purpose seemed to be little different from the National Confederation. The reason for this similarity was simple; it had been created specifically for the purpose of competing with the National Confederation.[37] The Central Association originated under the auspices of the Christian and liberal, nonsocialist Hirsch-Duncker unions, and was backed by prominent figures in the middle-class parties. Whereas the founding of the International League introduced the Communist–Social Democratic split into the ranks of the war-disabled, the founding of the Central Association introduced the divisions that existed in the German labor-union movement. Thus, in spite of their functional similarities and common goals, the socially oriented veterans' organizations, those concerned with the needs of the war-disabled and the families of those maimed or killed in the war, remained divided along social and political lines.[38]

In addition to new organizations devoted to the needs of the disabled, the First World War also produced another type of special-interest veterans' organization in Germany—the officers' associations. Whereas the former dealt with the casualties of the war, the latter in a sense represented the interests of the casualties of Germany's defeat and the revolution which followed. Before 1918 there were no officers' organizations, simply because there was no need for them. The German officer corps was recruited almost exclusively from the nobility and the upper levels of society. The professional officer enjoyed a position of enormous prestige in prewar German society and, upon retirement, officers were provided with pensions. In addition, since many were already independently wealthy or were at least guaranteed remunerative positions after their retirement because of their social connections, most former officers enjoyed secure and comfortable lives after their days of service were over. Assured of economic security and social prestige, they felt no need to unite organizationally to defend their interests during the empire. Not only was such activity unnecessary, it would have been considered demeaning in the view of the aristocratic ex-officers, most of whom refused to join the veterans' associations, for example, feeling that they were too plebeian.[39]

Germany's defeat and the revolution transformed the position of officers in German society and ended their reluctance to band together in defense of their common interests. The revolution was accompanied by a widespread wave of anger and revulsion against the old system and, as the most visible representatives of the old society and as symbols of both prewar oppression and wartime hardship and suffering, the officers were frequently subjected to harassment and abuse. Furthermore, the Treaty of Versailles limited Germany's postwar army, the Reichswehr, to 100,000 men of which only 4,000 were to be officers. As a consequence, a number of older officers were retired and scores of younger ones dismissed, so that more experienced officers could be retained. Faced with unemployment and a republic that appeared to be dominated by Social Democrats—their bitterest enemies before the war—former officers saw their future as precarious indeed. Consequently, they quickly founded organizations to defend their interests under the new circumstances. Although united in their suspicion, resentment, and hatred of the republic, as well as in their desire to secure their financial and social needs, the ex-officers were unable to unite in a single organization. Like those for disabled veterans, the postwar officers' associations were divided along social, political, and professional lines.

The largest of the officers' associations was the Deutscher Of-

fiziersbund (German Officers' League). The DOB was formed in
November 1918, literally on the heels of the revolution.[40] By 1922 it
numbered about 100,000 and membership remained around this figure throughout the republic. The DOB's purpose, in its own words,
was to serve as an "alliance of the officer class for the preservation
of its threatened existence and its violated rights."[41] In practice the
DOB concentrated primarily on securing economic and social benefits
for its members, which included active as well as retired officers. Although strongly conservative, nationalistic, and hostile to the republic, the DOB tried to avoid becoming openly involved in politics so as
not to endanger its effectiveness as an economic interest group or to
violate military regulations which prohibited active members of the
military from belonging to political associations. As a result of its
prudence, it became the foremost representative of the economic interests of the officer class and played an influential role in drafting
legislation relating to pensions and benefits for retired as well as
war-disabled officers and their families. Officially nonpartisan, the
DOB, once it had become established and the immediate threat of revolution was past, became less reserved in political matters. During
the middle and later years of the republic it began to cooperate more
openly with rightist radical organizations and purged what few republicans there were in its ranks.

Similar to the Deutscher Offiziersbund, but more limited in scope,
was the Marine-Offiziersverband (Naval Officers' Association),
which had about five thousand members. Like the DOB, the MOV, although hostile to the republic, maintained a nonpolitical stance, included active as well as former officers, and concentrated primarily
on obtaining economic and social benefits for its members.

To the right of these two organizations was the Nationalverband
Deutscher Offiziere (National Assocation of German Officers). Less
interested in economic and social questions than the others, it openly
devoted itself to antirepublican political activity. The NDO, which had
about ten thousand members, was formed in December, 1918, by a
group of diehard officers who rejected what they felt to be the opportunistic attitude of the DOB, i.e., its acceptance of the new conditions
in Germany and its emphasis on economic matters. According to the
NDO, the main task was not to secure economic advantages but to
carry out "the political fight against the conditions created by the revolution." After that, it was argued, "the problem of the
individual's [material] existence would take care of itself."[42] True to
its word, the Nationalverband Deutscher Offiziere waged an active

and open fight against the republic, rejecting any compromise with the new state and demanding the restoration of the Hohenzollern monarchy, as well as a return—with certain radical-conservative modifications—to the constitutional framework of the Bismarckian empire.[43]

The last of the major officers' associations was the Reichsoffiziersbund (National Officers' League), which numbered about ten thousand. The ROB was originally founded in October, 1919, as the Bund der Feldwebelleutnants (League of Sergeant-Major-Lieutenants) but changed its name at its first convention in October, 1920. While ungainly, the original name reflected the particular character of the ROB more clearly than the later one. The ROB's members were not former professional officers, but officers who had risen through the ranks or had otherwise been commissioned during the war.

The enormous drain upon manpower, especially among lower-ranking officers, had forced the German army to commission a number of enlisted men as officers during the war. One source of officer replacement was the one-year volunteers (Einjährige-Freiwilliger), who after a brief period of service were quickly trained in officer-candidate schools and then commissioned. In addition to these ninety-day wonders a number of noncommissioned officers and other enlisted men were promoted to fill the demand for lower-level officers. In order to maintain intact the elite social character of the officer corps, however, these men were rarely commissioned as regular officers. Instead, they were appointed to the temporary rank of *Feldwebelleutnant* (sergeant-major-lieutenant). While they served as officers during the war, it was always made clear that they were considered neither militarily nor socially the equals of the regular officers, and that once the emergency was over they were likely to be demoted.[44]

Discrimination against these officers continued after the war and naturally produced resentment.[45] The DOB's membership, for example, was limited to professional career officers. As a consequence, the ROB was founded. In addition to pressing for equality of treatment in officers' economic benefits, the ROB also demanded that former sergeant-major-lieutenants be recognized as lieutenants of the reserve *(Leutnant der Landwehr* a.D.). Once this demand was fulfilled, the social resentment of its members seems to have cooled somewhat. The republic's generosity in this matter, however, did not earn the ROB's gratitude or support, and it remained firmly antirepublican. The ROB officially maintained a position of political neutrality, since a large number of its members were state officials, who, like active military personnel, were prohibited from belonging to political organizations. In practice, however, it was far from neutral. Although it tried to avoid becoming openly involved in political questions, the ROB was heavily influenced by the NDO, to which a number of its members also belonged.

On the whole, the Weimar Republic was remarkably generous in providing for the economic needs of former officers—indeed, more so than the empire had been.[46] The same was true for veterans in general. The republic did the best it could and for the most part treated its veterans as well as or better than most governments. Yet in spite of this, as we have seen, many veterans remained alienated. Whether or not the majority of German veterans opposed the republic is difficult to say. One thing is certain, however: the overwhelming majority of *organized* veterans vehemently opposed it. In contrast to other countries (e.g., England), most German veterans' organizations were not primarily concerned with economic issues such as pensions, etc. With the exception of the organizations for the war-disabled (and even here political factors played a role), the mass-based veterans' organizations in Germany after World War I were politically, rather than economically, motivated. Ironically, the very concern and generosity of the republic in the matter of veterans' benefits may have contributed to this process of politicization by lessening the need for having to operate as economic-interest groups.[47] In any case, German veterans' organizations as a whole were among the most vociferous of the republic's many right-wing detractors. As with the officers' associations, however, there were differences in both the nature and the style of their opposition.

The Kyffhäuser-Bund survived the revolution and remained the largest single veterans' organization throughout the Weimar Republic. Like the army, which had for years exalted the emperor and proclaimed loyalty to him as the highest virtue, it quickly abandoned him in his moment of need. Convinced of the futility of a counter-revolution and terrified by the threat of a truly radical revolution, the Kyffhäuser-Bund accommodated itself to the new government, abandoning the monarchy in the hopes of saving its own organization. In response to a member's suggestion that the Bund should have proclaimed its support of the emperor and actively worked on his behalf, Westphal replied that although such action had been debated among the Bund's leaders, they had decided against it, and he continued:[48]

In view of the course of events during the past few days, we
feel that this decision was the correct one. . . . It [a more ag-
gressive policy] would only have caused confusion and harm,
and above all it would have endangered the future of our organization in a most serious manner.

Subsequent proclamations of the Kyffhäuser-Bund urged its members
to avoid any rash actions and to cooperate with the new government
in maintaining law and order.[49]

Germany's unexpected defeat, the collapse of the empire, and the
subsequent revolution nonetheless had had a profound and demoraliz-
ing effect on the Kyffhäuser-Bund and its leaders. In a letter of February, 1919, Westphal revealed his despair over the sudden change
of events:[50]

What we have had to experience is fearful and unbearable. . . .
For me the thought of the disgrace that has overcome us is so
terrible that I am sick of life. Only duty keeps me going. Be-
sides this, we have to engage in a difficult battle; we are experiencing a crisis such as I never could have believed possible. Daily there are reports of groups which have dissolved
themselves or left [our organization]. . . . It will take the most
strenuous effort to survive this crisis. . . .

The revolution has destroyed us and poisoned our
people. . . . What could [we] do when the proud German army
broke down and collapsed, when our own sailors betrayed the
fleet? What were the old men here, the only ones still left in
the veterans' associations at home, to do? It would have meant
the complete destruction of our cause if we had made the in-
sane attempt to stand up against the revolution. No, that would
have been impossible. Yet we will work on, rebuilding, and
our time will come again.

Although it survived the tumultous events of 1918–19, the Bund
was shaken and its recovery was slow. The previous obsession with
promoting the monarchy and combating social democracy had given
most people, including its own members, the feeling that this was the
Kyffhäuser-Bund's only purpose, and its belated entry into the field
of social welfare during the war had done little to dispel this impression. Faced with the prospect of an organizational collapse and
dwindling membership, the Bund's leaders launched a widespread recruitment program in order to win over new members from among

the returning veterans. Above all, efforts were made to promote the Bund's "new spirit" by emphasizing its new-found role as an organization devoted to serving the social and economic interests of veterans. In addition, local groups were urged to get rid of older, out-of-date leaders and replace them with younger, more dynamic men who would have a greater appeal to young veterans. As a final means of gaining new members, the Kyffhäuser-Bund opened its ranks to civilians who had served under military supervision during the war.[51] While purportedly this was done in order to make its membership correspond to "the circumstances of the Great War," a more likely explanation was the awareness that the changes would attract many lower-middle-class Germans who had served in such positions.

In spite of these efforts to modernize itself and to attract the younger veterans of the World War, membership declined and there were continued complaints over the defection of members and the dissolution of local branches. Nonetheless, the Kyffhäuser-Bund survived and eventually regained its prewar strength of between 2.5 and 3 million members.[52] In 1921 the Bund was reorganized and given a more centralized leadership, and in 1922 it changed its name to the Deutscher Reichskriegerbund "Kyffhäuser" (German National Combatants' League, *"Kyffhauser"*) or DRKB. Once consolidated, the Kyffhäuser-Bund returned to its prewar practice of excluding Social Democrats.[53] Similarly, its earlier tactical accommodation to the republic was soon replaced by open hostility to it, although the Bund generally tried to avoid direct political activity and continued to claim, as it had before the war, that it was politically neutral.

Although the Kyffhäuser-Bund eventually regained its prewar membership and was by far the largest single veterans' group in the Weimar Republic, it never regained the prestige and influence which it had enjoyed during the empire, and it was far from the most dynamic of the postwar veterans' organizations. The loss of state support and its former monopolistic position was without doubt an important factor in this, but an even more crucial cause for its relative decline was the failure to modernize itself and to appeal to the new generation of veterans.[54] In general, its activities consisted of building monuments and celebrating the anniversaries of great events in Germany's past. Wrapped in dreams of the golden days of the empire, the Kyffhäuser-Bund was unable to adapt itself to the present. Like the other prewar nationalist organizations, it was considered too old-fashioned, too "bourgeois," and too tame by the younger, more activist veterans. Instead, they were attracted to the more modern and radical organizations which emerged after the war, such as the Verband Nationalgesinnter Soldaten or the Stahlhelm.

The career of the Verband Nationalgesinnter Soldaten (Association of Nationalistic Soldiers) was short and stormy.[55] Originally founded as a veterans' organization in September, 1919, the Association soon became a radical political organization more dedicated to the overthrow of the republic than to the representation of veterans' interests. While its membership consisted primarily of ex-soldiers, the Association also accepted "nationalistic Germans," including women, who had not served in the war. The Association was closely linked to the ultraradical *völkisch* wing of the German National People's party, and its heavy involvement in politics eventually proved fatal. When in 1922 the *völkisch* wing of the German National People's party, which included a number of the Association's leaders, broke away to form its own party, the German-*völkisch* Freedom party, the ranks of the Association of Nationalistic Soldiers were split. The ultraradical *völkisch* faction retained control of the organization and began to steer it on an activist, putschist course. This alarmed the more moderate members of the Association, and in June, 1922, they seceded and formed a new organization, the Nationalverband Deutscher Soldaten (National Association of German Soldiers). As a result of its continued and virulent antirepublican activity, the original association was banned in late June, 1922, following the assassination of Walther Rathenau, the republican foreign minister. Shortly thereafter the National Association was also banned because of its antirepublican activity and the suspicion that it was merely a cover for the original association. Although both organizations continued to exist in some states and were later revived in others, neither played a significant role in the veterans' movement after 1922.

The largest and best-known of the postwar German veterans' organizations was undoubtedly the Stahlhelm, or Steel Helmet. By far the most dynamic and influential of Germany's postwar veterans' organizations, the Stahlhelm was founded by Franz Seldte, a former captain who had fought on the western front and had lost his left arm in the Battle of the Somme.[56] On November 13, just four days after the republic had been proclaimed, Seldte called some friends together in the laboratory of his mineral-water factory in Magdeburg in order to discuss his plans for founding a new organization for veterans who had served during the World War. His proposal found ready acceptance, and on December 25 another meeting was held, at which time the new organization, Der Stahlhelm, Bund der Frontsoldaten (The Steel Helmet, League of Front Soldiers), was officially founded. As indicated by its subtitle, membership in the Stahlheim was limited to soldiers who had fought at the front. According to minutes of the meeting, the new organization had three major goals: to promote comradeship among former front soldiers; to support the mutual interests of its members; to work for the maintenance of law and order or, as Seldte bluntly put it, to stop "this *Schweinerei* of revolution" from going any further. Although opposed to the revolution, the Stahlhelm was by no means a reactionary organization. Nor was it, at least initially, part of the racist, radical Right. True to its promise to promote the "true comradeship which had been practiced in the field" and to support front soldiers "regardless of differences of class or party," the Stahlhelm at first accepted both Jews and Social Democrats insofar as they had fulfilled the requirement of six months service at the front.

During the course of 1919 the Stahlhelm's role as a defender of law and order increasingly gained the upper hand, however, and this, combined with general political developments including the signing of the Treaty of Versailles, drove it further and further to the right. The shift in emphasis from the representation of veterans' interests to general right-wing political activity was reflected in a letter written by Seldte in 1920 in which he characterized the three main goals of the Stahlhelm as now being the "encouragement of the old comradeship, support of law and order, and reconstruction [*Aufbau*]." By 1920 "reconstruction" had become a general code word on the right for opposition to the republic, and Seldte himself noted that "the expression law and order" should be expanded "to include the protection of the entire economic and social system, as well as property, etc."[57] Like many other rightist organizations in the Weimar Republic, the political profile of the Stahlhelm was in large part formed by its activity as a paramilitary "self-defense" organization.

When Germany signed the armistice on November 11, 1918, it signified not only the end of the war but the end of the Imperial German Army as well. According to the terms of the armistice, Germany's military forces in the west were required to withdraw to positions east of the Rhine River within a month. Because of the number of troops and the distances involved, this withdrawal was a difficult undertaking. Nevertheless, discipline was maintained and it was successfully effected. Once across the Rhine, however, the obedience of the war-weary soldiers to their military superiors gave way to homesickness and the desire to be with their families in time for Christmas. Military discipline collapsed and the German army melted away. Consequently the plans of the Supreme Command to regain military control of Berlin with returning detachments of front soldiers in early December misfired, and when on Christmas Eve the few remaining detachments of regular soldiers were sent to dislodge insurgent leftist forces which had taken over the royal palace in Berlin, the troops threw down their weapons and either joined the rebels or fled. This fiasco marked the end of the Imperial German Army. It could no longer function as an effective power factor; realizing this, the Supreme Command ordered its demobilization.

Although the army had disappeared, the threat to the new republican government from its domestic enemies as well as Germany's newly independent neighbor in the east, Poland, remained. Consequently, the government needed to raise a military force that could maintain order and defend the eastern borders. Unfortunately, the new Socialist leaders of the republic proved incapable of creating one that was loyal to the new republic. Although there were instances of reliable and effective democratic units being formed, these remained few and far between. Lacking popular support or firm governmental direction, the various attempts to create a democratic militia remained abortive. Instead, the suppression of revolutionary outbreaks and the restoration of order were carried out by volunteer forces formed and led by former officers of the Imperial Army and recruited from elements in German society whose loyalty to the republic was dubious at best.

There were three basic types of volunteer forces: Free Corps (Freikorps), which functioned as regular military units and bore the brunt of fighting; Auxiliary Volunteer Units (Zeitfreiwilligen-verbände), which were only called up in emergencies and were more geographically limited than the Free Corps; and Civil Guards (Einwohnerwehren), which served primarily as auxiliary police units. The most famous—or infamous—were the Free Corps. Relatively independent and highly individualistic in character, these units were generally led by young ex-officers and recruited from former soldiers.[58] The Free Corps—as well as the other volunteer units—also attracted a number of civilian recruits, especially students, who joined out of patriotic enthusiasm, anticommunist zeal, or simply the hope of finding the military adventure which had been denied them during the war because of their age.

By the summer of 1919 the volunteer forces had essentially restored order in Germany, checked the Poles in the east, and made spectacular gains against the Bolshevik forces in the Baltic. All in all, nearly 1.5 million men were brought under arms in this manner, of whom approximately one-third belonged to the Free Corps.[59] Many of these volunteers, veterans and nonveterans alike, especially those in the Free Corps, hoped to continue their military careers in the new army—the Reichswehr—which was being formed by the republic. These hopes were dashed by the Treaty of Versailles.

Until the summer of 1919, Germans, including the members of the volunteer forces, had lived in what Ernst Troeltsch later called the "dreamland of the armistice period."[60] This "dreamland" came to an abrupt end with the signing of the Treaty of Versailles in June 1919, which, among other harsh and humiliating provisions, limited Germany's army to a long-term professional force of no more than 100,000 men, and the promulgation of the Weimar Constitution shortly thereafter. With these two events, the twin realities of defeat and revolution could no longer be ignored. As resentment and disillusionment grew, so did the forces of counterrevolution.

One of the most dangerous sources of discontent was the volunteer forces. For these men, the Treaty of Versailles shattered the "dreamland of the armistice period" in a very real and concrete manner. Combining genuine patriotic outrage with their own material self-interest, they attacked the republic for being weak in the face of Germany's enemies and ungrateful to those who had helped to save it. Feeling that they had been betrayed by the republic, they accused it of stabbing them (and Germany) in the back just as it and its leaders had presumably stabbed the old Imperial Army in the back in 1918. This resentment was adroitly exploited by counterrevolutionary political elements and in March, 1920, just before the volunteer forces were to be demobilized, the two came together in the ill-conceived and uncoordinated Kapp Putsch.[61] The attempt of the military and political outcasts of the republic forcibly to undo the changes wrought by the revolution failed miserably. Although hardly a clear-cut victor, the republic survived. The volunteer forces did not. After being used to suppress leftist uprisings triggered by the putsch, they were dissolved.

The volunteer units had provided a temporary shelter for many veterans while at the same time providing numerous young Germans who had not served in the war with a taste of military life and a "front experience" of their own. With the dissolution of the volunteer forces, these men, many of whom were unable, as Robert Waite put it, to "demobilize psychologically," were forced to return to a civilian society which they disliked and distrusted. Unable to find a permanent home in the truncated German army or the volunteer units, these militarily disenfranchised elements created substitutes in the form of paramilitary organizations. With the exception of the Stahlhelm, these were, strictly speaking, not veterans' organizations, since they included nonveterans as well. Nonetheless, they were recruited primarily from veterans, and their leaders were almost exclusively young former officers.

After the Kapp Putsch a young Free Corps officer about to leave active service wrote a letter to his commander outlining what he felt had to be done by the war generation. It contained the following words:[62]

The soldier has the courage to act, but he lacks political instinct. The politician has the instinct, but he lacks the courage and willingness to put his life on the line. We must enter politics and try to create a generation of leaders which unites the courage to act, the character, the firmness, the energy, and the composure of the soldier with the spirit, flair, cleverness, and snakelike cunning of the politician. This is the task of the generation of the trenches.

This desire to combine military virtues with political activity was embodied in the so-called military association (Wehrverbände), which combined open propagandistic activity with extensive programs of clandestine military training.[63] Unlike the numerous underground organizations which were founded after the dissolution of the volunteer forces, the military associations operated openly as patriotic associations dedicated to the national cause in general and, in particular, to the preservation and propagation of the German military tradition. Such open, legal activity was then supplemented with secret, illegal military training. Uniformed and organized along military lines, the military associations served as a surrogate for the army which had been denied by the Treaty of Versailles, while at the same time providing a vehicle for extraparliamentary, antirepublican political activity.

It was as a military association that the Stahlhelm first began to achieve prominence. The Stahlhelm was extremely active in the Civil Guard organizations which were formed in central Germany, and in its home city of Magdeburg contributed four companies to the local Auxiliary Volunteer Unit.[64] When the volunteer formations were dissolved in the spring of 1920, Stahlhelm leaders played a key role in the attempts to form a nationwide underground paramilitary organization, the Orgesch,[65] whose backbone in northern Germany was to be formed by Stahlhelm contingents. By the end of 1921, however, the Orgesch had largely ceased to exist, as a result of governmental action against secret military organizations—especially in Prussia. Instead of a setback, the government's action proved to be a boon for the Stahlhelm. Since it was officially a veterans' organization, the Stahlhelm was not directly affected by the prohibition of secret military organizations and subsequently absorbed many of the groups that were dissolved.[66] Although the progressive demobilization of the army had provided the Stahlhelm with a constant flow of new members, it was the dissolution of the volunteer formations, followed by the ban on secret military organizations, that provided its greatest surge in membership. In March, 1920, there were only thirty local Stahlhelm groups. By June, 1921, the number had risen to sixty-three and by the end of the year to three hundred. In June 1922 the Stahlhelm claimed five hundred local organizations and eventually reached a strength of around a half million members.[67] The rapid growth of the Stahlhelm was accompanied by an increasing radicalization caused by political events in general and, more specifically, the large influx of radicalized Free Corps elements. The organization's newspaper, *Der Stahlhelm,* which began to appear in September, 1919, reflected this change, as did the statements of a number of its leaders. By 1921–22 the Stahlhelm was no longer content merely to represent the needs of veterans or even to uphold law and order, but had begun to criticize the government with increasing bitterness and to demand that veterans be given a leading role in the state, a theme that was to be developed further in the coming years.

The Stahlhelm, at least initially, was concentrated primarily in central and northeastern Germany. In western Germany the dominant military association was the Jungdeutscher Orden (Young German Order), commonly called the Jungdo. Like the Stahlhelm, it was a product of the war and the revolution, as well as a continuation of certain prewar attitudes. Whereas the Stahlhelm contained elements of prewar veterans' organizations and postwar paramilitary formations, however, the Jungdo combined characteristics of the prewar youth movement with the postwar Free Corps tradition.

The Jungdeutscher Orden grew out of a volunteer unit that had been formed in Kassel on January 10, 1919, by a young Prussian officer, Artur Mahraun.[68] During the next year the unit, which comprised one to two hundred men, was primarily occupied in maintaining order in and around Kassel; later it also helped to put down the leftist uprisings in Thuringia which followed the Kapp Putsch. It was at this time that Mahraun founded the Jungdeutscher Orden. On March 17 he called together the leaders of his unit and presented a program for transforming it into a *bündisch* organization modeled along the lines of a medieval military order. According to Mahraun, the new organization was to be devoted to achieving a synthesis of the ideals of Potsdam and Weimar, i.e., the Prussian principle of leadership and obedience combined with the democratic-*bündisch* concepts that had characterized the prewar German youth movement. Mahraun's plans were enthusiastically accepted by his colleagues, and the Jungdeutscher Orden was born.

Although later developments were to prove the sincerity of Mahraun's more idealistic objectives, there were other, less lofty reasons for the transformation: on March 12 the Allies had renewed their demands for the dissolution of all German volunteer forces, and it was clear that if Mahraun was to save his unit a new organizational form was needed. Other volunteer units, such as the Free Corps Oberland and the Ehrhardt Brigade, were to employ similar tactics, but with less success than the Jungdo.[69]

In spite of some difficulties with the authorities because of its military origins and paramilitary character, the Jungdeutscher Orden, like the Stahlhelm, was largely unaffected by the government's crackdown on secret military activity. Capitalizing on its dual nature as a *bündisch* youth organization and a paramilitary force dedicated to "law and order," the Jungdo in the early 1920s rapidly expanded beyond its original narrow base of veterans, officers, and students and became a mass organization. By the end of 1920 it had grown from about ten local organizations centered in the state of Hesse to about fifty, located not only in Hesse but in Thuringia, Westphalia, and Hanover as well. By the time of the order's third anniversary celebration in January, 1923, it had nearly two hundred local groups and an estimated membership of about 200,000.[70] During the early years of the republic, the Jungdo was as large as, probably even larger than, the Stahlhelm, and though surpassed by the latter after 1924 it remained the second largest rightist paramilitary formation until the final years of the republic.

During the repbulic's early years, however, the cradle of paramilitary activity in Germany was not in the north or the west, but in the south, above all in Bavaria. During 1919 the Bavarian

Civil Guard under the leadership of Georg Escherich and Rudolf Kanzler had developed into a cohesive paramilitary force which numbered over 250,000 men.[71] The Bavarian Civil Guard not only became a state within a state but one hostile to the new state created by the revolution. At the time of the Kapp Putsch the conservative forces in Bavaria, aided and abetted by the Civil Guard, successfully ousted the Social Democratic state government that had been established in 1919 and replaced it with a conservative government headed by Gustav von Kahr. When, after the failure of the Kapp Putsch in Berlin, the Reich government moved to dissolve the volunteer forces, Kahr refused to comply. The Bavarian government successfully resisted the attempts of the federal government to dissolve the Bavarian Civil Guard for over a year, but finally had to give way. In June, 1921, the Bavarian Civil Guard, which was also the nucleus of the Orgesch, announced its dissolution. Instead of disbanding, however, it simply went underground and reemerged in early 1922 as a military association, the Bund Bayern und Reich (Bavaria and Reich League), under the leadership of Otto Pittinger.

Although the Bund Bayern und Reich was by far the largest of the paramilitary organizations in Bavaria, it was only one of many. The benevolent and protective attitude of the Bavarian government toward paramilitary organizations encouraged their growth in the south German state. While elsewhere in Germany the military associations were a nuisance which exacerbated political tensions and presented a vague threat to the state, they did not overtly influence political decisions. In Bavaria, however, paramilitary formations exercised a strong influence on the government and consequently were both a model and a source of envy for their counterparts in the north.

Supported by the Reichswehr, which felt the paramilitary organizations were necessary to supplement Germany's reduced armed forces, as well as by large segments of the middle class which saw them as an effective counterweight to the better-organized working class, the military associations flourished during the early years of the republic. Eschewing traditional political activity, they sought to achieve their political aims by means of military action. The ultimate goal was a war of liberation against France in the manner of the 1813 revival against Napoleon. Such a war against Germany's "external" enemies, however, was considered to be thwarted by the "internal" enemy, a term initially used to describe the communists but which soon came to mean virtually all those who supported the republic, above all the Social Democrats. The Military Associations' hopes of achieving their objective of freeing Germany from the bondage of both its "internal" and "external" enemies rested on two possible scenarios: (1) a leftist revolt—provoked if necessary—followed by suppression, the establishment of a military dictatorship, and a war of liberation against France and Poland; or (2) a foreign attack which would trigger a German national revival and war of liberation during the course of which the Left would be suppressed and a rightist dictatorship established. During the years 1921–23 both tactics were tried, but without success.

In spite of the troubled circumstances of the republic during its first five years and what appeared to be numerous opportunities to realize their objectives, the rightist paramilitary organizations were unable to transform their military strength into an effective political force. The hopes for a leftist uprising which would necessitate the government's calling on them for aid and thereby enable them to dictate political demands never materialized. When the Communists did rise up in a poorly planned and ill-timed attempt at revolution in March, 1921, the government was able to suppress them quickly without the help of outside forces. Similarly, attempts to provoke leftist uprisings through the assassination of prominent government officials also failed. The assassination of Matthias Erzburger in August, 1921, and of Walther Rathenau in June of the following year increased political tensions and aroused the wrath of the Left, but instead of providing opportunities for greater activity on the part of the rightist military associations, they only resulted in new and tougher laws against militant antirepublican activity.[72]

In 1923 the French occupation of the Ruhr rekindled the military association's hopes for a national war of liberation. These hopes were given further sustenance by increased support from Reichswehr leaders who felt the paramilitary organizations would be necessary to supplement the regular army in case the government's policy of passive resistance should escalate into open war. Riding the twin waves of inflamed nationalism and middle class fear engendered by the increased activity of the Left, the military associations made plans to deal simultaneously with Germany's "internal" and "external" enemies. Yet, once again the military associations failed to realize their ambitions. Lack of coordination, indecisiveness, political differences among themselves and, ultimately, the opposition of the Reichswehr all combined to frustrate their plans, and their hopes came to an ignominious end with Hitler's abortive Beer Hall Putsch in November, 1923.[73]

The shots of the Reichswehr and Bavarian State Police in Munich on the morning of November 9 marked more than an end to a stormy chapter in the history of the republic. They also signaled the end of the hopes for a forcible overthrow of the republic. In spite of its weakness, the young republic had withstood the assaults of its adversaries. Morevoer, the return of at least relative prosperity and stability after 1924 made it appear stronger than ever.

Discredited and weakened by the events of 1923, paramilitary organizations in Germany were forced to retrench and adapt themselves to the "threat" of stability. During the middle years of the republic the military associations underwent a gradual but distinct transformation. Realizing that a direct seizure of power was impossible, the leaders of the military associations began to reverse their priorities. Whereas previously they had put military activity above all and perceived political problems in a subsidiary and derivative manner, they now reasoned that before military action could again become meaningful the existing "system" had to be changed, and since force had proven unsuccessful the change would have to be made by other means. In short, putschism had to be replaced by politics. During the middle years of the republic, the military associations were transformed into what were called political combat leagues (politische Kampfbünde), which consciously developed political programs and sought to gain political influence. At the same time, however, military forms of organization, dress, and action were maintained. It was this mixture of military and political activity that gave the political combat leagues their special character in the following years.

The changeover to political activity was accompanied by a number of organizational changes. Once the hopes for an immediate overthrow of the republic had to be abandoned in favor of long-term political activity, the problem of providing reserves for the thinning ranks of war veterans became of pressing importance. In 1924 the Stahlhelm, which previously had limited its membership to veterans who had served six months at the front, created a special section (Landsturm der Stahlhelm) which accepted men who supported the Stahlhelm's goals but because of "age or other honorable reasons" had not served six months at the front.[74] In later years increasing numbers of nonveterans were accepted, and the distinction between veterans and nonveterans was even further reduced. Such measures not only reflected the Stahlhelm's transformation into a political combat league but also pointed to a basic difference between it and veterans' organizations in other, more settled countries; while veterans in England, for example, quickly abandoned what has been called "external aims" in favor of bread-and-butter issues such as pensions,[75] the Stahlhelm virtually neglected such activity and ultimately even sacrificed its character as a veterans' organization in order to achieve its "external aims," i.e., the overthrow of the Weimar Republic.

The primary means of creating reserves for the combat leagues was the formation of youth organizations. Here again the Stahlhelm led the way. Aware of the self-limiting nature of its original membership restrictions (in addition to six months front duty, members had to be twenty-one years old), it had considered the problem of youth organizations as early as 1922; desiring to retain its original character, however, it had refrained from founding its own youth groups, preferring instead to work through other organizations. In 1923, for example, the Stahlhelm developed close ties with the Wehrwolf, a military association founded in Halle during the French occupation of the Ruhr, which accepted men as young as seventeen. The Stahlhelm's attempts to gain control of the newer organization miscarried, however; by late 1923 the Wehrwolf, resenting the Stahlhelm's heavy-handed efforts at tutelage, moved off on its own. Consequently, the Stahlhelm began to form its own youth group, the Jungstahlhelm (Young Steel Helmet). During 1924 Jungstahlhelm units were formed throughout northern and southern Germany in conjunction with the new Stahlhelm sections that accepted older nonveterans.[76] The Jungstahlhelm accepted youths between the ages of seventeen and twenty-one, and its members upon completion of their twenty-first year and two years of service in the Jungstahlhelm were then accepted into the parent organization. These attempts of the Stahlhelm to provide itself with a constant flow of recruits in order to compensate for the inevitable decline of those who met the original membership criteria were not without success; by 1929 neutral observers concluded that 50 percent of the Stahlhelm's membership was nonveteran.[77] Positions of leadership, however, remained largely in the hands of older members, and this became a constant source of friction, especially in the Jungstahlhelm units.

During the middle years of the republic the other combat leagues, both large and small, also formed youth groups.[78] Through these auxiliary organizations the leagues were able to extend their influence to youths as young as twelve to fourteen years of age. In addition to producing a constant stream of recruits for the parent organizations, the youth groups also provided a source of well-disciplined "political

soldiers'' for the massive demonstrations that figured so prominently
in the political activity of the combat leagues. The major appeal of
the youth organizations was their military appearance and the opportunity they provided for military training. Military training, however,
was not all that their members received; they also received a massive
indoctrination of antidemocratic political ideas as well as an initiation
into political street fighting. In terms of the crucial problem of winning youth over to the ideals of the republic, the youth groups associated with the political combat leagues, like the leagues themselves, were truly negative schools of politics in which the major
subjects were hatred of the republic, intolerance, and violence.

While the rightist combat leagues were working to expand their
ranks, the supporters of the republic, in a belated response to the
events of 1923, sought to check the danger of the rightist paramilitary organizations by forming one of their own. In February, 1924,
the Right's monopoly on paramilitary activity was ended with the
founding of the Reichsbanner Schwarz-Rot-Gold, Bund der repub-
likanischen Kriegsteilnehmer (National Standard Black-Red-Gold,
League of Republican War Veterans).[79] As indicated by its subtitle,
the Reichsbanner was intended to serve as a republican veterans'
organization.[80] Yet the Reichsbanner was never intended to be only a
veterans' organization, a point that was later made more explicit
when its subtitle was changed to League of German Veterans and
Republicans. The Reichsbanner was not created to serve as a republican version of the Kyffhäuser-Bund, but as a counter-Stahlhelm.[81]
The main purpose of the Reichsbanner was to defend the republic
and to protect prorepublican organizations from attacks by the rightist
paramilitary formations.

The Reichsbanner was founded by Social Democrats, and although
efforts were made to give it a nonpartisan character (e.g., article 25
of its charter stated that its governing bodies ''must as far as possible
be composed of members of all parties which support the Weimar
Constitution''), its membership remained overwhelmingly Social
Democratic.[82] Nonetheless, members of the Democratic and Center
parties did pariticipate, at least initially. In the later years of the republic, however, when the middle-class republican parties began to
turn to the right, they increasingly disengaged themselves from the
Reichsbanner, and its Social Democratic character became even more
pronounced.[83]

Pledged to ''fight against and repel all attacks against republicans,
republican parties, republican unions, and all other organizations

which support the republic," the Reichsbanner adopted the same trappings as its rightist opponents. Indeed, it was often difficult to distinguish at first glance between a Reichsbanner function and one of the Stahlhelm. Military formations and commands, uniforms, flags, and marching bands were used by the Reichsbanner in the same manner and profusion as by the rightist combat leagues, a development that elicited complaints from the latter that the Reichsbanner had "stolen" their forms.[84] The Reichsbanner was also similar to the others in its organizational structure and method of selecting leaders, although here there were strong traces of Social Democratic traditions mixed with the combat-league characteristics. Like the other combat leagues, the Reichsbanner also had a youth group, the Jungbanner, and conducted marches, "maneuvers," and other miliary training exercises.

In spite of its similarities to the rightist organizations, there were significant differences, not only in its political goals but in its basic attitude toward things military. The wish to perpetuate the experience of the front or the belief in a special sociopolitical mission of the front soldier, for example, played a negligible role in the Republican Combat League. Furthermore, when such appeals were made, they were used to enlist support for the new state, not to mobilize opposition against it. Finally, the Reichsbanner's use of military forms and its military activity were not ends in themselves, as was frequently the case with the rightist organizations, but were strictly a means to an end. While the Reichsbanner utilized military forms, it never idealized them. In the qualitative confrontation between "soldier" and "civilian," the soldier was not the model and ideal. The Reichsbanner did not fight for a future state inspired by military ideals, but in defense of parliamentary democracy, a specifically civilian form of government.[85]

Given the circumstances of political life in the Weimar Republic, the formation of the Reichsbanner was a logical and understandable move on the part of the republic's supporters. Yet, while the motives of its founders were both good and defensible, the emergence of a Republican Combat League contained certain liabilities. First of all, it gave new life to the rightist paramilitary organizations precisely at a time when their further existence was in many cases being threatened by the onset of the prosperity and stablilty which began to make itself felt in Germany after 1924. Second, the emergence of yet another paramilitary organization unavoidably contributed to the polarization and militarization of politics. Finally, the formation of the Reichsbanner prompted the Communists to form a combat league of their own, the Rote Frontkämpferbund (Red Front-Fighters League), or RFB.

The first units of the Rote Frontkämpferbund were formed in central Germany during the summer of 1924.[86] The immediate and official cause for their formation was a bloody riot which took place between Communists and rightists in Halle in May. The underlying and basic reason for the creation of the Communist Combat League, however, was the success of the Reichsbanner. The Rote Frontkämpferbund appealed to veterans and served as a Communist veterans' organization, but, like the Reichsbanner, it never limited its membership solely to veterans. The RFB sought to attract veterans not because they were veterans per se, but because they provided the necessary core for effective paramilitary activity.

While in the streets the Rote Frontkämpferbund and the rightist combat leagues were violent political opponents, their aims were the same in one regard: both sought to discredit and overthrow the republic. There were also other similarities. As part of a militant, revolutionary movement, the RFB was not squeamish about its military charter. Unencumbered by the humanistic and pacifistic attitudes that frequently inhibited the Social Democrats, and armed with the theoretical props provided by the writings of Marx, Lenin, and, in particular, Engels, the Rote Frontkämpferbund considered itself not only a self-defense organization but the core of a red army that would in the future crush the German bourgeoisie and bring communism to Germany. The concept of being the cadre for a future revolutionary army that would some day liberate Germany from oppression was in many ways similar to the ethos of the rightist combat leagues, and the RFB's propaganda along these lines, as well as the elaborate ceremonial occasions at which allegiance was sworn to the Soviet Army, flags were dedicated, etc., often bore a striking resemblance to the activities of the Right. To be sure, the military aspirations and aspects of the RFB never even remotely achieved the importance for the Communist combat league that they did for the rightist paramilitary organizations, but there was a symbiotic relationship to such matters that never existed for the Reichsbanner.

Not surprisingly, the RFB also had a greater affinity for violence than its republican counterpart. In addition to fighting the rightist combat leagues (and the Reichsbanner), the RFB was also continually involved in clashes with the police. In 1929, after a particularly bloody incident involving the RFB and the Berlin police, the Communist Combat League was formally banned, and thereafter was forced to continue its existence as an underground organization. In the five years of its official existence (as well as later), however, the RFB contributed greatly to the militarization and violence of political life in the republic.

Meanwhile the politicalization of the rightist paramilitary organizations continued. By 1926 most of the former military associations had completed their transformation into political combat leagues. This change was expressed in a report drawn up for the Prussian minister of interior in October, 1926. Noting that the so-called nationalist organizations had originally concentrated primarily on military activity and left politics to others, it continued: "Since 1924 a change has been noticeable. . . . The organizations no longer—or no longer exclusively—limit themselves to the field of soldierly activity, but increasingly are becoming engaged in the political struggle and are seeking to obtain political influence and political power. . . ."[87] "Political influence and political power" proved to be as elusive for the combat leagues after 1923 as they had been for the military associations before. Once force had had to be renounced, the combat leagues were faced with the thorny problem of how they, as extraparliamentary organizations, were to influence political developments in a parliamentary democracy. For the most part, they were reduced to attempts to pressure the rightist parties into adopting more intransigent positions, a tactic that proved to be highly frustrating and ineffective.

Although the rightist parties welcomed the support of the combat leagues in the fight against the leftist parties, they soon became annoyed with the efforts of the "nonpolitical" politicians to meddle in their affairs. Moreover, the ill-concealed contempt of the combat leagues for the parties and the fact that the fulfillment of their demands ultimately would lead to the liquidation of the parties naturally limited possibilities for harmonious cooperation. "As long as the paramilitary formations simply functioned as recruiting organizations and supporters of the parties' work," complained a combat league supporter in 1926, "they were happily tolerated, [but] since they have made demands for political influence and a share in leadership, they are beginning to get on the nerves of the diehard party politicians."[88] In their efforts to bring the parties into line, the combat leagues frequently resorted to attempts at electoral blackmail, i.e., threatening to boycott elections unless the parties met their demands; yet fear of leftist gains always forced them to draw back at the last moment, and the threat was never carried out.[89] Similarly, there was periodic discussion among the combat leagues over the possibility of forming their own parties, but given their antipathy to parliamentary government as well as the hard-headed realization that they could hardly beat the parties at their own game, such talk remained for the most part conjectural and was intended more as a threat to the parties than as a serious alternative.

To the dismay of the combat leagues, politicalization proved to be no guarantee of sound or successful politics. Indeed, the effort to develop positive political programs and effective political tactics frequently produced divisions among the combat leagues themselves which made unified political action—the fundamental prerequisite for success—impossible. The debates between the various combat leagues which took place in the pages of their newspapers and journals, whose proliferation after 1924 was one of the most tangible expressions of the leagues' politicalization, at times reached a level of acrimony that was little different from that usually reserved for attacks on the Left. In particular, there were often sharp differences between the more *bündisch,* youth-oriented organizations and the Stahlhelm, which was composed of older, more established men and consequently was, relatively speaking, more conservative and restorative in its outlook. In a typical attack, for example, the Jungdo in 1925 charged that the Stahlhelm harbored a great number of reactionaries in its ranks, was closely tied to plutocratic financial interests, and selected its leaders by virtue of their prewar social and/or military positions. Consequently, it was concluded, the Jungdo had more in common with the Reichsbanner than with the Stahlhelm.[90] But in spite of their differences, the rightist combat leagues remained united on one basic matter—their hatred of the republic.

During the middle years of the republic, the rightist combat leagues in effect reversed Clausewitz's famous dictum and made politics a continuation of war by other means. Based essentially on the negation of current circumstances, the political demands of the combat leagues were strong in criticism, but weak, vague, and utopian in their proposals of positive alternatives. The "new nationalism," a term widely used by the combat leagues to characterize their political programs and to mark themselves off from the prewar nationalists, was, as a contemporary observer remarked, "less an intellectual construct than an inner attitude."[91] Although the politicalization of the combat leagues produced differences, it also produced an ideology, the so-called Front Ideology, which had an extremely pervasive effect in postwar Germany, not only among veterans but on the political right as a whole.[92]

For many Germans, plagued by a history of disunity, the war—at least initially—had seemed to offer a unifying ideal. The enthusiasm which greeted its outbreak was graphically captured by Stefan Zweig when he wrote of the August Days:[93]

> And in spite of all my hatred and aversion for war, I should not have liked to have missed the memory of those first days. As never before, thousands and hundreds of thousands felt what they should have felt in peacetime, that they belonged together. . . . All differences of class, rank and language were flooded over at that moment by a rushing feeling of fraternity.

This feeling of unity and common purpose was continued and deepened in the trenches where in the face of the common danger differences in civilian profession and position in society were forgotten and men were judged on their skill as soldiers.[94]

During the mid-1920s the experience of the war was politicized and made the basis for a powerful antirepublican ideology. Disillusionment with the republic led to an idealization of the period immediately preceding it. The experience of the trenches was seen in retrospect as embodying all the virtues which were lacking in the present state and which were to be possessed by the ideal future state, which—unlike the republic—would be capable of reversing and avenging the loss of World War I.

The politicalization of the front experience, with its stylized and distorted rendition of a heroic past and vague, idealistic pictures of a better future, provided the basis for sharp and bitter attacks on the political and social realities of the present. According to the combat leagues, the liberal, parliamentary political system of the Weimar Republic was not only an outdated creation of the nineteenth century but particularly unsuited for Germany. Parliamentary government was castigated as being weak and corrupt and as a system in which only the inferior could rise. Moreover, the liberal concept of individual freedom and the consequent pluralistic arrangement of society were considered the root causes of Germany's weakness. In short, the needs of the individual were to be subordinated to the needs of the state. Claiming to be the true guardians of the nationalistic grail and the "true" state, the combat leagues and their ideological fellow travelers rejected the existing state. The Weimar Republic, it was argued, had to be replaced by a state that was "national, social, military, and authoritarian."[95]

Having risked their lives for the nation and proved themselves in the trenches, the former soldiers of the combat leagues felt themselves uniquely qualified to lead the nation which by chance and subterfuge had fallen into the hands of civilians, who, through their weakness, lack of commitment, or outright treason had been responsible for Germany's defeat and subsequent problems. The experience and achievement of the front soldier, it was argued, had created a new type of person who alone possessed the insight, strength, and resolution to save Germany from its present state of weakness and chaos. One expression of this theme of the special role and rights of the former soldier was the contention that the republic's system of universal and equal suffrage was a mistake, since only those who had performed a service for the state, above all the front soldiers, were entitled to full political rights.[96]

The experience of the front, as Franz Seldte, the Stahlhelm leader, put it, was to be "the starting point for the transformation of the German state."[97] The unity of the trenches, according to the ideologues of the combat leagues, had been the first step in the development of a strong, united society, which had then been interrupted by the establishment of the weak and divided republic. Before Germany could again become strong, German society had to be united again as it had been in 1914. The combat leagues were in effect an attempt to transfer directly into civilian life the discipline and comradeship of the front. The militaristic, hierarchical, and *bündisch* organizational form of the combat leagues was to serve simultaneously as an example and a means of overcoming the pluralistic and divided society of the Weimar Republic. The combat leagues felt they were the political vanguard of the new state not only because they strove for it, but because they incorporated the new political order in their own being.

Although the virtues of the future state envisioned by the combat leagues were widely advertised, its particulars for the most part remained vague. One thing, however, was clear. It was not to be a return to the prewar empire. Never established in the empire, most of the young veterans and other members of the combat leagues who had reached maturity during or after the war had little reason to mourn its passing. Many, in fact, had already expressed their aversion to Wilhelmine society before the war as members of the German youth movement, and the empire's collapse had only further confirmed their conviction that the empire and those who ruled it had been corrupt and outdated.[98] Indeed, the young activists often attacked the new republic not so much because it had destroyed the old order, but because it had not. The republic, they charged, was nothing more than a continuation of Wilhelmine society with all its faults.

Foremost among these was the failure to win over the working class to the national cause. During the empire, it was claimed, the ruling and propertied classes had failed to see this, and it had cost Germany the war. The bitter class antagonism which still divided Germany, argued the combat leagues, had to be removed before Germany could ever successfully wage the hoped-for war of liberation. The proponents of the Front Ideology claimed that the war had been a watershed. The front generation, forged in the crucible of the trenches, had overcome the divisions which had separated Germans in the past. The "storm of steel," it was claimed, had obliterated the old social distinctions. All that mattered now was devotion to the national cause. In their view, the nation had been reduced to nationalists and internationalists. In order to induce the working class to forsake its previous alignment with the latter and to join the former, argued the young nationalists, real social reform, even social revolution, were not only permissable but necessary. The national revvolution, however, i.e., the overthrow of the republic and the Treaty of Versailles, was always to have precedence over the social.

The naive political conceptions which were associated with the Front Ideology had an enormous appeal for many young veterans. For many, the war had been, and would remain, the decisive experience in their lives. Politically unschooled before the war and faced upon their return with a situation that offered them little in the way of political or social security, many saw in military forms and virtues the solution to the republic's problems. While many of the aspirations connected with the Front Ideology were idealistic and honorable, the attempt to use the front experience as a basis for concrete political activity was unrealistic. The attempt to transport the "community of the trenches," a product of the completely abnormal situation of total war, into the postwar world and to make it the basis for peacetime civilian society, was not only impossible but dangerous. Such hopes betrayed a complete lack of understanding of political and social reality. In the trenches, where all men were united in the simple struggle for survival, all else was secondary, and the normal divisions and differences between men were either suspended or suppressed. In a peacetime society it was inevitable that differences would again arise. To refuse to acknowledge this and to try to return to the simpler circumstances which prevailed during the abnormal conditions of the war ultimately had to lead to dictatorial and to-talarian solutions, since all those interests that seemed to conflict with what was defined as the common good would either have to be forced into line or eliminated.

In fact, it soon became clear that the Front Ideology was highly selective and instead of promoting consensus only helped to justify further division. Not only were the "cowardly" and pacifistic civilians of the home front excluded from the new elite, but so were those front soldiers who had failed to draw the proper conclusions from the war experience itself. Ultimately the "true" war experience became limited to those on the right who opposed the republic and eventually even encompassed persons (e.g., youth) who had not even participated in the war. Moreover, the division of German society into "nationalists" and "internationalists" instead of bourgeoisie and workers did little to change existing class divisions. For the most part, only the labels had been changed. In practice, the old class antagonisms which had ostensibly been obliterated by the war experience and the "storm of steel" remained. The political combat leagues of the Weimar Republic had indeed broken with the past. They rejected Wilhelmine society and genuinely desired to come to terms with the working class. Yet the conditions for reconciliation were overwhelmingly one-sided. Socialism, ultimately, was to be no more than "the savior of nationalism."[99] The non-Marxian brand of socialism proffered by the combat leagues, be it "national" socialism or "front" socialism, was in fact little more than an ideological appeal for the total mobilization of German society for the war of revenge which they some day hoped to lead.

The combat leagues and the other rightist veterans' organizations in postwar Germany never were able themselves to achieve directly their hopes for a militant authoritarian state or their dream of a nation totally mobilized for a war of revenge. For this they had to wait for Adolf Hitler and the Third Reich. Not all veterans supported Hitler. Certainly those in the Reichsbanner did not. Nor, for that matter, did all those in the rightist organizations. Many of those in the old-line conservative groups, such as the DOB and Kyffhäuser-Bund, felt that Hitler was too coarse, too radical, and his movement too plebeian, while significant numbers of the more *bündisch* organizations such as the Jungdo, Wehrwolf and Bund Oberland felt that the Nazis were too "party-political," too opportunistic, and not sufficiently committed to a thorough moral regeneration of Germany. Nonetheless, the overwhelming majority of their rank and file either went over openly to Hitler and the Nazis or enthusiastically applauded their success. During the final years of the republic, the rightist combat leagues, with the exception of the Stahlhelm, declined and were essentially subsumed into the Nazi movement. Even though the Stahlhelm was able to hold its own in terms of members, it too came increasingly under the dominance of the National Socialists, as its leaders, mesmerized by the rising political power of the Nazis, sought to manipulate Hitler for their own ends. The campaign against the Young Plan of 1929, the formation of the Harzburg Front in 1931, the presidential elections of 1932 and finally Seldte's inclusion in Hitler's first Cabinet, all marked the progressive subjugation of the Stahlhelm to Hitler, not, as its leaders had hoped and expected, the reverse.

As in the case of so many other organizations which flourished during the republic and substantially aided both its downfall and the rise of Hitler, the rightist veterans' organizations and combat leagues were destroyed or absorbed by the Nazis once they came to power. Like the republican organizations and institutions which they detested, they too were *gleichgeschaltet* or "coordinated."[100] In May, 1933, the Kyffhäuser-Bund announced its unconditional support of Hitler and in September initiated a number of organizational and personnel changes that quickly brought it under National Socialist control. In February, 1934, all the officers' associations were united in the Reichsverband Deutscher Offiziere (National Association of German Officers) headed by Graf Rüdiger von der Goltz, the former commander of the Baltic Free Corps. During the summer of 1933 the rightist combat leagues, with the exception of the Stahlhelm, either dissolved themselves or were forced to join the SA. Because of the size of the Stahlhelm and Seldte's position as a minister in Hitler's Cabinet, National Socialist efforts to undercut the Stahlhelm were slower and more subtle, but no less effective. During the spring and summer following the Nazi takeover, its autonomy was progressively limited. In November, 1933, the Stahlhelm's backbone was essentially broken when it was subordinated to the newly created SA-Reserve. Thereafter it had only a shadow existence until it was formally dissolved in November, 1935.

The final step in the *Gleichschaltung* of the German veterans' movement came in March, 1938, when the Kyffhäuser-Bund was transformed into the N.S.-Reichskriegerbund (National Socialist

League of Veterans), which then assimilated the National Association of German Officers. Membership in the National Socialist League of Veterans, now the sole veterans' organization in Germany, was made compulsory for every German who had completed his military service, and in the following years the organization became little more than an organ for National Socialist military propaganda.[101] Thus, almost ignominiously, the veterans' movement, which had been one of the most independent and implacable foes of the republic, became a docile tool of Hitler's totalitarian Third Reich.

Whether or not they supported Hitler and the National Socialist movement directly, the rightist veterans' organizations and combat leagues all contributed to the coming of the Third Reich. Their constant vilification of the republic and its leaders helped greatly to undermine the republic's prestige and to discredit its political institutions. Their organizations provided both encouragement and a haven for antirepublican forces, preventing them from coming to terms with the republic on the one hand, while recruiting new adherents to the antirepublican cause on the other. The rightist veterans' organizations and combat leagues in effect institutionalized instability; they held the antirepublican forces of the right in a stage of semimobilization during the years of relative prosperity and stability in the late 1920s, thus preparing the way for Hitler's mobilization of them in full after the onset of the depression. Unable to seize power themselves, the rightist veterans' organizations and combat leagues contributed greatly to the republic's inability to wield it effectively; for this, if for no other reason, they were a significant factor in the Weimar Republic's collapse and the National Socialist seizure of power.

NOTES

1. Elie Halevy, *The Era of Tyrannies* (Doubleday, Anchor ed., 1965), p. 222. The statement was originally made in 1929.

2. The terms "forces of movement" and "forces of order" as well as the general analytical framework for their interplay during the war are taken from Arno J. Mayer, *Political Origins of the New Diplomacy, 1917–1918* (New York: Random House, Vintage ed., 1970).

3. For a concrete and crucial example of the importance of soldiers and the efforts of contending political factions to win their allegiance in Russia, see Alexander Rabinowitch, "The Petrograd Garrison and the Bolshevik Seizure of Power," *Revolution and Politics in Russia: Essays in Memory of B. I. Nicolaevsky*, ed. Alexander and Janet Rabinowitch (Bloomington: Indiana University Press, 1972).

4. For a more detailed account of efforts to gain control of German veterans dur-

ing the war, see my article "The Organization of German Veterans, 1917–1919," *Archiv für Sozialgeschichte*, Band 11 (1971).

5. On the early history of German veterans' organizations and the formation of the Kyffhäuser-Bund, see Alfred Westphal, "Die Kriegervereine," *Deutschland als Weltmacht: Vierzig Jahre Deutsches Reich*, hrsg, v. Kaiser-Wilhelm-Dank (Berlin, Kameradshaft 1911); and Wilhelm Reinhard, "Der N.S.-Reichskriegerbund," *Das Dritte Reich im Aufbau* (Berlin, Quelle & Meyer 1939), Band 3.

6. Eckart Kehr, "Zur Genesis des Königlich Preussischen Reserve-Offizers." repr. in Kehr, *Der Primat der Innenpolitik: Gesammelte Aufsatze zur preussisch-deutschen Sozialgeschichte in 19. und 20. Jahrhundert*, ed. Hans-Ulrich Wehler (Berlin, de Gruyter 1965).

7. On the conversion of the veterans' organizations into a "bulwark against Social Democracy," see Klaus Saul, "Der 'Deutsche Kriegerbund': Zur innenpolitischen Funktion eines 'nationalen' Verbandes im kaiserlichen Deutschland," *Militärgeschichtliche Mitteilungen* (February, 1969). Also see Reinhard Höhn, *Sozialismus und Heer*, Band 3 (Bad Harzburg, Verlag für Wissenshaft, Wirtshaft und Technik 1969), and Martin Kitchen, *The German Officer Corps 1890–1914* (London, Clarendon Press Oxford 1968), chaps. 6 and 7.

8. Westphal, p. 762.

9. Ibid., pp. 768–69.

10. Kyffhäuser-Bund der Deutschen Landeskriegerverbände, Sitzung des Vorstandes vom 30. und 31. Oktober, 1915. NSDAP Hauptarchiv, folder 913. Most of the materials in the NSDAP Hauptarchiv (hereafter cited as NSHA—followed by the folder number) are currently in the Bundesarchiv in Koblenz, Germany. The material is also available on microfilm as part of the Hoover Institution Microfilm Collection. See Grete Heinz and Agnes F. Peterson (eds.), *NSDAP Hauptarchiv: Guides to the Hoover Institution Microfilm Collection*, Hoover Institution Bibliographical Service, vol 17 (Stanford, Calif., 1964).

11. Höhn, 3:460.

12. Josef Nothaas, *Die Kriegsbeschädigtenfürsorge unter besondere Berücktsichtigung Bayerns* (inaugural dissertation, University of Munich), p. 17.

13. See ibid., p. 50.

14. For a brief history of the Prussian three-class suffrage system and a detailed account of the struggle for reform during the First World War, see Reinhard Patemann, *Der Kampf um die preussische Wahlreform im Ersten Weltkrieg*, Beiträge zur Geschichte des Parlamentarismus un der politischen Parteien, Band 26 (Düsseldorf, Droste 1964).

15. *Vorwärts*, December 31, 1916.

16. *Vorwärts*, January 21, 1917.

17. *Vorwärts*, April 3, 1917. Bericht des Brundesvorstandes mit Protokill der Verhandlungen des 2. Reichsbundestages, Würzburg, 11–15 Mai, Reichsbund der Kriegsbeschädigten, Kriegsteilnehmer, und Kriegshinterbliebenen (1920), p. 18 (hereafter cited as BdB).

18. *Vorwärts*, June 4, 1917.

19. Erster reichsdeutscher Bundestag der Kriegsbeschädigten und ehemaligen Kriegsteilnehmer, Verhandlungsbericht *Weimar, Ostern 1918* p. 15 (hereafter cited as ERB).

20. *Vorwärts*, June 4, 1917.

21. *Vorwärts*, January 21, 1918; ErB, p. 15.

22. On the origins and purpose of the Fatherland Party, see Dirk Stegmann, *Die Erben Bismarcks: Parteien und Verbände in der Spätphase des Wilhelminischen Deutschlands* (Kön and Berlin, Kiepenheuer & Witsch 1972), chap. 10.

23. *Vorwärts*, November 12, 1971.

24. *Vorwärts*, January 8, 12, and 18, 1918; ErB, pp. 12, 53.

25. BdB, p. 33.

26. ETB. See the proposed charter, pp. 19–20, and the one finally accepted, pp. 118–19.

27. Niederschrift über die Sitzung des Vorstandes des Kyffhäuser-Bundes der Deutschen Landes-Kriegerverbände vom 2. und 3. Juni, 1917, NSHA/913.

28. ETB, p. 73; *Vorwärts*, May 22 and June 4, 1918.

29. *Vorwärts*, September 21 and December 15, 1917.

30. *Vorwärts*, June 22 and July 23, 1918.

31. *Kriegervereinvorstand*, March, 1919.

32. See below, p. 156.

33. On the development of the stab-in-the-back legend, see Friedrich Frhr. Hiller von Gaertringen, " 'Dolchstoss'-Diskussion und 'Dolchstoss-Legende' im Wandel von vier Jahrzenten," in *Geschichte und Gegenwartsbewusstsein: Festschrift für Hans Rothenfels*, ed. Waldemar Besson and F. Frhr. Hiller von Gaertringen (Göttingen, Vandenhoeck & Ruprecht 1963).

34. The percentage of nondisabled veterans in the National Confederation was only slightly over 12; the increased emphasis on the problems of the next of kin of those killed in the war was made evident when shortly after the end of the war its name was changed to Reichsbund der Kriegsbeschädigten, Kriegsteilnehmer, und Kriegshinterbliebenen (National Confederation of War-Disabled, War Veterans and Next of Kin).

35. BdB, p. 6. For further details on the following, see ibid., pp. 45–48, and Nothaas, passim.

36. On the origins of the International League, see *BdB*, pp. 12–18.

37. On the origins and development of the Zentralverband, see ibid., pp. 22–27; and *Vorwärts*, June 28, 1918.

38. In 1922 the various organizations representing the war-disabled were proportionately represented in the National Committee for the Welfare of the War-Disabled as follows: Reichsbund, 13; Zentralverband, 5; Einheitsverband, Internationaler Bund, Kyffhäuser-Bund, 4 each. In 1921 an attempt was made to unite all the groups, but it failed, and the record of the negotiations provides a revealing insight into the differences between them. See Protokoll über Einigungsverhandlungen der Kriegsbeschadigten- und Kriegshinterbliebenen- Organisationen am 16. und 17. April in Weimar (1921).

39. On the unwillingness of ex-officers to join the veterans' organizations before the war, see Saul, "Der 'deutsche Kriegerbund,' " and Höhn, *Sozialismus und Heer*.

40. Brief sketches of the DOB and other officers' associations can be found in Dieter Fricke, et al. (eds.), *Die bürgerlichen Parteien in Deutschland: Handbuch der Geschichte der bürgerlichen Parteien und anderer bürgerlicher Interessenorganisationem vom Vormärz bis zum Jahre 1945* (Leipzig, VEB Bibliographishes Institut 1968), 2 vols. (hereafter cited as *Die bürgerlichen Parteien*).

41. *Berliner Tageblatt*, May 24, 1925.

42. Quoted in *Die bürgerlichen Parteien*, 447.

43. See the reports of the Nationalverband's yearly convention (generally held in March or April) in *Deutsche Zeitung*.

44. On the promotion of enlisted men to officers and the attendant problems, see Robert G. L. Waite, *Vanguard of Nazism: The Free Corps Movement in Postwar Germany, 1918–1923*, (New York: Norton, 1969) pp. 46–47.

45. See, for example, the article on the ROB by Oberleutnant a.D. von Stolch in *Preussische Zeitung*, January 19, 1922.

46. For a biased but essentially correct account of the republic's treatment of former officers, see Hans Ernst Fried, *The Guilt of the German Army* (New York, Macmillan 1942), pp. 98–161; also cf. Waite, p. 262.

47. In this connection, the formation of the National Confederation may also have

GERMANY: VETERANS' POLITICS UNDER THREE FLAGS   183

played a role. The National Confederation's persistent and effective representation of the economic interests of disabled veterans and their families undoubtedly helped to permit other veterans' organizations the luxury of devoting their energies to other, more political, matters. For more on this, cf. below pp. 168–69.

48. Westphal to Hermanni, November 13, 1918, NSHA/916.

49. See, for example, the official proclamation of the Kyffhäuser-Bund of November 14, 1918, NSHA/916.

50. Westphal to Gravenhorst, February 10, 1919, NSHA/916.

51. *Kriegervereinvorstand,* March, 1919; also see *Krieger-Zeitung,* August 3, 1919.

52. Of these only about ten percent were war-disabled veterans, a figure that clearly reflects the Kyffhäuser-Bund's failure—or lack of interest—in this field of activity in spite of its propaganda to the contrary. Also cf. notes 38 above and 54 below.

53. Karl Rohe, *Das Reichsbanner Schwarz Rot Gold: Ein Beitrag zur Geschichte und Struktur der politischen Kampfverbände zur Zeit der Weimarer Republik,* Beiträge zur Geschichte des Parlamentarismus und der politischen Parteien, Band 34 (Dusseldorf, Droste 1966), 126–127.

54. On the eve of the First World War, the Kyffhäuser-Bund claimed over 2,860,000 members. Of these approximately one-half were recalled to active duty during the war. By 1921 the Bund's membership had returned to nearly 2,200,000 and by 1929 had risen to over 2.5 million. Although the Kyffhäuser-Bund was therefore able to achieve a postwar membership that was nearly equal to its prewar membership, in view of the enormous number of new veterans created by the war the Bund's postwar record was at best only a relative success and clearly reflects a failure to appeal to large numbers of the new generation of veterans.

55. The following account of the VNS is based primarily on material in R431/766, Militärvereine 1921–23, Bundesarchiv, Koblenz.

56. The best general accounts of the Stahlhelm are Volker R. Berghahn, *Der Stahlhelm, Bund der Frontsoldaten, 1918–1935,* Beiträge zur Geschichte des Parlamentarismus und der politischen Parteien, Band 33 (Düsseldorf, Droste 1966), and Alois Klotzbucher, *Der Politische Weg des Stahlhelm, Bund der Frontsoldaten, in der Weimarer Republik: Ein Beitrag zur Geschichte der "Nationalen Opposition," 1918–1933* (inaugural dissertation, Erlangen-Nürnberg, 1964). Also see the entry in *Die bürgerlichen Parteien.*

57. Seldte to Georg Escherich, April 8, 1920, Bayerisches Hauptstaatsarchiv, Munich. Abteilung 4, Kriegsarchiv.

58. On the Free Corps movement see Waite, which although outdated in some respects captures the spirit of the movment, and, more recently, Hagen Schulze, *Freikorps und Republik, 1918–1920* (Boppard, Harald Boldt 1969). Additional worthwhile material can be found in Harold J. Gordon, Jr., *The Reichswehr and the German Republic, 1919–1926* (Princeton, Univ. Press 1957).

59. The exact membership of the Free Corps is hard to establish. Waite sets their number at between 200,000 and 400,000. Gordon accepts the latter figure, while Schulze concludes that the total figure was about 250,000. Membership figures for the auxiliary volunteer units do not seem to exist. A memorandum prepared by officials of the Civil Guard in late 1919 sets their membership at over one million. See Erwin Konnemann, *Einwohnerwehren und Zeitfreiwilligenverbände: Ihre Funktion beim Aufbau eines neuen imperialistischen Militärsystems, November 1918–1920*(Berlin [East], Deutscher Militärcrlag 1921), Dokument 23.

60. For a discussion of this phrase and the significance of the period, see Klemens von Klemperer, *Germany's New Conservatism: Its History and Dilemma in the Twentieth Century* (Princeton, Univ. Press 1957), pp. 76ff.

61. The definitive treatment of the putsch is Johannes Erger's *Der Kapp-Luttwitz Putsch: Ein Beitrag zur deutschen Innenpolitik, 1919/20,* Beiträge zur Geschichte des

Parlamentarismus und der politischen Parteien, Band 35 (Düsseldorf, Droste 1967).

62. Quoted in Otto-Ernst Schüddekopf, *Das Heer und die Republik: Quellen zur Politik der Reichswehrführung, 1918 bis 1933* (Hanover and Frankfurt a/M, Norddeutsche Verlagsanstalt O. Goedel 1955), p. 130.

63. A study on the activities of paramilitary organizations (Einwohnerwehren, Wehrverbände, politische Kampfbünde) during the Weimar Republic, based on my dissertation, *Paramilitary Organizations and the Weimar Republic: The Militarization of German Politics, 1918–1930* (Berkeley, California, 1972), is currently in preparation.

64. Kurt Finker, *Die militaristischen Wehrverbände in der Weimarer Republik und ihre Rolle bei der Unterdrückung der Arbeiterklasse und bei der Vorbereitung eines neuen imperialistsichen Krieges, 1924–1929* (Potsdam: Habilschrift, 1958), p. 66.

65. The term "Orgesch" was a contraction of "Organisation Escherich," which in turn referred to Georg Escherich, the leader of the Bavarian Civil Guard, which provided the forces in the south as well as the ideological base for the organization.

66. When the Reich government officially banned the Orgesch and other secret and/or military organizations in June, 1921, all that was required of the Stahlhelm was that it remove point three of its program—the upholding of law and order—from its bylaws. Although Stahlhelm members joined Civil Guard and volunteer units, it remained organizationally separate from them, a point that undoubtedly contributed to its survival. Cf. Berghahn, p. 17.

67. Klotzbücher, p. 13; Finker, p. 67; Berghahn, appendix 3.

68. For a general, though somewhat uncritical, account of the Jungdeutscher Orden, see Klaus Hornung, *Der Jungdeutscher Orden,* Beiträge zur Geschichte des Parlamentarismus under der politischen parteien, Band 14 (Düsseldorf, Droste 1958); also see the entry in *Die burgerlichen Parteien.*

69. The Free Corps Oberland was transformed into the Bund Oberland in October, 1921, and the Ehrhardt Brigade, after a period of underground activity, later emerged as the Bund Wiking. Both organizations remained rather elitist and somewhat conspiratorial in nature and never became true mass organizations.

70. Hornung, pp. 24, 27; Finker, p. 225.

71. Though highly slanted, the best history of the Bavarian Civil Guard is Rudolf Kanzler's *Bayerns Kampf gegen den Bolschewismus: Geschichte der bayerischen Einwohnerwehren* (Munich, Parcus & Co. 1931).

72. On political violence during the early years of the republic and the response to it, see the works by E. J. Gumbel, *Verschwörer: Beiträge zur Geschichte und Soziologie der deutschen nationalistischen Geheimbünde seit 1918* (Vienna, Malik-Verlag 1924), and *Verräter verfallen der Feme: Opfer, Mörder, Richter, 1918–1929* (Berlin, Malik-Verlag 1929); Wilhelm Hoegner, *Der politische Radikalismus in Deutschland 1919–1933* (Munich, Günther Olzog 1966); Howard Stern, "The Organization Consul," *Journal of Modern History,* 35 (1963); and Gotthard Jasper, *Der Schutz der Republik: Studien zur staatlichen Sicherung der Demokratie in der Weimarer Republik, 1922–30,* Tübingen Studien zur Geschichte und Politik, Nr. 16 (Tübingen, J.C.B. Mohr 1963).

73. The most recent and comprehensive account of the putsch, Harold J. Gordon's *Hitler and the Beer Hall Putsch* (Princeton, Univ. Press 1972), contains considerable material on the activities of paramilitary organizations in Bavaria both before and during 1923.

74. Berghahn, p. 33, 100; Klotzbücher, p. 41.

75. Graham Wootton, *The Politics of Influence: British Ex-Servicemen, Cabinet Decisions and Cultural Change, 1917–1957* (Cambridge, Mass.: Harvard U.P., 1963), p. 107; also cf. pp. 120-22.

76. On the Jungstahlhelm see Berghahn, pp. 32–33, 64.

77. Klotzbucher, p. 42.

78. In 1925 the Jungdo developed a two-stage youth organization: 16- to 20-year-olds were organized in Juggefolgenschaften and 12 to 15-year-olds in Jungtrupps. Even the Wehrwolf, originally expected itself to serve as a sort of youth organization for the Stahlhelm, soon found it necessary to create a youth group of its own, the Jungwolf, which accepted 14- to 16-year-olds.

79. Paramilitary self-defense units had been formed by the Social Democrats to defend their oganizations and the republic prior to the creation of the Reichsbanner, but they had been of a sporadic, short-lived, and local nature. The definitive account of the Reichsbanner, its precedents, founding, and development, is the work by Karl Rohe cited in note 53 above; also see Roger Philip Chickering, "The Reichsbanner and the Weimar Republic, 1924–26," *Journal of Modern History*, 40 (1968).

80. One of the Reichsbanner's goals, for example, was to "vigorously represent the interests of veterans," and its initial appeals were largely directed to veterans. See, for example, the excerpts from its bylaws reprinted in Ernst Posse, *Die politischen Kampfbünde Deutschlands* (Berlin: Junker und Dünnhaupt 1931), pp. 66–67, and the recruitment appeal quoted in Chickering, p. 526.

81. Rohe, p. 128.

82. On the composition of the Reichsbanner, see ibid., pp. 266ff.

83. On this see, in addition to Rohe and Chickering, Thomas A. Knapp, "The German Center Party and the Reichsbanner: A Case Study in Political and Social Consensus in the Weimar Republic," *International Review of Social History*, 14 (1969).

84. See, for example, the article "Das Reichsbanner," in *Wikinger* of October, 1924.

85. Rohe, pp. 115–16.

86. On the Rote Frontkämpfverbund see Hermann Dünow, *Der Rote Frontkämpfverbund: Die revolutionäre Schutz- und Wehr-organisation des deutschen Proletariats in der Weimarer Republik,* Schriftenreihe zur Fragen der Militärideologie und Militärpolitik, Heft 2 (Berlin [East], Deutscher Militärverlag 1958), and Helmut Lohse, *Die revolutionäre Traditionen des Roten Frontkämpfverbundes unter der Führung von Ernst Thälmann* (inaugural dissertation, Karl-Marx-Universität, Leipzig, 1955). Both these East German works, while informative, are naturally highly biased. For a contemporary middle-class account of the RFB, see Posse, pp. 66–67, and the recruitment appeal quoted in Chickering, 68–71.

87. A copy of the report entitled "Einigung in der Rechtsbewegung" is in the Grzesinski Nachlass in the International Institute for Social History in Amsterdam.

88. *Reichsflagge,* October 28, 1926.

89. See, for example, the article "Wahlenthaltung" in *Jungdeutsche,* March 11, 1928.

90. Hornung, pp. 61–66; also see the reports of the Reichskommissar für Überwachung der öffentlichen Ordnung (hereafter cited as RKO), Nr. 113, September 15, 1925, and Nr. 116, January 26, 1926.

91. Posse, p. 77.

92. On the prevalence and nature of antidemocratic thought, including the Front Ideology, see Kurt Sontheimer, *Antidemokratisches Denken in der Weimarer Republik: Die politischen Ideen des deutscher Nationalismus zwischen 1918 und 1933* (Munich, Nymphenburger 1962), and Armin Mohler, *Die Konservative Revolution in Deutschland 1918–1932: Grundiss ihren Weltanschauungen* (Stuttgart, Friedrich Vorwerk 1950).

93. Quoted in Harold L. Poor, *Kurt Tucholsky and the Ordeal of Germany, 1914–1935* (New York, Scribners 1968), p. 28. Zweig was referring to Vienna, but the description is equally valid for Germany.

94. For an interesting and sympathetic description of these feelings from a non-rightist source, see Erich Maria Remarque's *The Road Back.*

95. The phrase is Ernst Jünger's. Jünger was one of the most forceful advocates of

a state permanently and totally mobilized for war. See Walter Struve, *Elites against Democracy: Leadership Ideas in Bourgeois Political Thought in Germany, 1890–1933* (Princeton, Univ. Press 1973), chap. 12.

96. This belief was widely held among veterans of the radical Right. See, for example, Ernst Röhm's autobiography, *Geschichte eines Hochverräters*. (Munich: Franz Eher 1928/34) One group, the Frontkriegerbund in Munich, even demanded that votes be weighed according to the type and length of service performed during the war. RKO Nr. 117, April 1, 1926.

97. Quoted in RKO Nr. 116, January 21, 1926.

98. On the connection between the Combat Leagues and the pre-war youth movement in general see Posse. A particularly good example is Artur Mahraun; see Hornung, chap. 1.

99. Otto-Ernst Schüddekopf, *Linke Leute von Rechts: Nationalbolschewismus in Deutschland von 1918 bis 1933* (Stuttgart, W. Kohlhammer 1960), p. 102; also see pp. 166–67 and 261.

100. On the Gleichschaltung of the veterans' associations and Combat Leagues, see the monographs cited above and the articles in *Die bürgerlichen Parteien*.

101. On the formation and development of the N.S.-Reichskriegerbund, see the article by Wilhelm Reinhard cited in note 5.

INDEX

187

Spanish-American War, 42; veterans of, 46
Squadristic, 104, 125, 126
Stanley, E. M. C. (Lord Stanley), 15
Stavisky, Serge: scandal associated with, 81; Daladier's response to, 82
Steel Helmet: founding of and goals, 159–60, 164; as Military Association, 163–64; membership of, 164, 168–69; absorbs Free Corps, 164; as political combat league, 168; on overthrow of Republic, 169; creates youth league, 169; criticism of, 174; dissolved by Nazis, 179. *See also* Seldte, Franz
Sturmabteilung (SA), 179

Taittinger, Pierre, 77, 93
Tardieu, Andre, 75–76, 82
Taylor, John Thomas, American Legion lobbyist, 44
Tirpitz, Admiral Alfred von: as President of the Fatherland party, 146

Unemployment: among British veterans, 22, 30; among German veterans, 150. *See also* Employment
Union Federale des Combattants: membership and political alignment of, 70–71; on riots (February, 1934), 72, 73; as radical socialist, 96, 98
Union National des Combattants UNC: politics and, 70–71; on veterans' benefits, 71; challenge to government, 71–72; role in riots (February, 1934), 71–72, 80–84, 90–91; and Daladier's government, 91; Metz conference of, 96; praises Franco, 97; on popular front, 97. *See also* Goy, Jean; Lebecq, George
United Association of German War Disabled and Next of Kin, 151
United States veterans: opposition to neutrality, 41; legislative power of, 41–42; educating of Congress, 55

Unity of the trenches: unifying forces, 7–8; among British veterans, 33, among American veterans, 38; among French veterans, 59; among Italian veterans, 111; and Germans, 176. *See also* Front Ideology; Barbusse, Henri

Valois, Georges, 78–79
Vecchi, Ferruccio: and Arditi, 112–13; 116, 117, 118
Versailles, Treaty of, 106, 150, 153, 160, 162
Veterans, general: assessment of, 3–9. *See also* Unity of the trenches; British veterans, U.S. veterans, etc.
Veterans of Foreign Wars (U.S.): patriotism of, 39; 40–44 and *passim.*; pressure for bonus, 44; support of Rankin Bill, 47; on Disability Act, 1930, 48, 52
Volontaires Nationaux, 75
Volunteer forces: activites of, 161–63
Vorwärts, 140, 141, 144

Weimar Republic, 149, 160, 171, 176; toward veterans, 150; and demobilization, 150; on disabled care, 151–56; veterans alienation from, 156; establishes volunteer forces, 161; criticism of, 175
Wehrwolf: military association in Ruhr, 169; and Stahlhelm, 169; and Nazis, 178–79
Westphal, Dr. Alfred: founding of Kyffhauser Bund, 137–39; and land annexation, 149; response to monarchy, 156–57; on survival of Kyffhauser Bund, 157. *See also* Kyffhauser Bund
Weygand, General Maxime, 93
Wilber, Ray Lyman, Secretary of Interior, 45
Wilson, Woodrow: 38, 39 and *passim.*